UKIYO

浮世

Stories of the "Floating World"
of postwar Japan

Selected and edited by

JAY GLUCK

Personally Oriented, LTD, Ashiya Japan

TRANSLATIONS BY JAY GLUCK IN COLLABORATION WITH:
GRACE SUZUKI, MOMOI MAKOTO, SAKAGUCHI YUKIKO AND
BY HASHIZUME SUMIKO, KIMURA MICHIKO, GENEVIEVE CAULFIELD

Published 1963 in hard cover by THE VANGUARD PRESS, New York
and in Canada by COPP CLARK PUBLISHING CO., Ltd., Toronto
Second edition library paperback, UNIVERSAL LIBRARY, New York

Third edition revised, paperback, 1993 by
PERSONALLY ORIENTED LTD., Ashiya, Japan

Distributed in:
Western Hemisphere by WEATHERHILL PUBLISHING, New York
Canada by RAINCOAST-WEATHERHILL
Europe by SCORPION, London
Japan by YOHAN, Tokyo
Pacific Area U.S. military by STARS & STRIPES, Tokyo

LIBRARY OF CONGRESS CATALOGUE CARD NUMBER:
93-92624
(Original Edition: 63—21851)

Scanned and revised on Macintosh
Printed and bound in the United States of America
by McNaughton and Gunn, Michigan
on acid-free paper

ISBN 4-89360-037-0

Other books by Jay Gluck:
Ah So, Cartoon Misadventures of a Foreigner in Japan
Zen Combat, 1964; revised and enlarged 1993
With Sumi Gluck, *Japan Inside Out*, in 5 volumes, 1964
With Sumi & Garet Gluck, *Japan Inside Out* revised 1992
With Sumi Gluck & C.J.Penton, *A Survey of Persian Handicraft*

To

P A U L   Y O S H I R O   S A E K I ,   O . B . E .

(1 8 6 9 – 1 9 6 6)

teacher and friend

originally on his 92nd birthday
marking 75 years of "interpretation"

ACKNOWLEDGMENTS

The Imperial Rescript on Surrender is from The Nippon Times (now Japan Times) of August 15, 1945 (courtesy of Ogata Tamotsu, editor).

The following translations appeared in the original Orient edition of Ukiyo (Phoenix Books, Tokyo, 1954), © copyright 1954 by the editor and publisher, Jay Gluck: Revenge by Mishima Yukio, #*Woman Tarzan of Korea by Yuasa Katsuei, *Love in the Annam Jungle by Oka Masamichi, †*Black Out by Koyama Itoko, The Communist by Abé Tomoji, Black Market Blues by Koh Haruto, Ups and Downs by Shibaki Yoshiko, †The Only One by Nakamoto Takako, †Rice Weevils by Wada Den, *Sazanka by Kawachi Sensuke, *One World by Serizawa Kojiro. (Those marked "†" appeared by prior arrangement in Preview, Tokyo, those marked "*" in Orient Digests, Tokyo. "#" indicates story eliminated due to space limitation from 1963 edition and herein restored).

Also appearing originally in Preview and reprinted by arrangement with the publisher: Three Unforgettable Letters by Taguchi Shu, Captured by Americans by Fuji Seii.

Appearing originally in, and © copyright 1955 by, Orient Digests, Tokyo and reprinted by arrangement with the publisher: The Admiral That Davy Jones Didn't Want by Yokoi Toshiyuki, Homecoming 1945 by Akiyama Isa, #Korea through Japanese Eyes by Yuasa Katsuei, These Ten Years by Kon Hidemi, Please Not a Word To Anybody by Mizuki Yoko, The Affair of the Arabesque Inlay by Ishikawa Tatsuzo, A Date by Saisho Foumy, Bringing Up Mothers-in-Law by John Fujii.

Underground Escape from the book of the same name by Tsuji Masa-nobu, © copyright 1951, and *Damoi—Homeward Bound* from *Four Years in Hell* by Yamamoto Tomomi, © copyright 1952 by Asian Publishing, Tokyo, reprinted by arrangement with the publisher.

The Affair of the Arabesque Inlay by Ishikawa Tatsuzo appears in trans-lation by prior arrangement through *Orient Digests.*

Banshu Plain by Miyamoto Yuriko appears in translation by arrange-ment with the author's widower, Mr. Miyamoto Kenji, Secretary General of the Japan Communist Party.

The Sad Samurai from *Tears on the Tatami* by John Fujii, © copyright 1955 by Phoenix Books, Tokyo, by arrangement.

The Crane That Cannot Come Back by Seto Nanako, © copyright 1961 by The Committee for the Book, Hiroshima YMCA, reprinted by arrange-ment with The Committee.

Echoes from a Mountain School by Eguchi Koichi reprinted through the courtesy of UNESCO. .

Portions of the *Introduction* appeared by subsidiary arrangement in *Thought,* Delhi, India, 1962, © author.

Careful effort has been made to trace ownership of selections included in this anthology in order to secure permission to reprint © copyright material and to make full acknowledgment of their use. If any error of omission has occurred, it is purely inadvertent and will be corrected in subsequent editions, provided written notification is made to the publisher.

TRANSLATIONS:

JAY GLUCK: *Captured by Americans.*

GRACE SUZUKI and JAY GLUCK: *Revenge, Love in the Annam Jungle, Black Out, Black Market Blues, Please Not a Word To Anybody, Ups and Downs, The Only One, Korea Through Japanese Eyes, Lady Tarzan of Korea, Rice Weevils, Sazanka, The Communist, One World.*

MOMOI MAKOTO and JAY GLUCK: *The Admiral That Davy Jones Didn't Want, These Ten Years, The Affair of the Arabesque Inlay.*

SAKAGUCHI YUKIKO and JAY GLUCK: *Banshu Plain.*

HASHIZUME SUMIKO: *A Crane That Cannot Come Back.*

KIMURA MICHIKO and GENEVIEVE CAULFIELD: *Echoes From a Mountain School.*

AKIYAMA ISA (author): Homecoming 1945.

YAMAMOTO TOMOMI (author): *Damoi—Homeward Bound.*

Preview staff (Jay Gluck, editor): *Underground Escape.*

Three Unforgettable Letters, The Sad Samurai, A Date, and *Bringing Up Mothers In-Law* were originally written in English.

CONTENTS

x CONTENTS

INTRODUCTION

At the court of an emperor (he lived it matters not when) there was, among the many gentle arts, one which though not of very high rank was favored far beyond all the rest; as a result, the great looked with scorn and hatred upon the upstart. Thus, preponderant though it was, it was soon worn out with petty vexation, fell into a decline, and grew melancholy and retiring.

The Occidental newly arriving in Japan will often feign a Japaneseness by performing tea ceremony using powdered coffee, or sleeping on the floor alongside a perfectly good bed, or decking himself out in an ill-fitting kimono, secondhand and at least a decade out of style. Not wishing to go against such time-hallowed tradition, I open my maiden anthology with a paraphrase of the opening lines of what is probably the world's first novel, and certainly the greatest classic of Japanese literature, *The Tale of Genji* (11th century). Such invocation of an older and greater work was a favorite Japanese literary technique, although it is now even more out of fashion than the kimonos my tourist friends take home; however, this in no way detracts from their beauty or their practicality, or from the fact that novelist Lady Murasaki, by means of this technique, presents a concise history of a thousand years of Japanese fiction.

The Japanese term *sho-setsu* is usually translated as "novel"—however, its literal meaning is "small view," implying a narration of a life, or an account of living, which will take less time to read than to live through, and which might run, as *Genji*, some three-quarters of a million words (in English translation[1]) or, as some in this selection, a few hundred. The English term "novel" implies, according to Webster, "a compact plot and a point." The Japanese *sho-setsu* may very well have this, but it more than likely will not. The common Occidental understanding of the Oriental attitude that this phenomenal existence called life has no logical plot, and possibly no point to it either, should make further explanation unnecessary—just as the fact that some stories *do* have a plot, even a compact one, and do make or come to or have a point, should show that this Oriental attitude is not so simply stated and perhaps not so universally accepted. *Sho-setsu*, then, encompasses the whole of prose fiction. We should not expect it to conform to our standards or to our ideas or definitions. It is compartmented, perhaps more so than our own, but not always in the way ours is. This should only point out to us the utter arbitrariness of any such divisions.

The "gentle arts" are at least as numerous and probably more varied in Japan as anywhere else, and among them fiction has been "not of very high rank." Certainly that of highest rank has been the dance. It is an essential element in all of the Japanese performing arts, from pure dance, both sacred and at the other extreme (though "sacred" in use) very profane, through the various forms of dance-drama, which also run the gamut from sacred to most profane; the combat dances, from spectator sports like sumo-wrestling (whose performers are called literally wrestle-dancers), to the dance calisthenics of the martial arts of judo, karate, and various armament drills; the etiquette dances which ritualize the making and serving of tea, arranging of flowers, the reception at court or in a private home, the offerings to deity, the geisha's serving her client, the artist's warming-up rituals, and even that choreography of the artist's brush known as calligraphy. Like the plastic arts, the graphic arts have, in Japan as elsewhere, enjoyed "high rank" and imperial and noble patronage.

In literature Japan has differed little from other cultures in bestowing high rank on poetry and dialectics, the oldest records being a sanctified official history and an anthology of the poetry of emperors, nobles, and commoners. Both types were compiled by imperial command.

---

[1] The first translation by Arthur Waley, 1925-33; a more concise, less Victorian. version by Edward Seidenstecker in 1976 postdates this essay ,

In *The Tale of Genji* the hero discusses with the heroine the romances and popular literature. (Popular, that is, with those who could read—and though limited, a larger group than 11th century Europe presented). He questions whether these "are good things for a young girl to read;" he questions their relation to life—or the good life. This discussion indicates that these romances and the diaries, which we might term confession stories, were "looked upon with scorn" and read in the privacy of the bedroom—but "favored far beyond all the rest" of the literary and art forms in being so widely read and appreciated. Little of contemporary poetry and certainly none of the religious or pseudo-religious and statist dialectics ever enjoyed such popularity.

Prose fiction, then, enjoys a world-wide acceptance as being that which one takes to bed to read for other than its purely soporific qualities. Persians and Indians give equal recognition to their long poems, novels in rhyme; but Japanese literature has none. Even twelve centuries ago when Japanese tastes in poetry were broader and poems were of greater stylistic variety and length, a few minutes was enough to read one through. Perhaps the language is too staccato in structure; a long poem might rattle its characters and readers apart; or perhaps the same quality makes much of the prose poetic enough. A European can take his playwrights to bed with him, but most of the best Japanese theatrical literature is better not separated from its spectacle and dance and cacophonous instrumental accompaniment. Christian or Jew might take his Scripture to bed; the Japanese has spared himself the sanctification of his best old literature. But lives there a literate anywhere who does not take a novel of romance or adventure into his most private apartment?

The Japanese write in a script which is a mixture of the Chinese ideographs[2] and their own syllabary, the former used singly or in combination for the root of a word, with the latter indicating verb ending, adjectival or adverbial suffixes, and the like. Thus the verb "eat" might be written with character "X," so that "eaten" would be X-en, "eating" would be X-ing. To complicate matters, X alone might

---

[2] Simplest being barely stick-figure pictographs evolved from pictures, like a two-legged figure for "man," with his arms outstretched top mean "big" while abstract ideas—thus "ideograph"—are expressed in combinations, like the related series of one woman seated under a roof to mean "safe", with three under same roof for "noise" and two of course mean "trouble".

be read as eat, ate, food, cuisine, solely depending upon context; each ideograph having at least two ways to read it, one Japanese and one distorted Chinese, and often four or five (for Chinese of different eras when various usages of the term were imported—Chinese has but one reading of any ideograph). There are about 45,000 ideographs, but modern Japanese use but a fraction of these. Newspapers and popular magazines limit themselves to fewer than 2,000, expressing more complicated words in the phonetic syllabary. Foreign loan words[3], of which English is said to have provided some 7,000[4], mostly technical, are almost always written in the syllabary. Again, there are two dissimilar syllabaries, with thus two symbols for each syllable: thus a-i-u-e-o, ka-ki-ku-ke-ko, etc., for other consonant-vowel syllables. One of these, *katakana*, is a square-shaped series used today mostly for foreign words as we use italics, or on printed signs much as we would use a square, easy-to-read, Roman lettering. The other, *hiragana*, is a lovely flowing style, preferred by Lady Murasaki and used today for the root endings and native words not written in ideographs. And prior to World War II these two usages were reversed. As complicated as this sounds, it is a generalization and simplification of the actual state of affairs. Even the syllabary has odd readings and exceptions to its rules almost as maddening as English spelling.

The Chinese have been writing in some form for over 4,000 years. The script was developed to about what it is today perhaps 800 years before Christ. Confucius and Lao-Tse used it over 2,500 years ago. This script was introduced into Japan by hired Korean scribes perhaps a few centuries after Christ, but Japanese didn't really catch on to its concept until about the middle of the sixth century AD. And then, as they have done so many times, they exploded into action. The emperor ordered oral legends and annals of the imperial clan, along with some of those of others which did

---

[3] Early in the period of modernization in the late 1800s, both Chinese and Japanese adapted obsolete ideographs to new meanings, thus an old philosophical word *"den"* for a type of mystic dragon power, became the root term for the equally inexplicable "electric-" and *den* plus *wa*, talk, is "telephone". In 1952 when television was introduced there were long and heated debates about what to call it, and academicians favored *den-ga* or *den-ei*, variants on "electric pictures." But they took so long that the public came to use the English word and unable to pronounce either 'l' or 'v' came up with *terebijon*, shortened soon to *terebi* both written in *katakana* as foreign words.

[4] In 1963, perhaps double by 1993, though in the meantime many faddish colloquialisms have also faded.

not conflict too much, to be recorded. Under aegis of Regent-Prince Shotoku, scribes wrote down recitations of tribal memorizers to compose official histories: *Tennoki* (Emperors' Annals) and *Kokki* (National Annals) 620, later maliciously burned [though questionable remnant called *Kujiki* has attracted attention from late 1980s] then recreated from reciters as *Kojiki* (Ancient Annals) 712, and *Nihon Shoki* (Nippon Chronicle) 720, both available in English.

But the Japanese and Chinese languages bear no relation to each other and it was found to be easier to write in Chinese than to attempt to adapt to the highly declined polysyllabic spoken Japanese language the Chinese script evolved for a monosyllabic tongue. An anthology of some 4,500 Japanese poems by 450 different poets, *Manyoshu*, or Myriad Leaves, was compiled and recorded about 760 AD. (A selection of 1,000 were superbly translated and published in Tokyo in 1940 and scholar-poet Yasuda Ken has published other excellent samplings since the Pacific War). *Manyoshu* poems use the sound values of Chinese ideographs to record the sounds of Japanese words, in effect an intricate rebus writing. Imagine an Englishman writing in pictures using fractured French pronunciation: draw an eye, French *oeil*, and here indicating the English word "we," or two eyes, *yeux*, for "you."

Soon two syllabaries were developed by abbreviating certain ideographs beyond recognition and using them to indicate sounds only (much as our own alphabet evolved, "A" being an abbreviated picture of an ox, called in Semitic tongues *Aleph*, etc.). Chinese loan words came into the language along with the writing system, as well as an alternate Chinese way of pronouncing each ideograph. They were used grammatically as Japanese, with verb endings, in Japanese word order, and often with somewhat changed meaning. The script developed a great mystique and few could master it—which pleased the ruling elite. But practical women of the educated class simplified matters, writing in the everyday speech and using the simpler sound characters, or *hiragana* syllabary, almost exclusively. Personal diaries were kept in this way, romantic tales were jotted down, and the literature of fiction was born.

Most early novelists and romantic diarists were women of the educated court class, of whom the greatest was, of course, Murasaki Shikibu, Lady Purple, authoress of *The Tale of Genji*. The 13th to 17th centuries were marked by Mongol invasions and internal wars to which vassal lords brought combat artists and war correspondents to record their valor for posterity and to document their claims for expenses and in event of victory a share of the spoils from their liege lords. A parallel development was the war tale, which became more fictitious as time went on. *The Heike Story* is a modern chop-suey version of one of the greatest of these, and is available in English. The old diary styles continued, now written by men, often sage recluses, as *Hojoki* (Jottings from My Ten-foot-square Hut), of about 1212 AD, and *Tsurezuregusa* (Harvest of Leisure), about 1330—both available in English paperback. At this time noh-drama developed from old folk plays, *kagura* (literally "gods'-entertainment") and Buddhist miracle plays interpreted in Zen style. The best are by a father and son, Kannami and Zeami (active 1370 through 1443). From these, readapted for a merchant and plebeian audience and livened up in a snappy review style, evolved kabuki plays of the 17th and later centuries.

Japan closed herself off from the world in 1637. During the following period the flamboyant kabuki developed (originated as a female dance-review but soon limited to male actors as an anti-prostitution measure); poetry thrived as ever, but mostly limited to those short epigrammatic forms which had predominated in *Manyoshu*. Confucianism was rediscovered with a vengeance, and endless dialectic tracts with commentaries and critiques were turned out (the most important of which monopolize the English-language collection misnamed *Sources of the Japanese Tradition*), as well as popular colloquial Buddhist commentaries. But more important was the boom in books meant just to entertain.

Cheap printing from carved woodblocks had been introduced into Japan along with writing back in the 6th century. First used for re-producing Buddhist sutras, the technique was turned to producing the novels once laboriously hand-scripted. Competition increased as publishers and writers multiplied faster than the newly and rapidly developing plebeian literate class. Prices came down as cheap paperbacks were ground out. To increase sales appeal, illus-trators were hired, color techniques developed, and the ukiyo-e prints, "floating-world pictures", world-famed Japanese woodblock prints, blossomed as a great art in itself. These cheap novels were about the lives of the type of people who read them: gay blades of the city, shrewd merchants, professional women, actors and artists. They are a running commentary on city life of that gaudy Floating World, the *Ukiyo*, as it called itself from a Chinese poem. They are living, poignant, humorous, written in the snappy, slangy speech of the time (sometimes untranslatable even by native Japanese scholars). Best sampling of two of the best writers' works is Howard Hibbett's superb *The Floating World in Japanese Fiction.* These are often short stories which appeared in series, comprising an over-all long novel (shades of our later Dickens). The important aspect of these stories, as relating to our modern Japanese writers, is that these men wrote in concise language, rather than that painfully indirect, abstruse, verbose, erudite style of the dialecticians of "official" literature. From this popular tradition comes the modern Japanese newspaper style, and it almost certainly influences some of the seemingly Western modern writers.

In 1853 Commodore Perry appeared and demanded that Japan end her seclusion. By 1867 she had done so, again with a vengeance. Western literature was translated helter-skelter. The old-style cheap paperbacks went the way of similar booms in the West, getting cheaper and appealing to ever baser tastes. The men of vision and education were now learning Western languages in the new colleges, absorbing Western ways, translating Western literature (and pap), and very consciously affecting Western style in their own writing. But with these many "petty vexations" literature "fell into a decline, growing more melancholy and retiring." Failure of the new ways to produce quick solutions to Japan's problems, along with resurgence of those who wished to transform and readapt the old ways, brought on a clash between liberals with no tradition to bolster them and new samurai with an imported Prussian militarism to graft onto the old traditional warrior roots. The writers, melancholy beyond reprieve, retired. As novelist-critic Takami Jun noted, in a 1963 PEN club talk, Japanese literature of the past fifty years had been "a hermit's literature."

The literary archaeologist-cum-anthologist is prone to reconstruct an evolutionary chart, a family tree, in terms of his own experience. He would build or reconstruct the ruin of a paradise garden in the image of a shard of a willowware plate. He would clutter the world with *chinoiserie,* toast his world in Delft, a technique that is, of course, reciprocated—for exchange is a two-way street. What Western visitor to Japan has not looked with—what . . . a mixture of horror or shock, amusement or trepidation—upon some Japanese attempts at reproducing a specific style of Western building? (I am prejudiced, based on my own Japan experience, having once lived here in a typical example of Japanese campus Ameriquoiserie, a none-such version of Bible-belt barn architecture.)

Any anthropologist knows how dangerous yet essential it is to question a native informant. Ask an aborigine, "Who is your sire?" and he may point to the man who shot his totemic animal about the time his mother got her pains, or he may point to his mother's brother or, just possibly, the gentleman who made a habit of sleeping with mom. His concept of relation, of family, will not necessarily be yours. To the Japanese, spiritual continuity of family name is more important than blood (which may be thicker than water, but ink with which the family records are written is thicker yet). Great art and culture dynasties are maintained not only by childbirth but by adoption. In Kyoto I was introduced to the "family" from which a great lady from an ancient art family had reputedly come. There was no resemblance between daughter and "parent" beyond the superficial similarities of class. I learned later that she had risen from quite low estate through her ability, and had been chosen as a bride (by a family committee) to infuse new blood into the line. To give her a proper ancestry, she was adopted out to a good family in another city (who could use the forthcoming contractual link), then brought back to Kyoto as a "bride from a fine old line." Another time I was admonished by a Japanese friend who was afraid that my interest in a certain noted geisha was too serious and could jeopardize my future aspirations, yet she was his own natural half-sister. (To keep her as a hobby, of course, could have been helpful to such aspirations.)

Literature reflects a culture's soul. It is but one of several media by which culture expresses itself in our phenomenal world. If a literature is to reflect such a seemingly casual, yet ritualized, arbitrariness of approach to the product of sleeping on the floor, how are we to appreciate it from our padded pedestals? Roll off onto the floor and "ask an informant?"

"Japanese artist, from whence comest thou?"

"I am from Kyoto, the Paris of Japan" (or if America-oriented, ". . . Boston of Japan," or ". . . Florence of Japan," and I once heard a Japanese traveler disputing before a Persian guest whether to compare Kyoto with Isfahan or Shiraz). Artists are similarly compared. A Japanese painter hailed as the "van Gogh of Japan" saw his first van Gogh when his public relations manager posed him before one. One of the recent and last, supposedly, ukiyo-e artists of the old school is officially listed as heir to a great dynastic name, implying inheritance of a specific dynastic style. His accession to the title was based on convenience; he had not studied with any predecessor and in fact worked for the most part in Occidental watercolors, in Occidental proportion and perspective—and could not even claim to have been influenced by any of the French impressionists whom his own dynastic forebears had influenced. Work of another present-day Japanese painter, disciple of Matisse, bore no resemblance to that of his master except in the coloration and that, in truth, was the only aspect of his art heritage he had retained. Coincidentally, he used the same beautiful Japanese model.

Among Japanese writers, one drew acclaim from his American publisher: "Proust, a Japanese Proust . . . ." And when asked what he thought of Proust, replied, "Who?" Writing with a thrift and conciseness which critics attributed to the influence of Hemingway, another newcomer was in fact only reacting against the verbosity of an expatriate American professor of literature.

The attempt to cross catalogue the influences of writer upon writer has little importance outside of keeping the literary archaeologist busy. For the important influences to be brought to light perhaps a psychoanalyst might be of help. From the artist's point of view (not the archaeologist's) there are two types of influence. The artist may copy or emulate the form of another and adapt his techniques, but in dealing with translations we might well ask who it is that the translator would emulate. The influence which reaches deeper, and which may leave no telltale mound or even slightest carbon-14 trace, is that influence which most inspires. And this may just as easily be another art medium as a place or a person. But within his own medium a writer might be greatly influenced, say, by Faulkner's post-Nobel Kyoto lecture on the success of failure and his idea—how very Oriental—of the inevitability of imperfection,[5] and yet not be able to stomach Faulkner's writings. One might be inspired, say, by Selden Rodman's poetic biography of Lawrence of Arabia and strive to do what Rodman did—something comparable though not necessarily in the same form or style. Influences that count are those which contribute towards getting the "juice" (as

---

[5]*The Nobility of Failure* (USIS Kyoto lecture by William Faulkner, used as title for anthology of "Tragic Heroes in the History of Japan" by Ivan Morris in 1975.

Hemingway called it, perhaps that *ch'i* of Chinese art, philosophy and combat, or *ki* in Japan) to flow. It may be other writers (a translator from the Chinese whom I know uses Erle Stanley Gardner), it may be a bottle (we all know so many), it may be a painting, a joint, a pipe, a needle, sharpening pencils, walking up a mountain, esoteric shadow boxing, dance drills, or the pressure of due bills. Any sort of personal mandala will do just so long as it gets the head (or gut) spinning and produces detachment and associations for freeing the juice. The really important influence may be rather the vector or nature of the action—active, meditative, monochrome, polychrome, uphill, pointed, circular, shadowy, real. To truly plumb the effective influence would, I repeat, take psychoanalysis and a dissection thrown in. Any understanding this would give us of the artist or his art would not resemble that which he had hoped to convey and would be of as much use to us as his dead and dissected corpse, or the bleached skull on a psychiatrist's desk.

And you question again, perhaps angrily, perhaps justly so, "How are we to appreciate it from our padded pedestal?" Just by looking at it and trying to appreciate it for what it is, or what it has pretensions of being, with no preconceived notions, no mental forewords. (One should never read a foreword or an introduction till one has finished the body of the book.) The why and the how and the wherefore of it all is far less important. It is enough that these writers wrote when they did of what they did.

Turning again to Lady Murasaki, one is, with her, still "amazed at the advances which this art of fiction is now making," as Prince Genji exclaimed. "How do you suppose that our new writers come by this talent? It used to be thought that the authors of successful romances were merely particularly untruthful people whose imaginations had been stimulated by constantly inventing plausible lies. But that is clearly unfair. . . ."

"Perhaps," his companion answered, "only people who are themselves much occupied in practicing deception have the habit of thus dipping below the surface. I can assure you that for my part, when I read a story, I always accept it as an account of something that has really and actually happened."

Genji continued, "So you see, as a matter of fact I think far better of this art than I have led you to suppose. Even its practical value is immense. Without it what should we know of how people lived in the past . . .? For history books . . . show us only one small corner of life; whereas these diaries and romances which I see piled around you contain, I am sure, the most minute information about all sorts of people's private affairs . . . . But I have a theory of my own . . . this art . . . does not simply consist in the author's telling a story about the adventures of some other person. On the contrary, it happens because the storyteller's own experience of men and things, whether for good or ill—not only what he has passed through himself, but even events which he has only witnessed or been told of—has moved him to an emotion so passionate that he can no longer keep it shut up in his heart. Again and again something in his own life or in that around him will seem to the writer so important that he cannot bear to let it pass into oblivion. There must never come a time, he feels, when men do not know about it."

Writing 950 years later in *Preview*, shortly after we had initiated the *Ukiyo* project, critic Mukai Hiroo noted: "The Japanese short story or novel can be a window through which the West may see Japan as it is. Though vicarious, the picture thus seen should be more true, poignant and intimate than the result of any fleeting visit to the country." Yet though this should be so, the picture presented is somehow superficial: as Takami Jun has said, Japan's was a hermit's literature for half a century.

The sudden surge towards Westernization began officially in 1867. A few short pieces in the old popular paperback style successfully dealt with the new modes—such as *The Beefeater* and *The Western Peep Show*, available in several translations. The new, even cheaper lead-type printing and the expanding literacy set off a deluge of pulp writing. The first Western-style success, which dates the official beginning of the new literature, was the novel *Ukigumo* (Floating Clouds), 1888. This followed close on the heels of *The Essence of the Novel* (the term used is the broader *sho-setsu*), 1885, a critical work which became the bible of writers for decades. *Essence* denounced the moralizing that had been the moving force behind fiction with any pretensions and called for æsthetic realism. Discovery of the West permitted Japanese artists to rediscover humanity. At about the same time many writers, pioneered by Mori Ogai, rediscovered the Self under the initial impetus of the German *Ich Roman*, "I Novel." But the development was singularly Japanese, with moral dialectics rejected with, again, such a vengeance that the naturalists became uncritical reporters: there were no crusaders. The *Ich Roman* turns more introspective in the extreme tradition of the ancient hermit notebooks, a fixation with one's own petty experiences and idle thoughts. Whereas the old hermit notebooks had been meditations on life viewed with detachment, the Japanese I Novel became the product of navel-gazers, auto-voyeurs, who had forgotten why they were meditating. This was the main current of prewar Japanese literature, the most singularly Japanese, a natural product of the Thought Police State which developed, but also a great accessory to political development.

Japanese military victories against China and Russia at the turn of the century watered seeds of hope and encouraged the rise of a generation of Romantics. There was an Aesthetic School, first given impetus by Oscar Wilde, Maeterlinck, Baudelaire, which was divorced from social problems, yet less decadent or hedonistic than the European *fin de siècle* writers. Natsume Soseki, a writer of Chinese poems and student of English literature, returned from England with a British style of minimizing problems, with aloofness from privation the essence of his Leisure School. But the aloofness became confused by others with escapism. Natsume alone succeeded as the proverbial objective outsider, the man with the knowledge of experience used with the objectivity of detachment, and he wrote excellent satire (*I Am a Cat*) and penetrating analyses. A third romantic group exerted perhaps the greatest influence of any single band: the *Shirakaba-ha*, or White Birch School. This had a school tie origin, consisting mostly of graduates of the Peers School, Gakushuin. Their birthright entitled them to freedoms undreamed of by most other Japanese. They were idealists in the grand aristocratic tradition and they still maintain a faithful following among present-day "progressive" collegians for their fervor for human individuality and their concept of a humanity that transcends national and social categories. They are responsible for introducing much of the best of Western literature and art of the period.

Japanese literature of the generation that ended with the Great Earthquake of 1923 is dominated by this conflict between naturalists and romantic-idealists. But the situation of Japan and the world after World War I was intensely aggravated by the depression and further in Japan by the earthquake. The naturalists had tried to digest too much from the West and had turned into mere imitators. It was not enough just to record. Romanticism was fatally dampened by hunger pangs. A new confrontation developed: that of

Proletarian Writers versus Nationalists. It is a characteristic of Japan that foreign artists like Walt Whitman and Romain Rolland could be claimed as seminal influences for both the *fin de siècle* æsthetes and the later proto-communists.

The breakdown of feudalism had provided the original impetus for the Proletarian Writers, but the end of World War I brought them to the fore. Within a short time they virtually monopolized the entire generation of artists. It was during this period that most of the professional writers represented in this collection arose. (Biographical sketches of all contributors appear at the end of this volume.) Our selection is fairly representative of this conflict, though it was not consciously so planned. In brief, as in most of the industrialized nations, the various anarchist, socialist, and communist revolutionary ideas seized the imaginations of intellectuals. Marxists soon took the lead, but other factions maintained sufficient strength to prevent them from taking control. The great depression brought the Nationalists to power and Japan started on her overseas "experiment." Successes of the semi-autonomous overseas army strengthened militarism at home. Nationalism became the New Romanticism as old classics were disinterred for new worship, and often republished in heavily edited form. The Nationalists won out, not by greater literary showing, but by government control. Some of the better writers were caught in the middle, opposing both extremes. Most of those who published at all, and stayed out of jail, followed that old well-blazed path into personal hermitages. Strongest opposition was simply to withdraw from writing. Others engaged in a harmless literature of decadence. Still others hacked out inane war pulp, descriptions of battles, evidencing neither perspiration nor inspiration.

The end of the war in 1945 brought freedoms such as even the select White Birchers had not enjoyed, only this time for everyone. The American Occupation exerted control over the press, but left the fictioneers to do as they wished. The hordes of political prisoners released from jail included writers who had been arrested for harboring suspicious thoughts (one writer had been hauled off on account of "dangerous thoughts evidenced by his facial expression" when an official car drove by, whereas in fact he had never noticed it; he was just annoyed that his wife was keeping him waiting). The hermitages had been bombed out, the hermits forced out into the remains of the world. Japanese literature started from scratch after

1945, but the writers were for the most part older men and women; a whole generation had been lost to literature.

The *Bibliography of Showa Literature* 'from 1926 to the present,' published in 1959, fourteen years after the war, listed approximately 750 authors alive at the end of the war, of whom those 30 years of age or less (under 44 at time of publication) numbered a mere 39.

The three stylistic groupings of postwar literature are the old "I Novel"; the Fiction of Manners, another old school but one that did not attain fame until now; and the *après guerre*. The division is not clear-cut. An author may be categorized by his own personal preference or by a slight predominance of one quality. The I-Novelist draws only upon the shaving-mirror-reality of his own life for material. In the Fiction of Manners the author goes outside himself, dealing with events of everyday life, somewhat like American post-depression writers dealing with similar problems. The *apres guerre* writers return to the individual and the suffering of man caused by the gap between himself and social conditions. But the "I Novel" is little more than a well-turned diary, belonging more to the ancient diary tradition than to anything Western. The Fiction of Manners is of the stuff of the old picture scrolls, and rarely attains anything more than vignettes, and these are so much centered on one individual as to be as self-centered as the "I Novel." The *après guerre* rebel employs his version of Joycean stream-of-consciousness technique, Freudian psychoanalysis, illusion (when less successful, mere delusion), and a return to the interior monologue of the medieval hermit tracts, all exaggerated, preciously oversensitive.

It is all best described by Edward Seidensticker as "the posings of the autobiographers . . . seldom is an idea allowed to trouble the works." It lacks the depth the Westerner expects of literature, just as the Japanese lack, as William Lederer points out, the ability to take (I would prefer "the concept of taking") a moral stand. There is emotional journalism of apology or complaint, but little literature (or graphic art) of such grand-scale tragedies as Nanking or Hiroshima (which latter declined to establish sister-city relations with either Nanking or Dachau), or of the personal tragedy of the Kamikaze suicide troops, or the fate of an intellectual in a totalitarian society. Nakajima Kenzo points out that "the writers are afraid less of war itself than of the political repression which it brings," a fear that has become almost a conditioned reflex and which is as prevalent today as ever. This creates even in the "progressives" a nostalgia for the ancient national isolation from the world. But they have been thoroughly infected by the outside world and can never again successfully withdraw.

Modern Japanese literature was born of this mating of West with East. The seminal influences of the vigorous Occident cannot be underrated. The pioneers (and, as elsewhere, it seems that the great art was a product of beginning) like Mori Ogai and Natsume Soseki were thoroughly acquainted with the best of the West in the original. They were also equally at home in the classics of Japan and China.) All these professionals are widely read in Western literature, whether they reject it or acclaim it. More important, the part played by translation into Japanese must be considered. A surprising number of professional writers are products of university departments of foreign literature (as are a great number of the journalists from whom the more recent "City News Room" school of shock literature has come), but this may only provide a gloss. Of the twenty authors interviewed "in depth" in Nakano Yoshio's *Writers of Today,* almost all admit to having been first awakened to literature by some translation from the West. Even those earliest attackers of "West worship," Kitamura Takubu and Ishikawa Takuboku, were not traditionalists harking back to the old isolation, but modernists demanding absorption of the usable and creation of something new and native. Of the modern greats, Kawabata Yasunari may be rare in that he was never "intoxicated by the West," was from his earliest conscious days fond of Japanese classics, but he is well acquainted with Occidental letters and makes good use of what his genius finds nourishing.

One still perceives subtle shadows of Genji amidst Western ferroconcrete and traffic jams. Characteristic of classical Japanese literature is *mono no aware,* considered an "untranslatable term" but approximately explainable as the sighing acknowledgment of the "Ahness of it all," of an awareness of the inherent sorrow of things, appreciation of the implications of the moment of parting or of the fall of a leaf: but always applied to some moment or some outside object which might reflect a sparkle of enlightenment. At the hands of self-centered romantics in their hermitages it became soft-sell melodramatic mournful awareness of imagined futility of everything; any moment, and so all time, lost all power of projecting any implications. Now it is commonly evident only when the reader becomes aware of a moaning from the author: the cry of one drowning in the implications of the sinking of the old Floating World. This is not sarcastic criticism but simple recognition of the state of the intellectual as mirrored in professional literature of Japan. It is a technique the Occidental author might well adapt. It is one that our boy in the mountain school and our dying Hiroshima housewife use with delicacy, effectively, because as unpoluted amateurs they are still capable of experiencing. In spite of the physical similarity to the West, of imitative styles and literary fads, of simulating the way of life of the characters, the reader of modern Japanese literature will, as Mukai Hiroo puts it, "find exoticism in the thought processes which the stories describe or reflect, will become aware of the Japanese mind's dislike of scientific and analytical methods, the lack of objectivity, the predominance of emotion . . ." (which I would prefer to call sentimentality) ". . . over reason, the tendency to look inward . . ." (if with little of the Western novelist's inner searching or insight), ". . . rather than outward, and the quest for beauty in simplicity."

This "quest for beauty in simplicity" may materialize in a tendency to merely oversimplify, or even result in simple ambiguity. (There was difficulty getting the ending of the translation of Mishima Yukio's story right, if not clear, and while our present ending satisfied neither translators nor author, who, fluent in English himself could offer no better, we all accepted it as printed here). Japanese critics complain that translations of Japanese literature into English "make the meaning too clear." (However, letters to the editors of Japan's English newspapers constantly complain of the ever-present ambiguity). Other Japanese critics think that the literature, even the most avant-garde, is so rooted in traditional manners peculiar to Japan that it has been unable to rise above provincialism and has not produced independent works of art endowed with the universal appeal of kabuki or noh. Some feel that this rooting in peculiar mores makes it incomprehensible to anyone not already well versed in Japanese customs and history. [Subsequently, during the 1980s, this rationale was used by Japanese to claim exception from international norms, even immunity from accepted conduct not unlike more extreme apologists prewar].

The Western critic had not [until the 1980s rise of a new, if perhaps not improved, breed of foreign Japan expert] been so exclusive or pessimistic: *The Pacific Spectator* feels that "Japan has the most prolific publishing business in the world"; Dr. Donald Keene, that

".. . their literary output is among the worlds best." I feel that regardless of volume or quality, what Prince Genji said a thousand years ago is still true, that Japanese history, any history, must remain incomprehensible to anyone who does not flesh out the bones of historical outlines with the living tissue of literature.

Stories have been selected for this volume which fill in a section of the picture scroll of the Floating World of Japan during that drifting decade after the end of what Japanese call the "Pacific War." As editor of *View*, a *Life*-style monthly pictorial published in Tokyo (first Japan-published English magazine to attain 10,000 paid circulation), I had initiated a series of photo-and-text reports on typical, ordinary people—office girls, police patrolmen—usual city-desk feature stuff, but in a broad context, with an over-all book in mind. All of my associates were Japanese, yet the stories lacked veracity. We hunted through vernacular Japanese magazines to see how they handled similar situations. I was no more satisfied.

Then I rediscovered the *Genji Monogatari* dialogue on the essence of the novel which some graduate-school lecturer had referred to in passing and which I had jotted in shorthand in my notes. Perhaps oddly, the lecturer was Egyptian, noted Arab literateur, translator, and political exile, Ahmed Zaky Abushady, my professor of Arabic and modern Islamic thought at The Asia Institute in New York, who managed to instill in his students a sympathetic understanding, almost empathy, for the recent history of the Middle East through a selection of literature. There was also a book by another of my old profs recounting the history of early Islam through translations from ancient Arabic literature, records and religious tracts. It was also my good fortune that advisory editor to *View* at that time was Charles Cooke, multiple-O.Henry Award short-story writer and former *New Yorker* staffer, whose unselfish advice was invaluable. The staff was put to work scouting suitable material, and out of this my principal collaborators emerged: Grace Suzuki and Momoi Makoto. In May 1952 I took over simultaneous editorship of sister magazine *Preview* and the first test stories appeared in its pages. When I left the company and formed my own *Orient Digests* (soon to become first Japan-published English magazine to attain 20,000 paid circulation), by common consent the project moved with me. Several stories appeared in this magazine. Japan PEN Club gave a lunch to discuss our planned book, lent their generous cooperation, and eleven stories were published by Orient-Asia Grafix in book form for Japan-Korea circulation under this same title, *Ukiyo*, ten of which were reprinted in 1963, but all here.

We made no attempt to represent literary trends or representative writers. Indeed, at about the same time PEN Club had been called upon to nominate writers and stories for a UNESCO anthology, of which *Modern Japanese Short Stories* edited by Ivan Morris, is the product—[in a review of which we were referred to obliquely in stating that this UNESCO-backed book was not simply another "sociological" anthology but a truly "literary" one].

The first thin Orient edition of *Ukiyo* presented a picture of Japan that was far from complete, but the omissions were not ours —they were a product of the hermit tradition and the "posings of the autobiographers." No Japanese novelists had been leading militarists, nor had any writers yet risen out of the ranks of war children. Nor, did it seem, was any "autobiographer" going to sit down and do a deep character analysis of another person (a non-Oriental approach in any event), especially a former persecutor, in order to write a biographical novel.

Many of the short stories and excerpts from novels in this collection are barely disguised autobiography. They are fiction only in technique, and certainly far less fictitious than much avowedly factual memoirs. At *Preview* I had been in charge of another project: editing and rewriting ex-Colonel Tsuji Masanobu's *Underground Escape* and convicted war criminal Kodama Yoshio's *I Was Defeated* reminiscences of the war and its immediate aftermath. These had appeared earlier in garbled but nonetheless valuable translations. Alas, my new editions (from which this selection comes) were never issued. At *Orient Digests*, intending to show the Japanese view of the war, Momoi and I continued to express this idea by translating and publishing selections of this military nonfiction, which was at the time the most popular product of the Japanese magazine industry. From this project comes the Admiral Yokoi selection. [Momoi has since continued his writing on World War II, becoming a respected expert on military affairs].

Added since, to fill some still-felt lacunae, have been the amateur diaries, which today are still as much a part of the literature as they were in Genji's time.

Jay Gluck, Wakayama University, May 8, 1963

* Footnotes added 1993, as also minor text bracketed [-].

PREFACE TO THE 1993 EDITION

CRITICAL EXCEPTION has been taken to my use of the title *Ukiyo*, maintaining (not entirely incorrectly) that this term refers historically to the age of the *Ukiyo-e* "floating world pictures," for the most part (but not exclusively) woodblock prints, especially the flamboyant early 17th century.

This, too, was a period of postwar confusion—the wars that united the nation and established the Tokugawa clan as ruling shoguns in the new capital of Edo, now Tokyo—and it appeared to me much like that of the late 1940s through 1950s, characterized by a similar search for pleasure and new æsthetic and new standards. Our favorite theater critic and specialist in the flamboyant kabuki theater of that earlier era, Saisho Foumy, also refers to our period as "Ukiyo" in her 1954 short story "The Date." In both this classical kabuki and the cinema of the 1950s, heroes and heroines were of the *demi-monde*—gamblers, gangsters and professional beauties.

From Xmas Eve 1951 on I was adrift in this "Floating World." The final half year of U.S. Occupation I was one of only four foreigners in Kyoto to whom its ancient geisha areas were not off limits by Occupation edict, perhaps the only one who could take advantage. I lived at the pinnacle of Japanese æsthetic as house guest of tea master Sen Hounsai, former *kamikaze* pilot and now arbiter par excellence of the arts. I 'played,' as the Japanese say, in the Geisha quarters of Gion and Pontocho, drank in such as Ichiriki-chaya, 'teahouse' where the leader of the 47 ronin of the kabuki play *Chushingura* centuries ago in Ukiyo-I bandied.

And from there it was all downhill.

I moved to Tokyo the day before the great 1952 May Day Riot on the Imperial Palace Plaza—referred to in 'The Only One' and 'These Ten Years' and central event in 'The Communist.' I witnessed it firsthand as sole Caucasian on the "action" side of the police lines. In brief, it was the most beautifully choreographed tribal event I ever witnessed, and I still think back occasionally in begrudging admiration of the way it was all handled. Student dupes, like Izuta of our story, were 'managed' by pros of mysterious origin who through them kept the student mobs tightly pressed together in squads of about eight, shoulder to shoulder grasping a horizontal bamboo pole and jogging, knees high, sometimes in place, sometimes surging forth or being backed up—seemingly chaotic senseless —chanting "*washoi-washoi*," the meaningless cadence call adapted from hyperactive traditional shrine festivals. The foot stamping acted like goose-step marching, shocking the brain base, numbing brain function—robotizing. A sensual rhythm built up, the mob took on a life of its own like a great, writhing dragon. The leaders urged the numerous 'Izutas' on, praising them and raising them to leadership rank, maneuvered the mob to aim it at the police lines. Then they released it from its tightly controlled snake dance and, as in our story, the dragon surged forth.

Controller-cadres then quickly but unobtrusively slipped to the rear, removing their headbands and armbands of rank to dissolve into the mass of onlookers.

Many dupe-leaders like Izuta were rounded up by riot police— who had calmly held their ground unarmed, without the helmets and shields common today. Some 'student leaders' were still on trial in the 1970s, one generation later, their lives ruined. No real leaders were caught. Luckier kids like Ino drifted into anonymity and invented ploys like the one in the story, worked as free-lance agents like the good lone-wolf social and economic pirates they were—survivors—to become the engine of Japan's entrepreneurial 'miracle.' Were a sequel to 'The Communist' to be written today, it would probably see Ino running a successful international trading company, having hired his friend Izuta, both thriving bourgeoisie.

I drank "proletarian" *shochu* in dingy bars with *yakuza* and undercover police of the Second Section investigating foreigners, who once asked me if on that day I had seen a "mysterious Russian" circulating in the crowd. They described him. I filled in details—his crinkled red shirt, floppy blond hair, three-day stubble.

"Then you know him?"

"I guess so," I smiled and made the Japanese motion of pointing my forefinger and placing it on my nose, "*Boku-da*—me!"

I hobknobbed with Kodama-linked godfathers and their courtiers and diplomat buddies at night clubs. I wrote and cartooned for two English dailies and several Japanese periodicals—on one occasion my satirical column in *Asian Weekly* so annoyed the mob that I had to go into hiding in a different gang's red light district. I edited local magazines, in which the first of these stories appeared, then published-edited *Orient Digests*, and *Anoné*, pioneer entertainment magazine, meanwhile collecting rejects from America. I became involved in a long civil libel suit to clear my name, and my old drinking buddies of the Second Section proved their honor and testified on my behalf, assuring my final court victory.

My Nisei girl friend had come from New York to Japan on her Junior Year Abroad and stayed to co-edit *Anoné*—we married and moved to her ancestral farming village on the then-pristine Inland Sea near Hiroshima for a two-year writing-honeymoon. Our village mayor was the noted British-knighted scholar whose book on Central Asian Christians I had used in graduate school and to whom this volume is dedicated.

Wife pregnant, bank empty, we moved on to teach at radical Wakayama National University for over seven "fascinatingly-turbulent" years. Here I taught many the likes of Izuta and Ino, and like Taro of 'One World' and even a tattered few like Eguchi of 'Echoes from a Mountain School'—hungry, angry, confused, but basically apolitical and out for revenge against the situation they had been born into. During a 1958 reading class in *The New York Times International Edition* about the headlined Hungarian Revolution, they questioned how Americans could call this a "revolution" when it was against the "true Revolution." I asked one student to define revolution. His face went expressionless as he stood to attention—as students never did in my American-style classes—and recited by rote, "There are three revolutions: the American and French revolutions which were bloody uprisings of the bourgeoisie, and the Russian Revolution which was a peaceful revolution of the Proletariat." In the discussion that followed they were almost unanimous, they said, that "No, we do not believe this, that it was just what they were taught in high school," as well as in asserting that whatever 'history' happened before they were born was irrelevant, that history for them was limited to what they had experienced firsthand. Their fathers had advised them not to make the same mistakes they had, but offered no further positive guidance.

Several of these students went on eventually to manage overseas branches of major Japanese trading companies in America, Europe, Southeast Asia and Iran. They visit me, or I see these old men when I am abroad. It was seven years of fun and challenge. I resigned when the college president who had hired me, who taught Esthetics and Philosophy, was succeeded by a professor of French Law who could not speak French and who, with even less English, argued the fine points of language in contracts written in pidgin in a country where contracts take poor second place to personal relations and 'understanding'. And the students weren't any fun any more, I wasn't learning anything from them and so must not have been teaching them anything. Also, my two sons were growing up and my entire Education Ministry salary would not be enough to pay one tuition at the international school. I returned to the business world of publishing and art.

Thus, as one who, like Foumy, lived through it and experienced it personally in the trenches, so to speak, I make no apologies for my use of the term *Ukiyo*, then or now.

Jay Gluck
Ashiya, Japan
May 8, 1993

NOTES: All fully Japanese names appear in the Japanese manner (as in common with Chinese and Korean): family name first, personal name last. All vowels are pronounced as in Italian (b*a*r, b*i*t, bl*u*e, b*e*d, s*o*), but diacritical marks to indicate long vowels have been eliminated (two vowels together are pronounced separately—Ooka = O'oka), *g* always hard, *j* as in English, no syllable accented.

IMPERIAL RESCRIPT

H.I.M. Hirohito (Showa)

TO OUR GOOD AND LOYAL SUBJECTS:

After pondering deeply the general trend of the world and the actual conditions obtaining in Our Empire today, We have decided to effect a settlement of the present situation by resorting to an extraordinary measure.

We have ordered Our Government to inform the Governments of the United States, Great Britain, China and the Soviet Union that Our Empire accepts the provisions of their Joint Declaration.

To strive for the common prosperity and happiness of all nations as well as the security and well-being of Our subjects is the solemn obligation which has been handed down by Our Imperial Ancestors, and which We lay close to Our heart. Indeed, We declared war on America and Britain out of Our sincere desire to ensure the self-preservation of Japan and the stabilization of East Asia, it being far from Our thought either to infringe upon the sovereignty of other nations or to embark upon territorial aggrandizement. But now the war has lasted for nearly four years. Despite the best that

I

has been done by everyone—the gallant fighting of the military and naval forces, the diligence and assiduity of Our servants of the State and the devoted service of Our one hundred million people—the military situation has developed to Japan's disadvantage, while the general trends of the world have all turned against her interest. Moreover, the enemy has begun to employ a new and most cruel bomb, the power of which to do damage is indeed incalculable, and which has already taken many innocent lives. Should We continue to fight, it not only would result in an ultimate collapse and obliteration of the Japanese nation, but would also lead to the total extinction of human civilization. Such being the case, how are We to save the millions of Our subjects; or to atone for Our actions before the hallowed spirits of Our Imperial Ancestors? This is the reason why We have ordered the acceptance of the provisions of the Joint Declaration of the Powers.

We cannot but express the deepest sense of regret to our Allied nations of East Asia, who have consistently cooperated with the Empire towards the emancipation of East Asia. The thought of those officers and men as well as others who have fallen in the fields of battle, those who died at their posts of duty, or those who met with untimely death and all their bereaved families, pains Our heart night and day. The welfare of the wounded and the suffering, and of those who have lost their homes and livelihood, are the objects of Our profound solicitude. The hardships and suffering to which Our nation is to be subjected hereafter will certainly be great. We are keenly aware of the innermost feelings of all ye, Our subjects. However, it is according to the dictate of time and fate that We have resolved to pave the way for a grand peace for all the generations to come by enduring the unendurable and suffering what is insufferable.

Having been able to safeguard and maintain the structure of the Imperial State, We are always with ye, Our good and loyal subjects, relying upon your sincerity and integrity. Beware most strictly of any outbursts of emotion which may engender needless complication, or any fraternal contention and strife which may create confusion, lead ye astray, and cause ye to lose the confidence of the world. Let the entire nation continue as one family from generation to generation, ever firm in its faith of the imperishability of its divine land, and mindful of its heavy burden of responsibilities, and the long road before it. Devote all your strength to the construction of the future. Cultivate the ways of rectitude; foster nobility of spirit, and work with resolution so as ye may enhance the innate glory of the Imperial State and keep pace with the progress of the world.

(*Imperial Sign Manual*)
(*Imperial Seal*)

The 14th day of the 8th month
of the 20th (reign-) year of Showa*

—*translation as published in* The Nippon Times, *August 15, 1945*

* Reigned 1926-1989 as Hirohito; present emperor Akihito reign era is Heisei, 1989 – , (thus 1993 = Heisei 5th year; final year of old reign and first year of successor are same Western calendrical year).

THREE UNFORGETTABLE LETTERS

by Taguchi Shu

ON DECEMBER 7, 1941, when the report was flashed over the air that Japan had made a sudden attack on Pearl Harbor, I was engaging in jovial conversation with intimate American friends in my apartment in New York City. The report came like a bolt from the blue and suddenly made these dear friends enemies and me an enemy of theirs and I could not grasp the fantastic idea at all. Rather the fateful war that had then been set into motion appeared to me like an affair involving entirely distant worlds, with no relation to me.

A short time afterward I was placed under detention at Ellis Island. Whether the war between my country and America had ever occurred to me as an actuality or not, when at last I found myself incarcerated, it dawned upon me like a blast of icy wind that my status now was that of an enemy national. With this realization, I was overcome by indescribable feelings of loneliness, insecurity and despair.

There at Ellis Island more than two hundred of my fellow countrymen were detained with me. Each had his own world of worries, but over all there hovered demoralizing insecurity. As for me, isolated as I was from the outer world, it was wretchedness itself to gaze out of windows covered with meshed steel wires from morning to night, to see before my very eyes the massive and towering figure of Manhattan in whose galittering streets I had spent so many pleasurable moments. More than by a feeling of uncertainty and

4

hopelessness, I was crushed by the reality of my unhappy isolation from the world I loved so dearly.

It was at such a time that a letter came—a letter that gave me heart and made my feelings soar:

My Dear Shu:

After some time and effort, I have at last ascertained that it is not illegal to write letters to an enemy national and I now hasten to write this. My purpose of course is to try to give you whatever spiritual comfort I can, for your sudden change of environment and the sudden shock may have thrown you into an abyss of despair and also to show you that your American friends are not merely fair-weather friends. Friendship should not be a relationship maintained only in fair weather. People need an umbrella only when it rains. If friendship means merely going on picnics or to the movies together, the word "friend" is just a word and no more. And If anybody needed a friend now, you need one the most. Even if the whole world should become one's enemy and one is overcome with discouragement and despair, I know by experience that the mere knowledge that one has a friend— even only one—whose heart is true, supplies one with strength, courage and hope.

I believe without one iota of doubt that the censor who will check this letter and the Americans who surround you daily are people who have the right concept and consciousness of human equality, justice and freedom, and are people who will not look upon the individual with prejudice. It is because of this that I believe they will not prevent a letter written with a sincere motive from reaching you.

From the very first, I have never considered it irregular or unlawful for one to entertain friendly affections for another even if their respective countries are at war with each other. The ability to draw a clear line of distinction between individual sentiments and racial prejudice and national movements—that is the virtue and wisdom of American democracy. I have never, ever, doubted this fact.

I have so little spare time now. Even if I were at complete liberty to write to you, my conscience does not permit me to use the office typewriter during office hours.... It is a joy to know and to feel that by many small efforts I am contributing in some way to the cause of my country. Such being the case, I do not have much time. It is one's human obligation to write letters and to comfort a friend in unhappy circumstances.

For me, there is no greater joy than to write to you. And my conscience is clear. To enjoy life and help others to enjoy it without harming anyone—herein lies the whole of morality. These words which I read in some book at some time and left a deep impression on me have just occurred to me. If this humble letter of mine could give you some comfort and encouragement, nothing would bring me greater joy.

There are moments when a person feels utterly powerless. Especially now in a world which moves with such force as to be beyond our power to resist. It is difficult to foresee one's fate. But please do not ever lose hope. When one discovers how powerless he is in the environment in which he lives, it is said that he becomes truly aware of the meaning of Truth. It is seldom that those of us who are apt to be bewildered by social phenomena in our ordinary, everyday life are favored with such opportunities for meditation.

If we think of your present circumstances in such a light, we can say that you are not wasting time. Do not be disheartened and please continue to keep your spirits high and your courage unconquerable. It is my fervent prayer that you will have all the happiness possible under the present conditions.

Your American friend,

X–

Thereafter, during a long period of detention, I received several such letters from the same writer, full of friendly affection and inspiration. I need not say how these letters encouraged, taught and enriched my daily life.

After seven months of life under detention at Ellis Island, in Virginia and finally in West Virginia, arrangements were completed for our repatriation.

Those who had families in Japan and felt concern for them were overjoyed. But I was saddened by the thought that my repatriation would mean that these letters which had been the pillars of my strength might cease coming to me—forever. The departure of the repatriation ship was probably kept secret, for it was never reported in the papers. And so it pained me to think that my friend, not knowing that I had left, would keep on writing to me only to get letters back undelivered.

The time for embarkation came—a hot day in June. Across Manhattan on the New Jersey side was the Swedish liner, the *Gripsholm*, which was to take us as far as Lourenço Marques, Mozambique, in southern Africa. We boarded her on June 11, many of my fellow countrymen breathing a deep sigh as they looked at towering Manhattan for what might be the last time. Reluctant to leave the country where they had been born and brought up, the only one they knew, many of the teen-agers had tears in their eyes as they trod up the gangplank.

After the baggage inspection, I was escorted by a steward to my stateroom. No sooner had I entered it than a pink-faced, jovial man came in. He was the purser. "You're Mr. Taguchi, aren't you?" he asked. "Have you seen the letter under the pillow? I'm sorry, but because of censorship regulations we had to see it before you. You're a very fortunate man, I can tell you, to have such a good friend."

I immediately rushed to my cot, lifted the pillow and picked up the letter. It said:

My Dear Shu:

In the hope that this note will be delivered to you through the kindness of the purser, I am taking this opportunity to send you a few words of farewell. Now that you are about to leave for your country, I want you to go with the knowledge that your friends in America are ceaselessly praying for your happiness and our reunion, which we hope will not be too far away.

When you return to your country, a new life and a completely different environment will no doubt meet you. My present concern is that the thought conveyed to you through my letters might bring or cause you unhappiness and I fervently pray that my fears are unfounded. Until the day this sad and awful war ends, I intend to devote my heart and soul to the cause of my country. But I will continue to pray from the bottom of my heart for your happiness. When this war has ended and when mankind may again enjoy the blessings of peace and freedom, we shall be able to resume our friendship.

Whatever fate may unfold, I assure you that you will always be in my heart. Remember always, please, that your friendship and your trust have greatly enriched my life and my thoughts.

May God bless you and keep you until the day we meet again. I shall live for the day when I hear from you again.

Your American friend,

X–

For a while I stood still. My eyes felt very warm. How could this letter come to me when the sailing of the *Gripsholm* had not been made public? Probably it was here that my friend demonstrated his great intelligence, ingenuity and effort. Often the need to develop one's mind to the maximum, if it is to be useful at all, had been a subject of X's conversation.

Four years passed like a dream.

As a newsreel war correspondent, I had a busy, restless life. Lugging a camera, I went from one war theater to another—to Rabaul, which was under relentless air attacks all the while I was there, to Singapore, to Java, to the Philippines. My last two years at the war front were spent in the Philippines, where I tasted, as combat cameraman, the bitter hardships and tragedies of defeat. The sufferings I had to undergo were indescribable. Completely surrounded in the mountains of northern Luzon, subjected to daily torrents of bombs from the air, severe shelling from the ground, the situation of the army was hopeless. All avenues of escape were closed. Food supplies hardly existed. Sickness and starvation were taking a fearful toll. The dead and the dying were all around me. The living were too emaciated, too weak, even to look after themselves. I lost hope—how often I cannot say.

In these moments of despair, there was something that gave me the will and the desire to survive. It was the indelible memory of friendship, the warm sentiments which overflowed in the letters I received from my friend. Even in the chaos that followed the successive defeats, when morale was very low and the sense of human values had all but disappeared, when hopelessness and despair gripped the lives of the men around me, I did not lose myself. Those unforgettable letters sustained me. Though the whole world may seem to be blacked out and everyone appears to be an enemy, the mere knowledge that one has a true friend makes him feel that there are millions pulling for him.

In June, 1946, after nearly a year in a prisoner-of-war camp, I returned to my country. The cities were a mass of ruins. The people who walked the streets, their minds and discipline shaken by the defeat, aroused in me a feeling of desolation. Long absent from my country, I felt, when I stood among the ruins and among these people, as if I were alone, isolated, in a human desert.

One day, shortly after my repatriation, a friend informed me that an American officer who had come to Japan with the first wave of the army of occupation had been making frequent inquiries about me. Curious to know what I was wanted for, I paid the officer a call. He was a courteous, gray-haired gentleman with friendly eyes, a disarming smile and gentle speech. Just one look at him was enough to make one feel that he was a friend. When I told him that I was the person he had been inquiring about, he politely gave me a chair and immediately started to talk.

He took several letters from a drawer of his desk. They were all addressed to him from many of my American friends inquiring after me. Letters from an American wartime newsreel cameraman and from other old acquaintances, were there. Among the stack was one whose handwriting caught my notice immediately. It was the one I wanted to see most, even though it was addressed to the officer.

Dear Major—:

I have no words to thank you for your kind reply to the letter I wrote you immediately after the end of the war. I am deeply grateful, for I know you did this favor despite the pressure of your army duties.

I need not tell you how anxious I am to hear more about him in greater detail. Even though news about him may be of the worst, it would be preferable to know about it.

I am writing this letter with such care as to dispense with unnecessary details, because it may be censored by persons who would have no interest whatever in what is of great concern to us and I certainly do not want them to waste their valuable time.

It would be one of the mean tricks of fate that such a worthy subject as Shu should be deprived of life. However, I hope, for the sake of himself and his family, that he is still alive. And if it be the will of God that he lives, I know that he is contributing to the building of a peaceful world.

May I thank you again for your kind and considerate letter. The fact that you understand how I feel certainly gives me great hope, courage and assurance.

Sincerely yours,

X–

Tears welled in my eyes and vision became blurred. This letter deepened and strengthened all the more the faited h to which I had long continued to hold fast—faith in the fact that friendship is the greatest treasure anyone could have.

How wonderful to think that during the four horrible war years, when country fought country, when our peoples burnwith enmity and hatred, when a great gap—the field of battle—was created between us as a no man's land, there was someone on the other side of the lines who always thought and prayed for me; and when the guns became silent and peace returned, that someone would snatch the first opportunity to establish contact. It teaches one the greatness and goodness of friendship, it gives humanity limitless hope.

THE ADMIRAL THAT
DAVY JONES DIDN'T WANT

by Yokoi Toshiyuki

TO AN OLD-FASHIONED sea captain like myself, it was my duty to go down with my ship. But what was I to do when it sent me back up?

No matter how many years I spent at sea, I never got over the cranky-child feeling of foreboding which engulfed me the first time I gazed down into the impenetrable blue-green depths, from which all life in the beginning came, in which it still begins, and in which I knew mine would eventually end—to begin again into what? My past, my future and, for an unbearably long time, my present. That's probably why it's a rare seaman who swims for pleasure.

A ship is a psychiatrist's couch, and gazing into the tidal throb of the great mother sea is like staring at a tranquilizing metronome, ticking time backward, reflecting the past in its motion. And as an admiral of the Imperial Japanese Navy, I might just as well have been flat on my back in a clinic instead of on my bridge, surrounded by eight other aircraft carriers, five battleships, thirteen cruisers, and twenty-eight destroyers. We were the First Imperial Task Fleet out searching for United States Task Force 58 that lulling warm night of June 18, 1944.

My mind drifted back to December 7, 1941, when it had all started. It would be a modern war—complicated logistics, not living off the land as the Army had done for a decade in China. The generals wouldn't realize this. The Navy had supplies for only six months of full-scale warfare ready at hand, and sources of production were insufficient to appreciably extend it. Now three and a half years had passed since full-scale fighting had started in China. Full naval warfare had been avoided as much as possible, but the Navy was at the bottom of the supply barrel, and even the generals realized it.

The coming battle was the frantic poker player's last bet, our *whole* pile against our opponent's. And I could tell that it was a very long shot. The odds were too uneven.

It was a "sucker bet," but there was no other way out. It was the latest, and to be the last, chapter in our attempt to avenge the utter disaster almost exactly two years earlier at Midway, by destroying the U.S. fleet and with it MacArthur's island-hopping drive up through the Mariana Islands at Saipan.

Even so, both sides were opening the game cautiously. On February 11, 1944, anniversary of our imperial system's legendary founding 2,604 years before, our Japanese naval patrols had located an American Task Force of more than seventeen carriers. Against this we were moving our First Task Fleet, including my small carrier *Hiyo*. For months the two Task Forces had cat-and-moused around the Pacific.

Now, on June 18, our fleet was cruising some four hundred miles due west of the Marianas. We were completely undetected, we were sure of it; sure also we would sight the American fleet before it sighted us, and destroy it. Fighting morale was at fever pitch from supreme commander right down to lowest mess hand.

Vice Admiral Ozawa was in command of the fleet—an acknowledged expert in torpedo warfare but, in my opinion, inexperienced in full-scale naval operations. Ozawa was probably the most courageous officer in the Imperial Navy. He was a man who interpreted Horatio Nelson in terms of the Samurai Code and lived accordingly. His physical stature, over six feet, was giant for a Japanese, and may have overshadowed any weak points in his professional career. A nation which built a modern war machine on a feudal framework still preferred for its heroes those who looked like heroes.

Ozawa started the operation by breaking the first cardinal rule of warfare: he divided his force into three tactical units, each built around a core of three aircraft carriers. With the force extended in full line, thirty miles between each division, the plan was for the whole fleet to sweep the sea in search of the enemy. Ozawa banked heavily on what he considered "the proven superiority" of Japanese naval aircraft; he wanted to extend his effective range by pivoting his operation on the main air base in the Marianas, thus giving him the added advantage of heavier land-based bombers. "I will pound the American fleet with carrier-based planes, land-based bombers, and the guns of my surface vessels. I will give them no time to counterattack."

I was not as confident as Ozawa. Most of my twenty years of active service had been spent as a pilot. I had no illusions about what it took to make a first-class aviator, and I had fewer illusions about the fact that my present crews just didn't have it.

To me, a pilot needed the full Naval Air Training curriculum and at least two years of active duty aboard a carrier. My men were Jerry-trained wartime substitutes run through poorly equipped schools where ideological fervor filled the gaps in technical training. And few had even as much as four months aboard a carrier—weeks or months of inactive, fuel-conserving ready-room time was no substitute for on-the-spot practical experience.

Yet somehow, to my amazement, these men got their planes safely off the flight deck and, often as not, even got them back down —at least in broad daylight, on calm seas, and without the tension and distraction of being under fire. With these, Ozawa was out to challenge the most experienced naval airmen in the world, also vastly superior in number to our own forces. Either advantage in itself would have balanced out the scales, but both advantages on one side put the odds vastly in favor of the Americans.

Still, I realized the Japanese held one joker: the Americans were probably totally unaware of this Japanese weakness. And to play this card right, the Imperial Task Fleet had no alternative but to move in close, even to within visual sighting range of Task Force 58 —to give the green airmen every advantage of surface support and minimize chances of air-to-air contact.

I spoke to Ozawa, offering my own plan before the fleet had even set out, but I was brushed aside. It wasn't according to the books, Ozawa said. Ozawa epitomized the British military historian General J. F. C. Fuller's assessment of the Japanese tacticians who "on the one hand had . . . displayed a low cunning of incredible stupidity, and on the other had a lack of imagination of unbelievable profundity."

There would be a long-range attack, taking fullest advantage of the superiority of the Japanese aircraft—ignoring the fact that a plane is no better than its pilot.

At 0300, June 19, I despondently sent off my first scout aircraft.

The sun rose clear and sharp in the morning haze by 0630. Intelligence reports started to flow in. The American Task Force had deployed wide, west of the Marianas, and was coming in fast toward the center of the Japanese fleet. "Do they know we're here?" That was the vital question. The American vanguard was already within Admiral Ozawa's calculated range of attack.

The *Hiyo's* deck came alive. Semaphore men flagged the first planes off. I held my breath as successive fighters and torpedo planes made their run, drop, peel-off, and climb departures.

By 0830, Task Force 58 was within three hundred miles of Imperial Task Fleet One. The last of the attacking force of 260 Japanese aircraft faded below the eastern horizon. At 1000 hours a second group of eighty-two followed them. All available aircraft were now airborne and not a single American plane had been sighted. Ozawa was jubilant. We had taken the Americans by surprise.

I sighed in relief. If the attacking Japanese air fleet could whittle down the U.S. carrier strength, then Japan had a chance. I looked up at the golden disc riding higher in the late morning haze, then over at its silken counterpart flying from my mast. "The fate of the thousand-year empire," I mused, "hangs on the outcome of the next few thousand seconds."

In the intelligence center of the flagship, total silence hung like an arrested breath. A thousand seconds passed like as many years. Then the staccato chirp of the complicated Japanese Morse code, "Attacked . . . [static] . . . enemy carriers . . . battleships . . ." then total silence like one long tortured, asthmatic gasp.

A second radio contact, this time with the second air group. They reported total failure in making any contact with enemy units. They were giving up the hunt and returning. One squadron reported the necessity of detouring to Guam for refueling.

Noon arrived and still no further report came from the first air group. I was puzzled. I gazed into the calm blue sea and felt it beckon. This kind of warfare was new to me. I wondered how Ozawa was taking it; no books ever spilled any ink over fighting like this—no news from one side, from the other no contact.

Lunch was a nervous torture. The rice was cold and I almost gagged on it. Then the code room called down—a message. I raced up the ladder way to have my worst forebodings borne out. The fifty planes of group two which had landed at Guam had been ambushed on the ground by an enemy they hadn't been able to find. Only one was able to take off.

I returned to the bridge and gazed deep into the blue again. Then a flicker of motion caught the corner of my eye and I looked over toward the eastern horizon. The first air group was returning under total radio silence—but not in any recognizable formation.

One by one.

One hundred two planes limped in—102 out of 342.

In the ready-room the American strategy took shape in retrospect. They had concentrated on defending their carriers. They had set their battleships out as bait, and when the slow Japanese torpedo bombers began their approach run from twenty miles out, the American fighter cover moved in from over the rear-placed carriers and swarmed over the Japanese. Few torpedo bombers survived the first attack to reach their targets. Only minor hits were reported, scored on two battleships. The carriers steamed on unscathed.

Ozawa's plan might just as well have been drawn up for him by Washington.

By now my *Hiyo* was some thirty miles in the vanguard of the Japanese fleet. I looked back. Utter despair swept over me as I saw great columns of black smoke rising from beyond the horizon where I imagined the flagship should be. Minutes later the code room received a message from the cruiser *Yahagi* notifying our division of the sinking of a carrier and instructing me to take on its planes. It was *Shokaku*, which with *Zuikaku*, had attacked Pearl Harbor—the Americans were having thei rrevenge.

As the *Hiyo* approached the rendezvous point where the *Shokaku* should have been, I saw nothing but wreckage and thick floating oil. Not far beyond, the newest carrier in the Imperial Navy, the 45,000 ton *Taiho*, flagship of Vice-Admiral Ozawa, lay at a 50-degree list under a mourning canopy of black smoke. Immediately after the *Taiho* had sent off all its planes with the first attack group, she had taken a torpedo in her port bow from an American sub. As it was not considered serious enough to cripple the great carrier, no one was unduly alarmed; hours later it was found that the shock had split the seams of the main gasoline storage tank and fumes were playing havoc between decks.

At 1432 hours, as my 30,000-ton *Hiyo* hove to within a mile of the stricken flagship, I was thrown violently against the bulkhead by shock. The *Taiho* had rolled over on its port side and exploded.

The next morning, June 20, the remaining units rendezvoused with their tankers for refueling. At 1045 they were still linked to the tankers by the great serpentine fuel lines when the message came in, "Two enemy capital ships, one cruiser, several destroyers sighted . . . 20 degrees . . . five hundred miles off Peleliu . . ."

The expected American counterattack, but Imperial Fleet Headquarters now aboard the carrier *Zuikaku*, seemed to ignore the warning completely.

Minutes later the radio room reported picking up air-to-surface radiophone of approaching American planes. I ordered general quarters sounded and watched the former cocky overconfidence of my green crews give way to tenseness.

All day we waited. Had they been only scout planes? Had they missed sighting the Japanese fleet altogether? An hour before sunset, approximately six miles to port, over the haze and what I imagined should be Carrier Division Three, antiaircraft puffs appeared. I ordered all aircraft up and climbed into the antiaircraft fire control tower. The last plane had barely cleared the *Hiyo* flight deck when silver specks appeared overhead in the dying sunlight, elevation about 9,000 feet. Far from the ring formation, the carrier was covered by four of our destroyers, they immediately commenced fire. Futile at such range, I thought but, as if to accommodate them, the silver specks peeled off and arced downward.

I ordered hard a-starboard and full antiaircraft barrage. The first column of water spewed into the air one hundred yards to port —right where I would have been. Others blossomed around me, but the *Hiyo* took no hits. The barrage was perfect and deflected later attacking planes that had any chance to correct for the evasive action. The last dive bomber peeled over, broke through the canopy of tiny man-made clouds, corrected its dive and released. It was a certain miss, but a close one, the way it was arced. Then, angling in, it hit the tip of a mast and was deflected downwards right into the control tower where I stood.

When the smoke cleared, the navigating officer lay dead at my feet, but I could barely make out the body through the curtain of blood that covered my eyes. I wiped the blood away; my left eye was gone, I could feel the sting of shrapnel all over me. A voice nearby cried out, "Torpedo planes, off to port." Six squat TBM Grumman Avengers sped in on the last stages of their 5-degree downhill approach dive. The *Hiyo's* guns put up a withering barrage. Two disappeared. A third seemed discouraged by the barrage and released its torpedo out of range.

A fourth seemed favored by the gods. He kept coming in—500 meters . . . 400 . . . 300 . . . then he disappeared in a brilliant yellow puff, but a long black sausage appeared below the billow and dropped perfectly into the water—a sight I have never been able to forget, a perfect release, a feat I have held in admiration ever since.

At this range it was too late to evade. A white streak slashed toward the *Hiyo.* I felt toward my very self. There was a tremor from port, somewhere near the engine room. White steam poured from the funnel. All motion stopped. The sudden cessation of the noises I had grown so accustomed to was like a deafening rush of wind. Even the guns stopped. I staggered off, half-blind, for the bridge. Two more torpedo streaks appeared to port. Both hit astern, one in communications and one below the volatile oil tanks. Gasoline flowed out through cracked seams and ignited. Heavy fire-fighting equipment failed; hand pumps were useless. Flaming oil flowed toward the magazine.

I ordered all available men to carry the wounded onto the flight deck. The flag officer struck the Imperial battle flag and took down the Imperial portrait and important documents for removal to a destroyer. The wounded were placed on rafts and put over the side. All hands were mustered on deck to abandon ship. As they came up and took their stations, I made a brief farewell speech and all cheered, "Banzai! Ten thousand years' life to the Emperor!"

As they filed over the side, someone near me struck up the old sea chantey, "Seafaring may we lay our bodies deep . . ."

When the last officer left the deck, I saluted as smartly as my smarting wounds allowed, then sat down on an empty shell box and lit a cigarette. My blind left eye began to throb. With my good eye, I watched my men pull away, then stared down at the approaching deep. It would soon no longer be impenetrable for me.

The refrain, "lay our bodies deep," carried over the water. The last thing I remember thinking to myself was, "Now is the end . . . And the beginning?"

The deep blue momentarily veered away as the bow of the *Hiyo* lunged up, paused, and with a great sigh of escaping air, slipped silently back into the blue. I vividly remember the rushing water, the debris swirling past, the strange world of dancing corpses, boxes, pirouetting wreckage, approaching sleep. Then, a jolt from below froze all motion, dangling wreckage and corpses in eternity— a sharp pain in my left side—bubbles, swirling—and oblivion.

A wave slapped my face and brought me back into consciousness. Above were stars. Somewhere beyond the mass of wreckage the underwater explosion of the magazine had thrown me free to the surface. I could hear the soft refrain, "Seafaring may we lay our bodies deep . . ."

But the hands that pulled me out said, "Not yet, Admiral."

EDITOR'S NOTE: This was the greatest naval air battle of the war. Japan lost 395 of the fleet's 430 aircraft. The remnant of the Combined Fleet withdrew. Spruance wisely declined to follow up and concentrated on air cover for taking Saipan, which fell July 9. Prime Minister Tojo resigned July 18. Japanese armies in China overran U.S. mainland airbases. Saipan became the hub for a year of long-range bombing of Japanese cities. August 5, 1945, the *Enola Gray* took of from Saipan for the first atomic bombing.

CAPTURED BY AMERICANS

by Fuji Seii

THE JAPANESE traditional Boys' Festival, May 5, is the anniversary of my repatriation from Australia and my release from one and a half years as a prisoner of war. I make it a rule to celebrate my health and luck on this date, and to summon up memories of the past war.

Whenever May 5 comes and the carp pennants are floating on the breezes of my homeland, I feel eager to find a chance to get in touch with those who saved my life, the crew of an American submarine. I don't know their names, however the only name I still remember is Captain Hess, and I'm not even sure that this was the real name of the submarine skipper. Perhaps I had been told false names for security reasons.

The only way I have of identifying myself to the crew members who may chance to read this story is that I was a sort of artist who drew many portraits and cartoons of them. I signed them Fuji, and reminded them all that it was the same pronunciation as the mountain. We prisoners were three—a Lieutenant Shima, nicknamed Tojo because he so closely resembled the war leader, a Sergeant Nishikawa called Snafoo, who looked very strong even though he couldn't have been more than twenty-two, and myself.

This is the story of my adventure, told in the hope that one of its readers may happen to be of the crew who saved us, and that he will look me up so I may thank him for being alive and happy today.

19

It was October 16, 1944, when our ship was torpedoed. We were part of an army convoy en route to Borneo from Manila. I had just finished my turn at the anti-submarine watch and was about to descend the hatch to my quarters. A dazzling flash illuminated through the blinding rainstorm one of the crammed troopships off to port. With Nishikawa at my side, I dashed to the handrail and saw, to our horror, the white wake of a second torpedo headed straight for our ship.

Despite our shouted alarm, there was no time for evasive action. The blast of the torpedo in our sister ship was still ringing in our ears when we felt the sickening death shudder of our own craft. I was in the water before I knew it and no sooner had I caught hold of a life raft than the silhouette of our ship disappeared beneath the waves. Ten of us clinging to the raft barely survived the sucking power of our sinking ship. The rain was so heavy that even breathing was difficult. Two days and nights the storm continued unabated, and all that time we clung to the sides of a raft too small to hold us. One seriously wounded soldier died the second morning.

On the third night the storm passed and the water became as calm and as smooth as a pond. We realized that we were completely exhausted and fatigue forced us at last into the sleep we had been fighting off for fear of drowning. At one time we all climbed up onto the raft together, vainly seeking a place to sleep. Our combined weight sank the raft and it bobbed up again yards away. We swam frantically to regain it and unsuccessfully tried the same thing again and again.

I am not sure that we were all fully awake. We talked of how the others had fared. Someone ventured that rescue ships had saved all the others. Another claimed our ship had not sunk, but that we had been blown overboard by the blast and that it had continued on its way. The men spoke as in dreams, but we believed one another in our own befuddlement. Then Lieutenant Shimazu cried out, "How foolish I am to think that we are here. Why, an M.P. launch has just visited us and it took me to Headquarters to report on the damage to the ship." He added that he had just come back on the same motor launch and he had just come from Manila. We believed him and flapped and kicked our legs frantically, urging the raft on in the direction that Lieutenant Shimazu said was Manila. How long we continued, I cannot tell, but when no land appeared and darkness fell, we stopped and agreed to wait till morning.

When the fourth morning came and the day dragged on, nothing could be seen but sea and sky and puffy white clouds. That night two of the soldiers went mad and swam away from the float, laughing and sobbing in the dark. Their voices didn't last long.

By then everyone seemed devoid of sense. We argued ferociously which way to go. A cloud bank appeared on the horizon and we all thought it land. We all saw the white sails of fishing boats and believed with Shimazu that it was Manila. Then we saw a small canoe coming toward us. We could see figures rowing. Though it was still bright, they were seen only in silhouette. When we shouted, waving our hands, they also responded to us with raised hands. Excited with joy, we bellowed for help. But alas, when the boat approached us at about fifty or eighty meters, it suddenly disappeared. At the same time the white sails we had seen running on the horizon turned out to be an illusion.

It was not a serious disappointment for us, because soon after that we saw another boat, full of soldiers. We thought there would be no more chance to live if we missed this boat or if it disappeared. The boat approached us. We could hear shouting. We rowed the raft with the last of our strength. No sooner had we reached the boat than I fell down and fainted.

When I woke up after about ten hours' sleep, I found the soldiers in the boat still rowing. Nobody looked happy. Only the creaking of the oars echoed in the star-scattered night. Soon I realized that the people of the boat who saved us had also suffered shipwreck.

While days passed, we became uneasy and undisciplined. We drank salty water to wet our throats. I knew it could not do any good, but we could not help doing so. Sometimes we rowed. Sometimes we put an oar straight up, tying our clothes to it as a sail for our boat. This did not last long because we became uneasy, afraid the wind would change from day to night. Then we gave up everything, leaving our boat to run along with the tide. It was natural that my body, soaked in the sea for three days and nights, was badly burned by the southern sun.

The sixth evening presented a wonderfully beautiful scene, a magnificent sunset which I still remember vividly. By that time everybody was so tired that no one tried to stand up. At first we had talked about the time when we would land or be saved by a ship But the last day of our life in the sea we uttered very few words, and just lay down in the boat.

It was October 22, 1944.

A soldier found something on the horizon of the scarlet-tinted sea. A rescue ship?

Up from despair, we shouted and waved our hands, even though our voices could not reach the ship. The ship, glittering in the reflection of the setting sun, was coming straight toward us. How we admired the triumphantly approaching ship! The drowning man will catch even at a piece of straw. I loudly recited what my parents used to pray in front of the Shinto shrine. I did not know what to do. The ship was still coming straight, raising white foam by its bow. But wait, it was not a ship, but a submarine. The submarine approached until I could see the complete shape. No, it was not a Japanese submarine.

The submarine suddenly stopped near our boat with a blow of steam. (I thought it was steam, but maybe I was wrong.) A pair of steel plates that looked like radar twinkled to and fro. Abruptly a manhole burst open and a bunch of sailors jumped up with tommy guns and pistols. Some of them dashed to the deck gun and loaded swiftly.

Our boat was floating toward the submarine. I thought we would soon be killed. I could see even the bore of the gun that was directed at us. Then I realized I was thirsty.

A soldier murmured, "I can't die until I get a sip of water."

There was a tense moment. Nobody breathed, expecting a blast in the next instant. How could I die and why should I die after the week's struggle against death? I could not help shouting "water' in English. "Give me water!" Nishikawa followed me.

An officer, who turned out to be the captain of the submarine, whispered something to a crewman. "Is there anybody who can speak English?" was the first voice I heard from the enemy. I noticed warm sympathy in the voice of the crewman. A few minutes later, Lieutenant Shimazu, Sergeant Nishikawa, and I were on the deck of the submarine.

Shimazu and I, in broken English, asked them to give us water, because we'd had no water for a week. We just wanted water, even if we were to be killed.

The captain, who looked kind and generous, ordered something to a crewman who saluted and disappeared into the conning tower. Soon, two men emerged with two big cans of water and one big sack of canned foods. They threw them down into the boat.

I did not feel it was war. What I saw was nothing but peaceful and godly acts of mercy. The captain told us to stay; we were captured. I said good-by to the soldiers who remained in the boat and told them to report us dead and not to expect us to come back alive. We had been taught all prisoners would be killed. Even if we were not killed, it was the most shameful thing to become a prisoner of war. The submarine began to move, leaving the rest of the soldiers in the boat alive, set free.

The captain led us to the bridge. I stepped through the hatch and smelled—it was the smell of humans which I had forgotten for so long a time. I had forgotten human life, especially since I had become a soldier. Smoke of cigarettes, music, the soft atmosphere of living people—I felt I heard falling off me the crashing sound of chains that had tightly held me in a lifelong yoke. It was paradise even though everything in there was a weapon. How sweet the water was! I drank seven cups straight.

My story seems to have come to its end. The entire crew of the submarine was very kind. I cannot forget the two weeks' life in the submarine. The captain, whose name was Hess, was a gentleman who treated us kindly. He promised us to return what we had in our pockets, a watch, pencils and other things. I still have the watch, which is no longer usable because it had soaked in the sea for a week, but I keep it as a memento.

The gunner was kind and I felt as if he were my elder brother. I usually met him at the mess room, where a Spanish cook became one of my best friends. I taught him some Japanese and he was very glad when he found that bread in Japanese was *pan* because its pronunciation was very similar in his language.

They showed no hostility, certainly no cruelty toward us. A Swedish sailor told me that he became an American because he loved democracy. Nobody forced us to learn democracy, but I noticed they loved and enjoyed it, as if by nature.

The submarine anchored at Perth, Australia. We were sent to Brisbane by airplane. It was a nice trip, though we were afraid what would happen next. In Brisbane we joined the camp for Japanese prisoners of war. I was repatriated to Japan on May 5, the Japanese traditional Boys' Festival day. Since then, I have been happily working. Recently I married.

I want to show a picture of my wedding to the crew of the submarine. I am afraid they may not be able to recognize me, because I was so sunburnt and thin when they rescued me. And my hair was also much longer. I also fear that I, in turn, may not recognize them because they had handsome mustaches then and now must have returned to well-shaven faces and neat civilian suits. But still I am very eager to correspond with them.

The signature attached to this story of mine is the one I signed my drawings with. Perhaps it will help friends and former captor-saviors to recognize me. I hope so.

THESE TEN YEARS

A STORY OF SEVEN EX-SOLDIERS

by Kon Hidemi

AUGUST 15, 1945: The Emperor for the first time addressed his people over a nationwide radio hookup; then Japan for the first time admitted a victorious enemy to its shores. News of Japan's unconditional surrender, however, did not reach the ears of a great many Japanese soldiers, particularly those who had fled deep into the mountain jungles of the Philippines.

In the wilderness on both sides of the Canganyan Highway, many soldiers were scattered and isolated from their units and headquarters. In a secret lair in Canganyan, General Yamashita, the "Tiger of Malaya," and his staff awaited the final act, without any hope of reversing the tide of the war. In fact, it was not like war at all. To live for the day was the best one could expect. The one-sided situation brought U.S. tanks and airplanes everywhere, on and over the all-encompassing battlefields. Looking down at the star-marked tanks on the highways, the beaten soldiers would murmur, "*Chikusho*—beasts! They're probably eating good food!"

These same men thrust from their thoughts the fact that when they were found they would fall victim to the tanks' flame throwers, as they had seen many comrades incinerated—it was food they talked of. The soldiers that lived through tonight never thought of tomorrow. The simple fact that they were living was enough.

Naturally, food was scarce. Or rather, there was no food in any real sense. Anything edible was devoured. Lizard was a delicacy even this soon became hard to find. Corporal Kihara and the six other soldiers were always faced with imminent starvation.

25

The seven soldiers, however, somehow managed to live on—thanks to Corporal Kihara's talent. Before he was drafted, he had a criminal record. In the army he had a peculiar MOS (Military Occupational Specialty)—stealing; when the war was lost he became a hero because his specialty now saved his comrades' lives. Whenever he came back from hunting he always carried something that joyfully surprised the other six men. Unhulled rice was one of his most surprising offerings.

The farmers' houses were empty—all the food stocks had either been taken away by the farmers or looted by the withdrawing Japanese soldiers. Nevertheless, Corporal Kihara could sniff out secret hoarding places. With looted boxes of U.S. K-rations in his hands, he looked like an angel.

Human beings can live if they have only fire, rice, and salt. Luckily the men had kept aside a little salt when they were separated from the main force. For the other two necessities—rice and fire—they depended solely on Cpl Kihara. In addition to being an excellent thief, he was a master fire-maker. Without him the seven soldiers could not have survived more than a week, while others around them were dying of fatigue and hunger.

The tiny nipa-house in which the seven hid themselves was located in a narrow crevasse between steep mountain sides. Low-flying P38s would fly past but never strafe the house or any of the seven soldiers, so they used to look up and whistle at the planes, assured of perfect safety.

Among them was Odaira, formerly a journalist. He hated the war the most. Every time he sighed "We're finished," Pfc. Nara retorted, "That's what an intellectual believes. That's defeatism. You're trying to discourage us!"

Nara was every inch a soldier. Each morning he got up and led the others in reciting the Emperor's Commandments to Soldiers. He seemed firmly to believe in the day when he would recapture Manila. Looking at the enemy tanks and airplanes, seeing no counterattack from our side, he still denied reality. Strangely enough, however, the other six were more influenced by Nara than by Odaira. Whenever Nara shouted "Get up—all of you!" they simply followed his words and bowed in the direction of Japan, as they used to in the routine life of the barracks.

Pfc. Takeuchi held a special status because of his young age. Whenever the others were involved in a discussion, he always stayed silent. When he did speak, he associated himself with the general point of view. Whenever the seven tried to decide a matter by voting, he was always the last to cast his vote. Consequently, he gave the impression of deciding everything.

"He is another Kihara—but intellectual," criticized Odaira, whose opinion was always voted against by the others. Odaira insisted that the Japanese Army would give up very soon, making further food conservation unnecessary. Nara and Narazaki vehemently opposed this. In such cases, Takeuchi always agreed with Nara, though he ate up his own reserves by himself, thus tacitly backing Odaira's prediction.

One day as usual Kihara went food hunting. In a few minutes he hurried back and told them breathlessly, "I saw a white-flagged car carrying officers down the highway." This seemed to fit in with a mysterious silence they had noticed the last few days. No airplane roared. No artillery blasted. They had, in fact, been wondering if a cease-fire was in order. They were excited at the news.

Confused, they looked at Odaira for his opinion.

"There's nothing to say. The war is over," he said.

Even Nara could think of no reply. As no tanks passed by, Narazaki suggested they send out a scout to find out what had happened. Pvt. Taguchi voiced agreement.

"I will go," Pfc. Tobo offered. But everyone shook his head disapprovingly to the half-starved private. Narazaki spoke out, "You must stay here and conserve your strength. I'll take the job."

He went down the mountain with Pfc. Odaira, where they learned of Japan's unconditional surrender, now five days after the fact. This news—the first authentic information they had received in the past six months—made Nara cry.

Every one of the seven belonged to a different unit whose fate nobody knew. They had lived thus far only by relying on their own unity—dividing scanty food among themselves. But now that the war was over there seemed little reason for them to keep on doing so. In the American camp, they could sleep with arms and feet stretched, without the worry of food hunting, and P38s. Odaira gave his usual optimistic forecast.

"You beast!" Nara shouted, "Can't you realize we'll be chained by the enemy?" He could have hit Odaira, if he had had the strength.

Nevertheless, when the sun went up next morning, all seven descended the mountain for the first time to an open road. Truck after truck with American drivers rolled past carrying full loads of Japanese soldiers. The seven waved at their compatriots. But nobody answered them back.

"Goddamit! They behave like total strangers!" They spat on the ground.

The seven soldiers were finally picked up by a passing truck. For the first time in eight months they went out of the Canganyan Valley, emerging on flat land under the glaring sun. As they passed by, they were threateningly stared at by the natives who had already come back.

At the northwest end of the highway stood a temporary camp headquarters. With the help of some Nisei enlisted men, several American officers had already started assigning POW work to the Japanese soldiers who silently waited in a long line in front of the camp. At the gate of the camp, the seven soldiers were separated according to the units to which they had once belonged. Tobo and Taguchi were hospitalized, their conditions had grown worse on their way to the camp.

A minute before they bade farewell to each other, Narazaki said, "If we ever get to Japan safely, how about meeting every August for dinner together?"

"You idiot! How can you say such a thing—you're a prisoner of war. You'll never go back to Japan," Nara retorted, almost shouting.

They were separated before they could argue further or agree on a place to meet, encamped in different groups, not knowing each other's whereabouts.

Odaira became editor of a mimeographed newspaper for the camp POWs. Pfc. Nara did not know this, but one day he was startled to find in the POW paper the news of the repatriation ships he had never expected. In the camp, he was treated in a way that seemed, by comparison, almost heavenly. The letters POW painted on his back and pants did not bother him in the least. Labor was light: digging latrines for GIs, sticking in fence poles and other such work, could hardly be called "labor." Without any strict watch and with the small quantity of porridge which seemed rather appropriate for undernourished men, he—as the men around him—was quite satisfied.

As the living grew better, each man became, however, more anxious to know about the homeland. The news trickled in slowly. Knowledge was painful. Almost all the cities were reduced to ashes.

Nagasaki and Hiroshima were wiped out by hell bombs. Then the men knew they'd had better luck than the people at home.

Soon, Japanese repatriation ships anchored in Manila Bay, where capsized hulks still lay with their red bellies sticking out of the water.

It was 1946—when Generals Homma and Yamashita were sentenced to death—that Nara finally landed in Kagoshima. He was shocked to see the shattered homeland, aghast at the horrible sight of Hiroshima as the train passed by. He went straight to Kawachi, his home town, which looked almost strange to his eyes after eight years in the Army. To his surprise, his mother and sister-in-law were safe in his house. His brother was working in the pig-bristle factory, already an expert brush maker.

Nevertheless, life for Nara was miserable. To feed an extra mouth was difficult in those days. Demobilized Nara Hachiro turned out to be an unwelcome guest. Nara dreamed of the Philippine mountains where he could depend on Kihara's loot. No fresh fruits or vegetables were available. Potatoes and pumpkins were staple foods. Even these were in short supply, hunted by many Osaka citizens who daily swarmed to the Kawachi area. Nara Hachiro became acutely aware of how desperately the urban areas were hit by food shortages. Daily the newspaper spread photos of beggar-like citizens under their burned tin-plate shacks.

On the unlit roads there roamed vagrant dogs looking for things to eat or at least bite. Gang robberies became a common affair. The homeland he had so longed for in the Philippines now became a place where there was nothing to admire.

Nara wanted to go to Osaka for a job, but how could he find a job in a destroyed city of debris and ashes? He finally decided to stay on in his house, no matter how his brother and sister-in-law might show their disgust with him.

Hachiro tried to help and went out into the rice fields early each morning. His brother liked this and spoke more friendly, "To tell you the truth, farming was best during wartime. Rice was so precious. Everyone respected us. But no fieldhands, you know, after you were drafted. I was also mobilized into the factory. Nobody could take care of the fields . . . ."

In the fields Nara Hachiro felt strangely easy. But day after day the monotonous life in the farmhouse grew more vacant and dry. He had seen a world that no one in his family could ever even dream of. In the Philippines he used to look at the natives toiling in the rice fields, planting tobacco seeds, and bearing so many children. He thought they were foolish. But now, looking at his brother's way of living, he could hardly find any difference.

"I saw a colored movie in Manila. That was beautiful – – ," he began one night.

"You mean, they have a better culture than ours?" the brother asked.

"Yeah, direct from America."

"But it's in the south—you can't stand heat—don't you ever go crazy with a climate that never changes?"

"It's hot. But the movie theaters and hotels have air-conditioning. When it's hot, it's better to get inside the movie house —you get pretty cool," he explained.

"Yeah? With what do they make it cool?" The brother was curious.

"Electricity of course."

Then the sister-in-law burst into laughter, "Wherever can you mean? Electricity is for warming things. How can you cool things with electricity?"

Hachiro avoided answering. He thought his sister-in-law was ignorant. But he himself also knew little of how such technical contradictions could be worked out.

Odaira Shuntaro succeeded in securing his old job, thanks to the city editor who had been bureau chief in the Philippines. But back in the office he found that men who were once his juniors were already at the "desks" exercising control over the younger men. It was as if an old veteran non-com were at the mercy of green young officers. Moreover, the men at the desk seemed to embarrass him by showing an air of constraint.

After four years in the Army, he was accustomed to organization. He himself did not regard the matter with as much concern as others did. He was rather happy with the simple fact that he could return to his old job. Settling himself in the company's dormitory in Yoyogi, he felt there need be nothing to worry about.

In contrast to the days before Odaira was drafted, the newspaper business seemed to be growing into a full-fledged profession. According to editorial policy the reporters could now write anything.

In the dark days of wartime, however, they had been simply messenger boys who carried around the stinking official announcements of the General Staff Headquarters or of the Information Bureau. No evening editions. No more than two pages. The several thousand employees of the company were a great financial burden.

When Odaira Shuntaro landed at Kagoshima, he could see everywhere flowers in full bloom. But the towns and cities had been reduced to ruins that extended as far as the eye could see. Human beings had become lost, but nature was in full bloom. Shuntaro could thus still believe that eventually life would rise again from these ashes.

But now Odaira had become very realistic, and therefore very pessimistic. Back in the newspaper office, where things went along most realistically, he did not realize that his once flexible way of thinking had changed into almost a stiff-necked tenacity. In the year the war ended, people seemed simply to give up in the face of the hardships that came from a scarcity of food and housing. In 1946 the Higashikuni cabinet was succeeded by the Shidehara cabinet, which ignored the mounting inflation. People began to criticize the government, particularly after April when the new constitution restored freedom of speech. People took advantage of privileges obtained through the sacrifice of others.

Among governmental officials and newspapermen, there was speculation that a riot might occur in the autumn. They pointed to various signs that seemed similar to conditions and situations in post-World War I Russia and Germany just before their revolutions.

Shuntaro daily frequented the black-market area near Shimbashi to have a sip of *kasutori*, a Japanese calvados. People paid little attention to the taste of things. Anything drinkable was welcome. *Kasutori*—with its strong after-effect—charmed people who had but little spending money. Mostly moonshined by Koreans in Japan, it was extremely dangerous. Odaira knew this, yet as evening came on, he could not stand a minute without a glass of *kasutori.*

One night, he was staggering out of the narrow lane of the market, when he was suddenly accosted. "That's Odaira, isn't it?"

At first glance he thought a black-marketeer was approaching him. It crossed his mind that the figure was a thief carrying loot on his back. That sun-tanned face with elephant eyes quickly reminded him of someone familiar.

"Oh, Takeuchi!" Shuntaro shouted.

Takeuchi was wearing a pair of khaki pants, a patched-up shirt, and a combat cap—a complete black-marketeer's uniform.

"How's everything?" Odaira asked.

"I'm selling frying pans here. Good sales, though," said Takeuchi with a big smile that made him look younger. Bachelor that Odaira was, he could not understand why so many people would buy frying pans.

Looking at Odaira Shuntaro's bewildered face, Takeuchi explained rather proudly, "These are made very cheap by a former munitions plant." A former armament plant haf become a frying pan factory! A most becoming outcome of a defeated economy, Shuntaro thought. But he also wondered how long Takeuchi could continue selling frying pans, for sooner or later the public would have enough of them.

"Say, how about a drink?" Shuntaro asked.

"A *kasutori?*" Takeuchi responded very quickly.

"Until good drinks appear, *kasutori* will have to do. Then, you'll give up selling frying pans?" Shuntaro asked as a glass was placed on the counter.

"Naturally, why not? So long as they sell, I'll work at it. That's all," Takeuchi said matter-of-factly. He was still following the majority. In whatever circumstances he might be, Shuntaro thought, Takeuchi would never change his character. He was a man who could nonchalantly accept even these confused and tired days.

"I guess someday you'll be a big shot," Shuntaro said.

"Hah, hah! Here, again, you're fortune telling. You used to tell us the future of the war. Now we're in peace. For that prediction I'd like to buy a drink," Takeuchi said, wiping his mouth with his dirty right hand.

"A *kasutori?* "

"No, of course not. Say, by the way, I sent a letter to old Nara Hachiro—"

"Where's he now?" Shuntaro asked, reaching for his glass.

"Farming in Kawachi. I told him he'll never be satisfied with farming. I think I can teach him how to sell these frying pans. He is an honest fellow, you know. If I tell him to sell, he will certainly sell as I say – –"

"Okay, then, when you two fellows sell everything, let's have a big drink," Odaira said.

The bill was on the table. Takeuchi, however, made no motion to pick it up despite his talk about big sales. Finally, in disgust, Shuntaro picked up the bill. When he paid, Takeuchi simply said, as if he had not noticed it before, "Sorry, I'll buy next time."

In May 1946, Yoshida Shigeru formed his Cabinet. The muchfeared riot did not occur—not because Yoshida's policy was appropriate, but because the people knew riots would never bring forth food and better living. On the other hand, several violent incidents occurred between labor and management. Following the first authorized May Day, a so-called "Food May Day" was held on May 8.

As Shuntaro went out to cover the story, he was surprised to see the furious way the crowds were shouting in front of the premier's residence. "Come out, Yoshida!" "We want Yoshida!" And some 200,000 people cried "Down with the Yoshida cabinet!" as they paraded past the Diet building.

Odaira remembered the wartime days when the military hierarchy allowed no criticism. People were trained to follow the imperative order blindly. In postwar days, people's reactions led them to oppose anything imperative. But once trained to obey orders, people accepted the orders of the Occupation Forces without question.

The Occupation Forces least expected such peaceful and obedient behavior, as they knew well the stubborn resistance of the Japanese armies over the previous four years. But they knew little about the Japanese psychology of obediently accepting orders, even those of the conqueror. The so-called 2:1 (February First) Strike in 1947, therefore, was quickly subdued by a word from MacArthur's Headquarters. People's dissatisfaction, however, was bound to explode somewhere, sometime. Japan was an unstable country where there was no assurance even of being able to live. The general public, therefore, became easy victims of the Communist campaigns. Legal strikes occurred as a daily routine. Strikes, thefts, and robberies filled almost every page of the dailies. Minor crimes such as pickpocketing and stealing were virtually ignored by editors who were too busy following up the big stories. Even police and justice authorities could not spare time for minor crimes.

Under such circumstances, Tokyoites were terror-stricken when they read of a bank robbery that resulted in the death of eleven bank clerks. A middle-aged man walked into the Shiinamachi Branch of the Teikoku Bank one dull day in January, 1947.

Somehow he persuaded all the clerks to take a drink of poisoned "medicine," then calmly walked out with 110,000 yen, a fortune.

This was a crime big enough for all newspapers to follow, but Odaira Shuntaro picked up a small and strange crime story. From a Metropolitan Police detective he heard of a thief who stole only from foreigners. As the crimes were repeated, the police authorities were increasingly criticized.

In those days, most of the fashionable foreign-style houses in Tokyo had been commandeered for the use of VIPs, high-ranking Allied officers and their families. The elusive burglar was reported to have succeeded in sneaking into even the most strictly guarded houses. When he broke into a major general's house in Azabu, however, he committed the serious mistake of making a noise that awoke the general, who came downstairs with a Colt automatic in his hand.

The general fired two shots as the figure jumped over a high concrete wall. No fingerprints were found. Nothing was left behind. The story itself was interesting, at least to Shuntaro's journalistic sense. In the story Odaira wrote he also added that the Metropolitan Police Board would be harshly criticized unless they could nab a thief who preyed on and baffled the Occupation Forces.

The story when it appeared in the paper received a surprising response. In the Occupation days, people use to look at the foreigners as "special personages" who rode in comfortable off-limits-to-Japanese railway cars while Japanese were sardine-packed into dirty, crowded coaches. The Occupationaires gave the general public a feeling of oppression. The story, therefore, created a modern Robin Hood who invaded the "Occupation houses" when everyone feared even to talk about his feelings.

The editor, however, called in Odaira and warned, "Watch out, Odaira. The newspaper section of GHQ seems to be displeased with your story." Shuntaro nodded, but did not try to comment or express an opinion.

The story was a scoop. Other reporters congratulated Shuntaro. But he was not pleased with their flattering words, as he knew well he would not be able to write good stories any more if GHQ were watching him.

While he was in this dismal mood, a letter arrived from Take-uchi, written in a clumsy square hand. It was an invitation to a party which Nara would also attend. Shuntaro, however, could not make up his mind, remembering how Takeuchi had stuck him with the bill, but on the designated day, he received a telephone call from Takeuchi, who assured him "strictly no charge." Shuntaro then decided to go.

At Yaeko's House in Suitengu, Odaira was glad to find, besides Takeuchi and Nara, former Cpl. Narazaki, Pfc. Tobo, and Cpl. Kihara, who had saved his comrades' lives by "surprise presents" in the Philippine days. Yaeko's House was actually a high-class restaurant disguised as an ordinary house—a black-market restaurant sake shop, a product of MacArthur's "Dry Days." Odaira was dumbfounded not only by the house but also by beautiful Yaeko, the hostess. Clad in a fashionable kimono that would have been hard to find even in prewar days, she was entirely out of place, even with Takeuchi, who was also wearing a brand-new suit giving no hint that he had ever worn an old khaki black-marketeer's uniform.

"Now that Odaira-san is here, let's start the party," Nara said with the dignity of a master of ceremonies, his sun-tanned, rough farmer's face beaming.

Ushered into the next room, the guests were again astonished at the gorgeous set-up of the table.

"Takeuchi had always been smart in grabbing opportunities," Narazaki murmured. "But I never dreamed he could do this much."

"No, no. I haven't done anything yet. I simply wanted to ask your assistance for my future and show my thanks for the past," Takeuchi replied. "You see, I once bumped into Odaira-san in a Shimbashi black-market. That's the hardest time I ever experienced. I didn't have dough enough to buy drinks. Odaira-san bought a drink for me. I never forgot his kindness. Ever since I've wanted to do something to repay him. Right now I'm selling tiles for foreign style toilets. Mr. Kihara is working for me as a repairman. With your assistance, I'm planning to be a more useful man in this society." Takeuchi's speech finally came to an end.

As he poked his chopsticks into one of the dishes, Odaira could not but remember the days in the Philippines when he had least dreamed of such a day. The soldier who once dreamed of Manila's recapture by the Japanese Army was now making handsome money supplying tiles, riding high on the current building boom.

"Kihara, you were always good at everything. But I didn't know you were with Takeuchi," Odaira said. Kihara simply smiled off the remark, while Takeuchi took over.

"Yes, Kihara is good at repairing foreign-style toilets. He can even climb up to high footholds when we have to measure the number of tiles necessary for the outer decoration of the building. But he is too good at everything. That's his trouble. He can't stick to the same job for long."

"You mean your talent kills you?" Odaira turned to Kihara. "So, what are you doing now?"

Kihara still did not answer. Takeuchi again began to speak in a boss-like way. "This fellow is now mad for photography. He's really good at it. I wonder if your newspaper company could hire him – – ."

Then Tobo, who had been silent, said, "Narazaki-san – – you were our commander – –."

"Ya – – a very bad one," Narazaki said, as if in scorn of himself. And he explained he was working as a salesman. With his poor eloquence, he was apparently making little money. Everyone recalled how he had insisted on the uselessness of fighting when he brought back the news of Japan's complete surrender.

Tobo said he was teaching at a primary school in a small town on the northern tip of Honshu. "In my town, people are so poor that I can't just be a teacher to the school kids – –. I registered in the Communist Party because I know I have to work for the poor," he said, full of the passion of a young man.

Hearing his old buddies' remarks, Odaira noticed the maids who were serving sake to the guests. Their hands and fingers were extremely white—different from those of ordinary maids. "What kind of house is this?" Odaira whispered to Nara.

"Oh, this house?" Nara made a forced smile, saying, "Ah . . . a sort of a company dormitory."

That was enough. It seemed rather stupid to ask who the mistress was. Takeuchi had done really well taking advantage of the disorder. Odaira could not help wondering at these strangely changing times that caused such tremendous shifts in people's fortunes.

"Say, how about a picture?" Takeuchi asked Kihara, who brought out a German-made camera—too expensive a camera for the hobby of a latrine repairman. Kihara took pictures of the guests from various angles.

The editorial room of Odaira's office was always filled with confusion and shouting, as if reflecting the world's movement. Social chaos gave birth to many like Takeuchi while igniting political consciousness among the young who tried to mold churning chaos into revolutionary movement.

The strikes that had occurred recently seemed to Odaira to be symptomatic of something different from the ones that had driven the workers to walk out because of desperate need for higher wages to meet the rocketing cost of living. Now the strikes reflected political colors.

On July 5, 1949, Mr. Shimoyama, President of the National Railways, was found dead on railway tracks in the southern outskirts of Tokyo. Police sought clues in the then-prevailing dangerous atmosphere among the railway workers' union, but the vague announcements of the police led all the newspapers into confusion. It was thought that the president might have committed suicide—from the excessive strain of negotiating with the union. The newspapers were divided in their opinions. And the controversial views never crystallized into any collective conclusion. There appeared nothing to prove the truth.

While this case remained wrapped in mystery, the second incident happened. On July 15, a driverless and empty train suddenly surged down the tracks and went off the rails near Mitaka Station into some private houses, killing ten persons and seriously injuring seven. A witness reported to the police that he heard a railway worker shout just after the train started to run, "Watch this! Revenge on those who fired us!" Certain suspects were arrested, but no concrete evidence was produced.

The next month, another train was derailed in Matsukawa. After the train was overturned, the police frantically looked for evidence only after the spot was completely trampled by the crowds that thronged around it.

In all these incidents there was one common element: none of the arrested confessed to anything the police were seeking. No one admitted any knowledge of the incidents—of the first run-away train, the second derailment, the resulting deaths. All took advantage of the right to keep silent to any questions that might tend to incriminate them. This otherwise "most humane" right given by the new Constitution baffled the police in their effort to find the truth. Without scientific investigation methods far more advanced than those then available, there was little chance of solving these mysteries and the general public grew impatient.

Whatever the truth might have been, the Communist Party and its followers objected loudly to the official attitude that openly suggested that secret party movements were behind the incidents. Whether true or not, the authority's announcements gave the public an impression of treacherous and villainous behavior on the part of the Communist Party.

The Party that was liberated by MacArthur and that had secured over 2,140,000 votes to win six seats in the Diet in the 1946 General Election, increasingly lost popularity after a series of bloody incidents. Odaira could well imagine Tobo's perplexed state of mind, since Tobo had enthusiastically engaged in Party activities in a lonely mountain town as a freshman Party member, apparently driven by an urge for justice in the midst of a disorderly society.

The Party line, however, underwent no changes until May Day of 1952.

In the meantime, Odaira was busy answering phones and assigning cub-reporters. One day, Narazaki came into his room. As an automobile salesman, he had been trying hard to sell cars to Odaira's newspaper company. But he succeeded only in making contracts for a few motorcycles. He had no talent as a salesman, lacking the necessary eloquence and smooth appearance—the last things Narazaki ever could attain.

"It's not so hard to sell cars, but the trouble is how to get paid," Narazaki said half-musingly.

"Even this office?" Odaira asked.

"No," Narazaki said quickly. "Your company has a good reputation. So I don't worry about payment; in this case, it's the competition that's tough."

Narazaki confessed that he was a "grade C" salesman receiving instructions from a younger man who handled the actual negotiations. Consequently, he had to be satisfied with a minor share of commissions.

"But anyway, I have to thank Takeuchi. He bought several station wagons from me." Narazaki sighed. "I really owe a lot to him."

"That's good that Takeuchi will buy. He's got a knack of getting ahead of the others," Odaira said.

"Yeah, the guy who makes money always makes money wherever he goes," Narazaki murmured, and got up to leave.

Narazaki looked too downcast for Odaira to let him go that way.

"Say, Narazaki, how about a drink?" Odaira asked.

They went to the black-market area behind Yurakucho Station.

"They built restaurants first," Narazaki mumbled to himself. "Say, about a restaurant, I've been trying to bring that Kihara to his senses. You see, he's no good."

"But, that camera, you remember? That was a very expensive one. If a person sold it, he could build a little house," Odaira said, his cheeks rosy-hued after two glasses of synthetic sake. "Anyway, it costs one or two hundred thousand yen." Odaira stared at his partner.

"Yeah?" Narazaki suddenly changed his tone, "Then – –" He paused a moment and said, "I hate to say this. But I wonder if he has resumed his 'special line of work.'" Narazaki seemed really puzzled. "He saved our lives in the Philippine mountains, but he shouldn't do that here in Tokyo," he said, raising his voice.

Odaira laughed. But soon his journalistic sense reminded him of something. He dared not mention it to Narazaki. Instead he asked, "Narazaki, are you still associating with him?"

"Yeah. That stupid Nara wants to marry Kihara's sister," Narazaki replied.

"How is he making a living?"

"Not magnificently. Kihara's always playing around, but still he lives far better than I do. He says he can sell his pictures."

Odaira did not ask any more questions. But Narazaki continued, "You know Kihara's sister-in-law? She's been working in Takeuchi's restaurant. She has a very bad reputation. Even Takeuchi doesn't think much of her. But that poor Nara is crazy about her, though I told him to give up such a woman—a thousand times!" Odaira simply nodded, as Narazaki went on, "Kihara says nothing. But she looks hopelessly homely even after living in Tokyo so long. Only a farmer like Nara could see anything in her."

"That's too bad," Odaira said.

"You think so, too?" Narazaki said half-questioning.

"I don't know her. So, I can say nothing about the marriage. But Kihara's sister must be like Kihara, I think. What does she say?"

"Oh, she's willing, of course. But we know she can't be a good wife for Nara."

After they talked on, they finally shook hands and said, "Let's wise him up!" They said farewell in front of Yurakucho Station.

Despite severe food shortages, housing problems, and high commodity prices, certain privileged and wealthy classes lived fantastically well. Bribery became a part of daily life between Government officials and the seekers of special privileges. One such scandal was finally exposed and it was a great surprise to most of the people when they first learned that the Showa Denko Company extended its "hands" to Cabinet members. Even Socialist Premier Ashida Hitoshi was suspected of receiving excessive "party contributions" from Hinohara Setsuzo, President of Denko. Ashida expelled the men implicated from the cabinet. The surprised general public showed some slight indignation. Some people even sent letters to the editor: "Those who were exposed are just the unlucky ones. There are many who don't get caught . . ."

In September, 1950, *Lady Chatterley's Lover* was indicted as an "obscene publication." Literary circles protested en mass, on the ground that there were thousands of other erotic or pornographic publications wrongly set loose by the postwar liberalism.

Moral delinquency permeated almost all ranks and walks of society. Politicians and businessmen tried to approach the powerful officials of the Economic and Scientific Section of SCAP (Supreme Commander Allied Powers), which held almost unlimited authority over economic affairs in defeated Japan. Takeuchi, of course, used every possible means of taking a part in, and winning, the bidding for contracts for the construction and remodeling of buildings. Odaira made a secret check through his own sources: Takeuchi had done so much that once indicted he could have little chance of acquittal. Takeuchi was safe only because the police authorities were too busy catching up with crimes of greater magnitude.

Under such circumstances, the Communist Party had a great advantage in its anti-government campaign. The Party obtained twenty-five seats in the general election after the collapse under scandal of the Socialist Ashida cabinet. The third Yoshida Cabinet was formed. The revolutionary force was becoming a serious threat to the conservative camp, when suddenly in June, 1950, war broke out in Korea.

The Korean war lasted a long time and brought with it a great inflationary boom through the magic of *tokuju*, Special Procurement. This was a heavenly manna that artificially resurrected the otherwise suffocated Japanese economy.

America also tried to reverse its policy towards Japan. The punitive policy was now shifted to a baby-sitting policy so that Japan could be kept comfortably in the buggy of the Western camp.

The constitutional renunciation of war was surely now to be declared a failure, and become virtually a dead letter.

All these sudden changes were so dazzling that Odaira almost forgot Taguchi, one of his old pals. Odaira phoned Takeuchi, but it was Nara who answered the phone. "I sent a postcard to you. Taguchi died in a TB sanitarium near Kamakura. He died miserably. Had he informed us earlier, we'd have done something . . . if only we had known a little earlier . . ."

Odaira Shuntaro went to Zushi to attend the funeral ceremony of Taguchi. He found Nara and Narazaki already helping. Taguchi's father complained meekly, "If only we could have bought butter—or something nourishing." For Taguchi, stricken with tuberculosis, there had been no nourishment or medicine. His death had been like the melting away of a candle.

After the ceremony all three kept silent, feeling a strange vacancy of mind. Finally Nara said, "How about dropping in at our place in Suitengu for a drink?"

But neither Odaira nor Narazaki accepted the offer.

Instead, Odaira hurried back to the office. He called in a junior reporter who covered the Metropolitan Police Board.

"Say, about that Jesse James Jr.—guess you should track it down again."

"Is there any new angle?" the reporter asked.

"Positively, it's one of my friends," Odaira said.

"Your friend? Oh, no."

"Yes. I haven't got any concrete evidence yet. But this guy can climb up a high fence quite easily. You said the thief usually enters through a washroom. This guy is an expert repairman of flush toilets," Odaira calmly said.

"Well, you think I should track him?"

"Yes. Somehow I am in debt to him, I mean I was. But now I can't help. He's too slimy and going too far. I've just been to a friend's funeral and really felt I shouldn't let a crooked friend run around loose in this society when an honest but weak and poor guy simply dies. If he comes back to his senses—maybe after serving a term—I will shake his hands, of course," Odaira said rather emotionally.

Giving a detailed description of Kihara, Odaira added, "Try to make him give himself up, if you can."

A few days later, the reporter came back to report on the progress of the Jesse James Jr. case. He found several suspicious points but they weren't enough to indict Kihara, who seemed to have committed a series of almost perfect crimes.

"Unless he strikes again, we can't nab him," the reporter concluded.

"A lucky fellow!" Odaira sighed.

But he wasn't. Kihara's luck came to an end. He moved into the Yokohama area. Though he succeeded in sneaking into a foreigner's residence, he got caught on a barbed-wire fence. While he tried desperately to get loose, a bullet from a pistol got him in the leg.

"I should have stopped him earlier!" Odaira clenched his fists with frustrated regret, but felt strangely relieved that he had not caught Kihara with his own hands.

Kihara's arrest was worth a three-column spread in every newspaper. One day, Odaira received a letter from Narazaki:

The news really upset me. Kihara was Jesse James, Jr.! I now remember so well how we praised his stealing ability. It saved our lives. But actually I'm relieved to hear about his arrest. Things are different now and under this present, more normal life situation his habitual stealing should be punished. I've had the suspicion for a long time that he might be the culprit. How many times have I thought of informing the police about him! Now he's been arrested! I know we owe our lives to him, but I feel "justice has longer arms than our poor sentiments."

Odaira chuckled. Narazaki's line of thinking was practically the same as his own. He was greatly encouraged to have such an honest, righteous, and warm man courageously fighting against the disorder of the present society.

Then he remembered Nara, who was so taken with Kihara's sister, Asako. When Nara visited his office, he disclosed an amazing story. He was going to open a bar in the Ginza. Odaira couldn't help thinking that Nara—the farmer—would be a sure victim of some sharp practice or other.

"Are you serious about this crazy idea?" Odaira asked.

"Sure, of course. I bet the business'll be a success, if you bring in lots of friends." Nara seemed completely certain that his venture would succeed.

"The Ginza is not any place we can afford to go," Odaira said, giving up the idea of dissuading him.

"Don't think that way. Soon beer will be on the market. Foreign liquors, too. From now on bars should not be limited. I'll try not to limit the customers to the wealthy class."

Odaira was suddenly aware of the contradiction that prevailed almost everywhere in society. After the breaking up of the Zaibatsu and promulgation of the Anti-Monopoly Law and the Economic Decentralization Law, the peers and nobles lost their powers and became the "has-been" families. Their houses and 'mansions,' Japlish term for condominiums, were bought up by upstarts and black-marketeers—a complete social upheaval.

Of the seven warriors who had shared their scanty food in the deep mountains of the Philippines, Taguchi had died, Kihara had been arrested, leaving only five survivors in the whirl of this confused society. Even the remaining five were now living entirely different kinds of lives.

One night, Odaira was invited to the Foreign Correspondents' Club, where he could drink beer to his heart's content. Here there was none of that arrogance usually found among "conquerors." Equality and liberty prevailed. Odaira treasured this atmosphere such as that he could hardly find in any other place.

As he passed by Yurakucho Station, he saw gaily attired "angels of the street" swarming around the station. They looked like flowers blooming on a scorched land.

Totally devastated Japan had quickly absorbed the fashions of the world. Girls were using American cosmetics and wearing costumes straight out of Vogue regardless of their dimensions and coloring. He remembered a "Letter to the Editor" that had come in that morning. It severely criticized the recent stylishness of the Japanese girls on the ground that there were so many war-suffering people even among the victors. The letter was full of bitter words against frivolity and flippancy. That much was understandable but Odaira could hardly think it entirely wrong that Japanese girls wanted to cast off the wartime *mompei*—the dull-looking blue cotton farmer's pantaloons.

"As soon as the girls become prettier, the men start working harder"—that old saw, Odaira thought, could be applied to every one but that lone wolf Narazaki—though he had looked busier in his most recent visits. Then one sunny afternoon in a coffee shop near his office, Odaira eliminated Nara as an exception to the rule. A very modern girl was sitting beside Narazaki, who abruptly asked "Haven't you met this girl before?"

Odaira struggled with his memory.

Then Narazaki startled both Odaira and the girl by saying, "She was Mrs. Taguchi, don't you remember?"

The girl blushed. Odaira quickly flashed back to the day of Taguchi's funeral. Yes, there was a girl who was wearing a black mourning kimono.

Narazaki told all about his new bride. She was formerly a nurse in the sanitarium where Taguchi died. Competing with several rivals, Taguchi succeeded in winning her hand, probably because of his naiveté.

"We've already started living together," Narazaki frankly confessed.

Odaira simply said, "Congratulations." The couple looked completely mismatched—at one end, the rugged simplicity of Narazaki; at the other, the modern winsomeness of Katsuko.

In the early postwar days there was no one who could openly criticize MacArthur and his policy. Naturally, there was no such freedom under the Occupation administration. But a powerful additional inhibition was also operative—Japanese nature was accustomed to obeying blindly the ruler's words. MacArthur did not understand this blindly obedient nature. He seemed to believe that Japan was full of militaristic nationals. When he realized his misconception, he tried to alter his policy. The general public, however, was scarcely aware of changes taking place far above them. They were simply following the orders that came out of the SCAP (Supreme Commander Allied Powers) in the Daiichi Building through the Japanese government, always carefully muffled with showers of beautiful modifiers.

The people, therefore, were completely stunned when they were confronted with the unexpected news that MacArthur—the almighty five-star general, foreign Shogun—had been fired by Truman. After MacArthur's departure, there sprang up an interesting phenomenon—an increasing anti-Americanism. Japanese began publicly criticizing the foreign nationals who had been strutting through their country. The citizens of Kyoto and Osaka attacked their municipal authorities on account of local regulations that prohibited Japanese drivers from passing Occupation vehicles.

This tendency was given further impetus by the Communist Party. They claimed that the democracy the Americans had brought to Japan was suspect; it provided liberty and freedom only between the Japanese but not between Japanese and Americans.

The Communist leaders who had been purged by MacArthur in June 1950 went underground, whence they apparently maintained command over their followers. "Red" students started riots on the campuses. Professors could not control their students. Some professors even tried to get on the bandwagon by making themselves look "pink," if not completely "red." The Teachers Union of Japan started to make political announcements, while the core Communists prepared operation "Y" for armed uprisings. Pistols were smuggled in from "nowhere." Molotov Cocktail bottles were secretly prepared for military operations. "The Communist Party that should be loved by the people" had disappeared.

In the late afternoon of May Day 1952, Odaira was on his way to the Ministry of Education to cover a story on the "6-3-3 System" of six years primary school and three each of junior high and high school, adopted after defeat from America. His car was passing near the north entrance of the Hibiya Park when the driver pointed toward the Imperial Palace Plaza and shouted, "Look, Odaira-san, something must be up!"

A cloud of dust was rising high, suggesting some serious trouble.

"Let's go back . . . to Babasakimon, if we can," Odaira ordered, though he began to doubt whether the car could get through the crowds that now swarmed around. The car, however, somehow managed to get through. Every window of the Daiichi and Meiji buildings was full of American faces looking down curiously.

A photographer was coming back from the plaza. His torn shirt and bloody face clearly reflected the seriousness of the trouble. Then a group of students gathered around the American cars parked alongside the road. The cars were turned over and set afire, one after another.

"That's outrageous," the driver yelled.

As Odaira looked around, most of the Occupation cars parked around the Hibiya-Babasakimon area had either smashed windows or were being turned over and set afire. From the direction of the plaza could be heard the sound of flaming bottles exploding. A rescue squad of policemen were running from Hibiya. The students scattered as the policemen tried to grab them.

"It's getting too dangerous. Let's go back," Odaira said. At that moment he saw a pale young man staggering toward the car. He could not see the man's face, which was covered with dust and bloodstains. But Odaira noticed something familiar.

"Tobo! Here!" he shouted with a slightly suppressed voice, hopefully to be heard as far as Tobo and no farther, gesturing to the half-opened door. The man collapsed on the floor.

"Let's go back!" Odaira said, as he closed the door.

"Where to? The office?" the driver gasped.

"No! To the Ginza! Quick!" An idea flickered in Odaira's mind.

Parking the car in front of a bar in West Ginza, Odaira carried Tobo to the rear entrance. "Nara! Are you there?" he shouted.

Down the staircase came Asako, clad in pajamas.

"Asako-san, is he out? Well, this fellow is our mutual friend. He's hurt. Could you do something to help him?"

Tobo's face was ashen when he was laid down on the tatami in the attic. Tired but excited, Tobo looked seriously hurt.

"What happened?" Asako asked.

"Oh, he just got messed up in the May Day celebrations. He'll be all right with an hour of sleep," Odaira answered.

"Is he also a friend of my husband?" she asked. "He looks so courageous for his age, doesn't he, Odaira-san?" She was intently looking down at Tobo's closed eyes. Odaira looked away from her heaving bosom, lifting almost out of her pink pajamas.

Soon Tobo opened his eyes, looked mysteriously around, and tried to raise his head.

"No, no. You should be a good boy and be quiet!" Asako patted Tobo's shoulder.

"Where am I?" Tobo meekly asked.

"You're in Nara's house. This is Mrs. Nara," Odaira said.

Tobo smiled a wryly, as if he were ashamed of being helped by a "running dog" of capitalism and "a poison seller of capitalism."

"I must go." He raised his upper body.

"Where to?" Odaira tried to push him down.

"To the Imperial Plaza, of course."

"Nonsense, May Day is over," Odaira said, almost harshly.

"I won't be defeated! War isn't over," Tobo murmured and collapsed.

Odaira left the bar, asking Asako to keep an eye on Tobo. When he came back to his desk, however, he received a telephone call from Asako, who told him that Tobo had left the bar saying he would give himself up.

That day, he learned later, about five thousand policemen had been involved in hand-to-hand fighting with five to six thousand members of the All Japan Student Association, the Daily Workers' Union, and the Korean Federation in Japan. Many people had been seriously injured. The police had used tear gas, which finally dispersed the rioters.

Odaira, however, could never trace the whereabouts of Tobo. Possibly he was among the rioters arrested. He was shocked at what happened that day. But there was another person who was further —and in an unexpected fashion—shocked by the effect of the May Day riot. It was Nara Hachiro.

A few days later he came to Odaira's office and explained with tears in his eyes. His wife, Asako, had not been unfaithful since their marriage. But on May Day she had kissed Tobo when he could not move. "That's why Tobo left our house," he said. "I'm deeply sorry for what my wife has done to my old friend."

Odaira could remember Asako looking down at Tobo's closed eyes. Now in front of him was Nara also with closed wet eyes, murmuring that he would divorce his wife.

"If I should keep on with this life, I would be most miserable," Nara sighed. "Anyway, I will think it over," he said and left.

Takeuchi Renpei seemed to be most prosperous. Amid the deflation, buildings were being constructed one after another. His business, naturally, increased.

Odaira received an invitation to a party from Takeuchi. When he arrived at the restaurant in Tsukiji, he found Nara, Narazaki, and Takeuchi already sitting around a large table.

"Tonight is the Old Comrades Get-Together Party and also the farewell to Nara. He is going back to his farm," Takeuchi declared.

Nara bowed twice or thrice to every toast.

"That's good," Odaira said and quickly reflected whether his remark was fit for an occasion where Nara had divorced his wife and was going back to farming.

"Well, I think farming is the best job I can do," Nara said, almost delightedly.

"But it took lots of money and time before you realized it," Takeuchi jokingly teased him.

"Yet, you're lucky, you drank lots of liquor when I was simply sipping that atomic-bomb bootleg," Odaira joined the kidding.

"Well, I'll never drink foreign liquor again in my life," Nara replied seriously.

"Say, let's stop talking. Let's drink!" Takeuchi shouted and gestured to the waiting Geisha girls, suggesting they pour more sake for every one.

Taguchi dead; Kihara and Tobo in the custody of the police, though for different charges; Nara now going back to where he came from.

Ten years had passed so quickly—or so slowly, in a sense—Odaira was musing, when suddenly Takeuchi said: "Let's the three of us find a bride for Odaira! Otherwise he will be simply drinking sake until he passes away!"

"Never mind my business! You've two or three mistresses. That'll cover my share. I don't need any dame around me!" Odaira shouted, but was soon ashamed as every Geisha looked curiously at him.

He poured himself some sake and gulped it down—trying to swallow something, some thought, that he felt somewhat vaguely he should rather forget.

HOMECOMING 1945

by Akiyama Isa

NO ONE was at the station to meet him. He hadn't expected anyone,
of course; but still he looked around hopefully searching the milling
crowds for some familiar face, some anchorage to the past. Instead
he saw the empty, hulking, roofless remains of the station, the
shaky walls propped up by boards, and next to the ruins of the
building, the hastily constructed plywood barracks that now served
as the station.

A black quivering mass of flies papered the plywood walls. He
watched the lazily sunning insects, trying to ignore the knowledge
of what had made them suddenly so well-fed, but it was hard to
suppress a shudder.

Suddenly stepping over to the wall, he took his ragged military
cap off and began slapping and cutting viciously at the flies.
Mockingly, the flies escaped out of his reach only to swarm back
again.

People were gathering to stare at him. He dusted off his cap and
put it on, tugged at it, tightened the army pack on his shoulders, and
walked away. He did not understand himself why he had so
furiously attacked the flies. It was a foolish gesture and he felt
ashamed.

There were no buses. He started down the road toward his home
on foot. The road stretched out in front of him wider than he
remembered it, for the houses on both sides had been explosively

49

cleared; nothing remained but rubble: stones, bricks, tiles, pieces of corrugated tin, broken crockery.

Here and there a water spigot jutted nakedly out of the bare ground like some surrealistic sapling. He turned his head quickly away from the sight of tree trunks scorched by some terrible, unearthly heat, but paused and gazed, repressing a giggle for there was something humorous in the half of a porcelain bathtub and part of a toilet exposed to public gaze.

The pack on his shoulder grew heavy, but he plodded on. All around him there was an awful stillness, the quiet that follows a gigantic upheaval, as palpable as that of an ever-humming machine having been turned off. It seemed to him that he was alone in the vast dreamlike devastation surrounding him.

Then he saw a three-sided lean-to pieced together from corrugated tin and half-burnt planks that had been rescued from the debris. A woman in rags sat on the earthen floor inside, looking out at the road. He called out, "Do you happen to know anything about the people near Nikitsu?" The woman gazed at him blankly. He repeated his question as he approached nearer. Then he saw that one half of her face had been kneaded and twisted like soft dough, her exterior reflecting the twisting of her inner being from any sense of reality.

The woman remained silent, staring straight ahead, expressionless. She was beyond hearing or seeing, she was merely waiting for that final release. He mumbled an apology and walked on past her hut.

By the familiar curve of the road, he knew at last his home was now near. He had prepared himself, he thought, for what he would find, and yet he was in no way prepared. Ever since that dreadful day one month ago when official confirmation reached him, he had read and listened to every scrap of information he could pick up in the news and from the rumors. Every moment on the troop train had been spent in preparing himself. But even now he did not want to believe.

He found the location of his house; the stone lantern, leaning tipsily, was still standing in the space that had been garden. The foundation stones faintly marked the floor plan. He walked through —this had been the family room, this was his parents' room, this the dining room, the kitchen, his sister's room.

He put down his pack slowly and tried to think what he should do next. The dumb remains of what had once been his home were proof that the official report was true. No one in his family or in the neighborhood could have survived.

The compounded feelings of bitterness, anguish and loss swirled through him until he was unable to think at all. Aimlessly he kicked at a battered saucepan lying near his foot.

Something glittered amidst the heap of dark rubble beneath the pan.

He stooped to look closer. The glitter came from a small *juzu*, a rosary made of crystal beads. With trembling fingers he picked it up, marveling that a fragile string of beads had remained intact in the midst of all that wreckage. He knew the *juzu*, it was the one his mother used in her morning devotions to Buddha. He could see vividly his mother's serene face as she sat quietly before the small family altar softly intoning the sutra.

Very awkwardly he tried to slip the *juzu* around his clasped hands as he had done when he was a child in imitation of his mother, but the weakened string gave way and the beads clattered to the ground. Like a person coming out of ether, he was gripped by the pain of grief. He saw what had been whole jusr a moment ago disintegrate in an instant at the touch of his hands. He threw himself on the ground and wept.

Gradually he became calmer. He sat up and wiped his face with his shirtsleeves. His utter hopelessness and resentment and sorrow seemed to recede from him with the flow of tears.

Then he bent down, carefully picking up the scattered crystal beads. The beads could be restrung and made whole again. The links unifying individuals with one another were frail and transitory, constantly being strained and broken, but faith could relink all into one connected circle again. He wrapped the salvaged beads in his handkerchief and put it in his pocket.

Then he shouldered his pack and walked away toward the heart of the city, slowly, but with steady steps.

A CRANE THAT CANNOT COME BACK

by Seto Nanako

I must live through the realities of life
Too cruel and irretrievable,
Though I feel much pain in myself.
Supposing
That my days are numbered.

Aug. 25, 1958

Profuse bleeding!
How painful I've felt in both mind and body.
Words simply fail me in expressing myself to others.
Thinking I'd be lost, I stoutly stood it, even while I cried. Gritting my teeth, I stoutly stood it, telling myself that I must live. Then, at the very moment that I was feeling relieved, I burst into tears in the excess of my joy. Soon after a feeling of anxiety grew in me, a fear lest I should shortly be attacked once more by that horror, and again be lost.
I *must* think about it against my will. I do not belong to myself alone.
I must live as long as I can for the benefit of my daughter, my mother, husband, and brother, although I have become weak and disabled.
Oh, God, let me live, and in peace.

52

Nov. 12

I recall it was about this time . . .
Like terrible dreams . . . almost one year has passed already.
My throat has become swollen, it is clearly visible.
I have had a sore throat for several days.

Nov. 14

The bloody phlegm continues, though I am careful still to keep quiet.
Impossible for me to rid myself of a feeling of fear.
Unthinkingly, gave a scolding to Mami, my child, for her mischief. Now I repent.

Nov. 15

Mother has made a large purchase for me.
I feel very sorry for her.
I hear she has stopped smoking . . . only because of me.
How hard it must have been for you, mother!
I must live at any cost, for the sake of my family, especially Mami . . . poor thing.

A verse suddenly came to me:

> *I that am now sick in bed*
> *Do want to live as long as possible;*
> *I am fighting*
> *For my only daughter.*

A poor verse . . . just a passing thought. I'd be ashamed if anyone else saw it.

Nov. 16

Caught a slight cold. Mami also feels bad, being a little feverish.

Nov. 17

It makes me very uneasy to take so much medicine.
Another new disease would be fatal to me.
How long will it be until we can joyfully look at each other again?
I am weeping . . .

Nov. 18

Have a constant headache. My sore throat continues as usual.
Whenever I have a singing in my ears, I feel unable to endure it.
But I am trying to take as little medicine as possible.
Another person had died of pernicious anemia, it is said . . .
Recently, I get tired easily. Feel stiff in my shoulders, despite being
in bed.

Nov. 21

I'm very surprised to hear that there is something abnormal about
my chest.
Now I know the reason for the bloody phlegm, and also why I have
been given streptomycin continually.
Out of the frying pan into the . . .
I have symptoms of Basedow's disease. That gets on my nerves, too.

Nov. 22

I've got a slight fever all the time. I am always in fear that something else is wrong with me.
Last night I was terribly confused, because a disgusting arthralgia
began; however, it has now passed.
Feel relieved. May nothing be abnormal!

Nov. 23

Tears after tears,
Looking at the town by night,
Seeing Mami off from the hospital,
Longing for the time I shall recover from illness,
Fear grows that I may never be well again.

> *How long will it be*
> *Before the time I can lead a happy life*
> *With Mami?*
> *Listening to the sound of the peace bell*
> *Traveling over the autumn night*
> *Growing deeper and deeper.*

Nov. 26

Bleeding for five minutes . . .
Being caused by menses?

Nov. 27

Mother gives me so much food . . . I can't eat it all.
Filled with much gratitude.

Nov. 3o

Feel so happy when Mami comes here.
Feel so bad when Mami goes home . . . unspeakable sorrow.

Dec. I

Time flies like an arrow.
The last month of the year has stolen upon us.
It seems likely that my beauty parlor will be reopened.
I am a constant source of anxiety to my mother.

Dec. 2

Kikusada-san visits me. I speak too much about my illness and
have hardly time to thank him for his kindness.

Dec. 3

Feeling better these days. Because of my liver?
Hoping this good condition continues.

Dec. 8

Begin to put my pictures in order. They bring back pleasant memories of when I was in good health.

Dec. 10

We could manage to buy for my husband an overcoat, which he has
long wanted. Sorry for him having done without it until now.
I think that he himself will have to get the clothes he needs from
now on . . . little by little.

Mami's need for clothing is also pressing heavily on me; however, it seems to be hardly possible to do anything about it.

Have a vague bad feeling in my body and try hard not to tell others about it.

Shortly the light is turned out and I go to bed listening to the sound of the peace bell.

I feel lonely.

Dec. 11

The blood count of leukocytes is 4,500.

May everything go well, at least until the New Year, when I may visit home.

Dec. 12

Receive a small package from Tokyo containing a pair of pretty gloves for Mami. I kiss them impulsively.

Get tired watching TV again after such a long time.

Stiffness in my shoulders and pain in my back makes me so gloomy.

My only wish is that I may become healthy again, at least by the New Year holidays.

Dec. 13

I can't move my arms and neck today.

The doctor says that I may be out of the hospital in a few months if nothing abnormal interferes. God, preserve me!

On hearing that Shimizu-san is said to have cancer, I fall into low spirits as if it were my own disease.

Dec. 14

Am sorry for giving a scolding to Mami, and think, Mami, please forgive my thoughtless heart.

When she grows ripe for marriage, I am afraid, she will have to face many obstacles[1]. . . . Until that time, oh, I wish I could live on . . .

---

[1] NOTE Offspring of seriously ill parents, especially victims of radiation illness, are undesirable in matrimonial match-making and are frequently pruned out by premarital investigations.

Mami, please don't think ill of me, since only your father's uncontaminated blood runs in your veins. Thus, you must never consider yourself unfortunate, Mami. And so, get married to a person like your papa, you know.

Dec. 17

Feel many pains in the various joints of my body. My face appears to be a bit swollen . . . a reaction of Amipylo?

Dec. 21

My roommate has left the hospital.
Bedding and equipment have all been taken out of my room.
I'll be alone from tonight.
In my loneliness, tears stream ceaselessly down my cheeks.
Although thinking that I shall get used to my vacant room soon, tears come at once.
Make up my mind to ask my nurse, Shigehiro-san, to explain to me my medical record.
She advises me to take it easy for a few months so that I will make no failure of my life. I grit my teeth . . .
The count of leukocytes is 6,400. The doctor says that all the parts of my body which have been abnormal seem to be gradually returning to a normal condition.
Even with little or no blood transfusions, my condition should take no turn for the worse!

Dec. 22

I felt so lonely that it took much time to get to sleep last night.
I never hear the voice of Mami through the phone, or news about Mami from my husband, without tears.
When my husband had to go home, it was very hard for me to keep back my tears.

Dec. 24

The New Year is just around the corner. Many patients are leaving the hospital. I was at last moved into another room yesterday, in which I've been left alone again. I cannot stand such utter loneliness.

Whenever night nears, my feeling of solitude grows more and more.
It is Christmas Eve tonight. Listening to gay Christmas carols sung
under the windows, I become sad to tears, wondering how soon I can
return to good health and a happy life.
I hear that the patient who was operated on for his pancreas is
dangerously ill. When the doctor inclines his head as if in doubt at
seeing me, I always fear that I might be in the same situation as
that patient.
How long has it been since I saw Mami last? All day I think about
driving home without taking permission from the doctors, to meet
my lovely Mami.

Dec. 25

I did not expect anybody to come to celebrate the holy night, but my
brother, Hiromi, and his friends dropped in to wish me a *Merry
Christmas*, bringing a piece of Christmas cake they bought together
downtown. Weep for joy.

Dec. 26

Became feverish since last night. Seems I cannot quite feel comfortable about it when relapses occur.
Am making efforts not to think about my illness going from bad to
worse, but a feeling of uneasiness inevitably attacks me.
Hoping that blood transfusions will not bring on fever, and that my
temperature will not rise any more.

Dec. 27

According to thermometer at 6:00 a.m., I have 99°, though slept like
a log last night by the help of an injection.
Slight drop to 98.4° at noon.
May I never develop a higher fever than tonight's!
But, alas! I have an attack of fever of 100.4° although the pains have
been gradually abating.
Must I give up all hope of visiting my home?
What an irony of fate!
Patent medicine for a cold is liable to reduce a higher feverish
attack.
Take medicine, Ilotycin (erythromycin). I know it has a drastic side
effect.

I am simply dying to go home, only so that I can see Mami at play from my bed.

May I return home!

Dec. 28

I have had quite a weak appetite for a couple of days.

Urine suddenly decreased to a small amount today.

Received a slight feverish attack, because I broke into a cold sweat when the doctors took the blood from my chest.

I am not feeling much better.

Soon comes the hour of putting out the lights.

A sudden attack of unbearable solitude again.

Seem to be slightly feverish.

I catch at, and open every nerve to, any slight changes that happen.

I cannot possibly live long since I am a broken person.

I cannot know very well how things stand with Hiromi, however . . .

Poor fellow!

How can we help him find his life worth living?

Mother and I are being tormented by it.

Jan. 2, 1959

Began a new year of life in the hospital.

As nobody else is yet here—after going home for New Year's Day—there is much quiet and loneliness . . .

Gather up my courage, looking forward to the day of leaving the hospital.

About half the blood transfusions I've already taken before—100 cc.

Jan. 5

The highest fever is 98.6° for today.

Five days have already passed, too soon.

A patient in the next room has returned to the hospital.

Since the 27th of last month my fever refuses to go down to normal.

It seems not to be serious enough to worry about, but it is always weighing heavily on me.

Spend lonely the long-awaited New Year in the hospital.

How hateful to be tried by God!

Feel like sinking through the earth.

My husband is very kind to me in every way possible.
One more has died this morning. The second victim this year.

Jan. 6

Scarcely had the fever been reduced when it rose to 104° last night.
Lose the power of resistance and feel myself easily running down day by day. My husband leaves nothing to desire in nursing me.
I am much indebted to him.
I haven't seen Mami for quite a while. I hope she is fine.
I cannot help feeling depressed. 102.2° in the evening.

Jan. 7

One more has died. Third victim this year.
Am sorry for having wasted a lot of money on the medicine; about four thousand yen (about $11) just simply to go home.
Besides, I made Mami happy by promising to return home.
Want very badly to be in bed together holding her tight in my arms if only for one night.
Count of leukocytes was 5,300 on the 27th of last December.
But erythrocyte and color index rather decreased.

Jan. 10

Mami and I meet after a long separation.
Shed tears.
Knowing that I must not move, Mami never comes close to me.
Feeling of loneliness . . .
There are still white signs in my throat like diphtheria.
We have been having troubles that are a bit different from before since the day before yesterday.
We are all black sheep, including me!
Hiromi has finally left home to go to Tokyo. I can't help feeling uneasy about Hiromi. Speaking little, showing his feelings hardly at all, but I suppose he must be filled with much suffering. I'm sorry I couldn't meet him, for all his coming, before he left for Tokyo.
I that am already disabled cannot possibly do everything as I want.
I can't stand by myself.
Wish my earliest possible recovery not only for my sake but also for my lovely daughter, Mami.
Mami is now my only hope to get well.

Jan. 12

Much menses after two months.
The count of leukocytes was 1,100 on the 30th of last December, but fortunately returned to a normal 5,000 on the 10th of this month. Yesterday Mami and I had a merry time together all day long after her long absence. She says, "Mommy, shall we go with Papa to Fukuya Department Store, with its many facilities for play, in the day after sleeping for one night all together?" That makes me cry! May our happiest day come soon. I answered, "Mami, I wonder if that day will come after a lot of nights." Mami looked confused as she knew nothing about how long I must stay. Feel sorry for her. Shed tears.

Jan. 13

Spent the whole day all right without any sense of boredom.
Having a wonderful time with Mami makes me tired.
Bad headache. Feel very ill in my chest tonight.
I have never felt as sick as I do these days.
I am also out of sorts around my stomach.
Perhaps it might be my imagination.
Feel relieved to know that mother intends to come home and settle down.
I am anxious when I think about Hiromi; tears run down out of my eyes. Hoping that I may have enough sleep tonight and get up happily tomorrow morning.
Shadow of restlessness.
Writing this diary while in bed five minutes before the lights are put out.
It is now raining. That makes me very sad.

Jan. 14

The head consulting physician comes round to see me, and says, "Perhaps you may be able to leave the hospital around the end of March."
I was very glad to hear it. I wish I could pay a day visit, at least before March. But I fear that I may cause much trouble by catching a cold, since I am too sensitive to that. Unwillingly, I control myself.

May I feel quite well by the day when Mami enters kindergarten.
Opinions about my blood test sound pretty good.
I know it is not good to be so gloomy about everything.
The doctor says that there is no reason to worry about my chest trouble.
My face seems to be a bit swollen now; I have been growing stouter.
The blood transfusions are reduced to twice a week from today.
I am very happy to know that I am getting better than ever.
I have not seen my husband for three days.
Oh, yes, my body temperature has been returning to normal; besides, there is no need to test the urine quantity any more; the examinations of urine and feces become reduced to once a month from now on. I wonder if I am expected to go home around March.
May everything pass off quietly. And may I soon recover. . . .

Jan. 15

My husband kindly called on me after a long absence. He seems to be tired out. I never miss two days without seeing Mami.
I find her fascinatingly pretty hearing her voice through the phone "Mommy, see you again. . . . "

Jan. 16

Permission for bathing.
Dr. Ishida said only in play that I am leaving the hospital by the end of this month. I know it is not true, but my heart beats with joy. The doctor says leukocytes are normal. There seems to be nothing wrong.
Tears for joy. Pleased with myself.
The blood transfusions will be only on Monday and Thursday every week.
Please God, I will not be long in getting well for the sake of Mami.
In the evening Sanae brings Mami to the hospital.
Mami's little face looked very cold, but she didn't seem to be catching a cold. I was reassured by that. But I feel an unaccountable compassion for her . . .
I do not know, does Mami miss me and feel lonely?
I hope I may live long enough to protect my only daughter, as long as possible.

Jan. 18

It has been awfully cold for a couple of days. Through the windows I see many people in good health, and envy them very much.
Mami came in the afternoon.
Her hands were a bit swollen with the cold. I suppose she must have felt cold, but she did not mind at all. She was very fine.
I notice there have been some changes about Mami that she never had before, in her way of reading a book or doing something by herself.
Since she is now growing, she is eagerly asking me many questions. "Mommy, what is this? Well, how come —"
I am afraid, may my family be so kind as to answer her questions, though it takes much trouble to do so. It is now one of the most important times in her passage through life.

Jan. 19

Only three drops of kenacort (triamcinolone).
I pray to be back safely in March. I'm feeling better.
Mami has become simply mad in asking about everything lately.
People say that the future depends on the ages between three and four.
I hope everybody will kindly use easy language in teaching Mami.
May I be able to be back home around March as the doctor says.
And may what he says contain absolute truth for this one time.
Shige-kun, Hiromi's good friend, brought me a piece of pie yesterday.
He dropped in today again because he can't come tomorrow.
Thanks to him I spent the whole day without any boredom.
Remember Hiromi suddenly and think about him. I hope he may
not be discouraged by Miss Kuwada, who was one of his best
girlfriends and killed herself, and make some mistakes.

Jan. 21

The head physician—unexpected on Wednesday—comes around to see me. It is a pleasure for me since he shows me my medical record.
Leukocytes are 4,400. May this result be an error.
The test of my medulla taken yesterday appears to be not so bad.
Have a little too much fever in the afternoon. That is haunting me.

Besides, I feel a headache every day. I am worried because there still remain some white symptoms in my throat, which I hope will soon die away.

There is no use in thinking or in writing for the purpose of expressing myself. But mother and my husband who know me best are so busy that they have little time to talk with me.

Nevertheless, I do want to talk and to make myself heard— too much.

That is why I use my pen like this. By doing so, I drown my anxiety to a degree. No, I try to force it away . . .

It is a holiday today for my family. They are all bright and happy.

Their faces are full of the delights of working. I envy them very much.

Jan. 26

The day before yesterday I was so happy as to be moved to tears when I met Hiromi after a long absence. But I was very surprised to hear Hiromi left home again yesterday; mother called on me unannounced and told me about him, her face turning pale. What a foolish thing you have done, Hiromi!

I thought we had been leading our lives quietly and peacefully for these last few days . . .

What worries my mother has!

I don't now know how I can keep mother in good spirits, but I hope she takes enough care of herself at least.

Mami is always reading our adult faces. Please be careful of the influence of your moods on the child.

Mami is my only child. I greatly appreciate having her.

Jan. 27

I hope Hiromi may return home safely.

I have been restless since yesterday as there are some problems left in my mind. I never feel refreshed unless I work out my troubles. It might be enough to grow up spiritually for my age, though it will take a long time to be matured psychologically.

I will be relieved on one count if only Hiromi gets married and becomes a good merchant. Our family cannot afford even the time to say hello to each other every day since we are now living apart, individually.

But I firmly believe that we are, anytime and anywhere, always bound by the same spirit.

While I have been on the earth, I know mother, Hiromi, my husband, and Mami will have had some things to complain of about me. And I about them. But we have been too careful in our speech and behavior to each other. Mother is a woman born to be filled with troubles.

Besides, she makes herself more miserable by making plenty of worries of her own. Mother was born and bred in loveless circumstances. She has been striving extraordinarily to live, though being exposed herself to cold treatment. That is because she is a person of strong affection, as is not seen in everybody. Her precious affection is never closed to anyone, neither to her children, nor to those who have no connection with her.

To be frank, such a precious love can be considered at once her strong point and her weak point, because it is a blind love.

I know it will be almost impossible for my mother to grant my request to her to be more selfish or less kind to other persons. I wish she would not give her love so freely to everybody.

Perhaps I may express myself so poorly that nobody can follow me. But I shall be quite satisfied if she alone understands me.

Don't remain a miserable mother any more.

Mami has come three days running. I enjoy myself while she is with me, but after she leaves the hospital, I become too lonely to bear it.

"It is amazing that you should recover from your illness so fast," said the head physician.

My heart beats with joy.

I wonder when I shall be home?

Jan. 28

Leukocytes were 4,400 on the 20th of this month.

Whenever I have taken a blood examination, leukocytes have been increasing, 200 each time, and became 4,800 in all by the 27th of this month.

I hope my leukocytes may continue to increase like this. Then I will be able to leave the hospital temporarily around March.

Well, I should rather say "take a long stay out," instead of "leaving the hospital."

Anyway nothing can keep me in the hospital longer.

Mami, I'll be very happy to take you along to Tenmaya Playland on the condition that I leave the hospital.

Even if people think their marriage for the best, it does not always succeed.

But ours is an exception.

Being young, we thought only of ourselves, and at the same time were passionate. Nevertheless, we made a nice start.

As the time passed, our affection deepened, becoming more real. I sometimes believe there are few couples who feel as happy as we.

Our marriage is very wonderful.

But, too bad—this happiness is completely spoiled by my illness.

Jan. 29

The weather being rainy since last night, I feel a bit gloomy when I get up this morning.

Hearing Mami speaking, I become a little bright and happy.

According to my mother, Mami was crying while my mother went out for thirty minutes—poor thing.

If I am only in good health . . . I always think about it one way or another. It is said that children's character is influenced by such circumstances to a great degree.

I think of the future of Mami; I do want Mami to be a well-educated woman despite being a girl. She is my only child. And I do want Mami to be brought up with warm domestic affection. It reminds me that when my brother and I were little children, our mother was in bed for a long time. I do not want Mami to have such experiences as mine. I fear that family troubles are liable to complicate home life.

Being threatened with my illness, I am so sorry for not being able to give full play to my fondness for Mami. Dotage? Blind love? Well, call it either, but in any event, I wish I could embrace Mami in my arms with all my might.

However, I am afraid that Mami forgets me when I do not see her often.

Thinking so, I feel lonely and miserable sometimes.

Jan. 30

No blood transfusion since Tuesday. This way, I may perhaps leave the hospital around the end of next month.

I am so sensitive as to easily catch a cold, but I will be all right as far as that goes.

May nothing abnormal happen, and have mercy on me to live one day longer on earth. I exist not only for the sake of myself, but—

Feb. 3

I see visitor after visitor all day long: Shige-kun and Mrs. Morikazu, who have both come to see me four times, and Mrs. Wada, and Sanae.

How happy I have been today without any boredom, thanks to them. But when they must be going: left all alone, I feel all the more sad.

I have been not up to the mark from the day before yesterday.

Mami comes for the first time since we met nine days ago.

She has been so quick learning how to speak. I feel very sorry for Mami since I could not celebrate her birthday at all. Hiromi has not come back yet. It is surprising that he should have changed like this; he was so kind and meek when a little boy. I wonder if he has some trouble with being an A-bomb sufferer. Yes, he must have, I am sure. It seems to be a great problem for us to gain a better understanding about him physically and mentally. My home is full of black sheep! I feel like praying with folded hands to my mother and husband. My stepfather and my aunt are taking good care of Mami. Much obliged.

I am a bit tired today. Blood transfusions were stopped yesterday.

Feb. 4

There is still some fatigue left. Have a little high temperature this morning. Try to keep quiet today.

I will feel better again by tomorrow morning.

My body seems to be growing weaker day by day.

Feb. 7

Isolation becomes doubly acute. Tears stream down ceaselessly.

Receive an express package containing a style book from Hiromi. You silly fool, Hiromi!

Weep.

At last, yesterday, I got permission to leave the hospital on February 27, I am simply mad with joy.

I think the twenty days left till I leave much longer than they are.
Hoping time flies fast.
May nothing abnormal happen!
I feel uneasy to receive a letter from Hiromi in Hirano.

Feb. 9

I feel a bit feverish, but it is not much fever.
My top temperature has been 99° for today. So the more nervous I am the higher it gets. My pulse is pretty high, too.
At any rate, I am dying to go home; I'll stop thinking anything about my illness.
Time, fly, quickly, quickly!
Time, fly, quickly, quickly!
May nothing abnormal happen!
Shigeru-kun comes to see me.
A bit cold.
Send some money to Hiromi.

Feb. 12

Mami does not come.

Feb. 22

My sweet home! I have not seen it for almost nine months.
I entirely drown memory of my illness for a while.
Come back again to the hospital, after staying for one night at my home. Chilliness of the passage in the hospital.
I act selfishly to my husband in loneliness. Sorry for him.
Time to put off lights soon—lonely.
Tears. Tears stream down—ceaselessly . . .
Unfortunately, one more has died tonight.
I don't want to die.
Mami, my only daughter!
Nanako, Mami's only mother!
"Oh, this feeling . . .
"This lonely feeling . . . . "

(These are her last written words during her second experience in the hospital. She died at 10:45 A.M., April 10, 1959.)

UNDERGROUND ESCAPE

by Tsuji Masanobu

FROM THE RADIO came the high, halting voice of the Emperor.

"We have resolved to pave the way for a grand peace for all the generations to come by enduring the unendurable and suffering what is insufferable . . . We are always with ye, Our good and loyal subjects . . . Beware most strictly of any outbursts of emotion . . . ."

Thus, everything ended.

In the basement of the Bangkok headquarters, suppressed cries rose from the ranks of men standing at attention with bowed heads.

As I listened, I told myself, "I have no excuse. I have committed a sin for which ten thousand deaths cannot atone. It would be proper *bushido* to apologize by committing *hara-kiri*. However, the Imperial wish is that we disarm unconditionally and abide by the orders of the Allied Powers. To obey is the duty of a subject. It is not the wish of His Majesty that we, by our actions, should lose again 'our trust both at home and abroad.'"

I felt as if my very bowels were being torn into shreds. In the midst of this intense suffering, with cheeks still wet with tears, I attended the final conference in the commander's room. At this meeting, a certain high-ranking general said, "How can we bear to hand over our swords now hanging at our waists? We should return to Japan armed as we are and should be disarmed there. Unless we can do that, I'll cut the enemy to pieces or cut open my stomach."

Was there no one to refute the rantings of this officer? Unable to stand it, I said quietly, "The Imperial Rescript asks us to bear the

69

unbearable. If there is anyone who does not agree with His Majesty's wish, I see nothing wrong in his cutting up the enemy or committing *hara-kiri* on his own initiative. But it would be a mistake to have the attitude of the entire army decided by the emotions of one individual We must strive to send every last youth back home safely. Please go ahead and cut open your stomach in front of Loyalty Shrine."

It was a struggle for me to say what I did before a large gathering, especially to a superior officer who had looked after me and cared for me for so long; however, I felt there was no other way out of the difficulty.

Deputy Chief-of-Staff Hamada, who had listened with quiet composure from beginning to end, said detachedly, "Tsuji, I have one thing to ask of you. Japan must suffer for the next ten or twenty years. If possible, I'd like you to go underground in China and open up a new way for the future of Asia. I know a Taiwanese who is head of a group of pirates. If you want to go to Taiwan, I'll introduce you to him."

I answered, "Taiwan's not too bad. But, I'll try my hardest to go underground in Thailand, by becoming a priest."

And my resolution was complete.

There had been distributed to the Southeast Asia army a number of "special volunteers," seventeen-year-olds who had been hand-picked and educated to become "special attack corps," the so-called Kamikaze, chosen for Navy, army and Air Force duties from which there would be no return. Now, without any planes to fly, they had been parceled out among various ground detachments as so-called "strategic forces," to be used as spies and subversive agents. There were around fifty of these youths in Bangkok.

I spoke to these youngsters, none now older than twenty-two or -three, telling them I intended to go underground in Thailand by becoming a Buddhist priest. When they heard this, eight of these young men came and asked to go with me. All had been real priests in civilian life. I decided to choose two or three of the best, but all insisted on joining me. On their youthful faces was written the firm resolve to work for the reconstruction of their country with the same spirit they had subjected their bodies to in the rigid military training they had recently completed.

They were set on joining me in going underground. I had been with them for only a few lectures, yet for some reason I felt toward them a deep confidence and immeasurable love. When the majority of the older men had only one thought in mind—to return to Japan as soon as possible—here were youngsters competing for the right to stay in Thailand.

"All right. I'm asking you all to stay and die with me. We might have to stay underground for ten years, maybe twenty, but I want all of you to give your lives as foundation stones in the establishment of true Thai-Japanese friendship."

I, too, resolved that I would be ready to die with these youths, more like my own young sons or my own young brothers.

The memory of the Deputy War Minister came to my mind. He had been a Commander of the Army Air Force in the Philippines. There he had thrown hundreds of youthful "special attack corps" fliers into the teeth of death. But once the situation developed in favor of the enemy, he defied the orders of Commander Yamashita, abandoned his men, and fled to Taiwan.

I pledged to myself, "No matter what happens, I'll throw away this body of mine with these youngsters."

I immediately investigated the family backgrounds of these youths. I found that Probationary Sub-Lieutenant Tada was the only son of a widowed mother and already the head of a temple. I felt that I would have to send Tada home. I spoke to him of Karmic fate and said, "I want you to go home and get in touch with the families of the other seven men. Then I want you to start on the reformation of the religious world of Japan."

He did not utter a word of dissatisfaction and replied, "I deeply regret that I cannot be accepted. But I feel that what you tell me is also my proper task. I shall return as you order."

I next visited the embassy. I found the ambassador weighted down by the swift changes of the past few days. Suffering was written all over his face, but he greeted me in a quiet voice. "I'm very sorry. The future Japan must win back the trust of the world through her moral principles. Let us work toward the rebirth of a nation that will not contain even a single criminal."

"Today's situation is the result of the sins of us military men," I answered. "In the hope of atoning for even a part of this great sin, I want to stay in Thailand together with seven young men as foundation stones in the erection of a lasting friendship between Thailand and Japan. Could your excellency not ask for the understanding of the Thai leaders for this venture?"

"Very good. As my last service to my country, I shall immediately ask for permission for your venture from the Thai Minister of Education and the Prime Minister. I know you will do your best and act from high principles."

The British forces had not as yet arrived in Thailand. Although I had not heard of my being designated as a war crimes suspect, I was fully ready to meet such a fate. If the British army were to start a search for me, I knew that I would be causing undue trouble to the ambassador. Although he was a civil servant, the ambassador did not pause and think of his own position. I felt that he showed himself to be a true patriot by granting my request.

If this man had become an army leader, he would surely have been like General Nogi. I could not but feel admiration for Ambassador Yamamoto when I compared his soft-spoken determination with the arrogance of those high-ranking officers who took full advantage of the power of their military uniforms. Ambassador Yamamoto had showed himself ready to give up everything out of his deep concern for his country.

I felt that Ambassador Yamamoto was a true diplomat and true patriot. I shook hands firmly with him and soon left. In all probability, this was a final farewell. I could not halt the streams of tears that flowed down my cheeks.

Priestly garb for eight men were prepared. The tailor's customer was Maruyama Kamito of the Hikari Mission, a priest of the Nichiren Sect, and the dressing room was an inner suite in the Thailand Hotel.

Taking care not to disturb my army colleagues, who were deep in slumber, I tiptoed out of my room. Just as I reached the car that I had readied in secret, I noticed Sub-Lieutenants Akutsu and Shirakura waiting, shoulders slumped in despondency.

"Thanks very much for everything. Please take good care of yourselves," I mumbled.

We exchanged our final farewells. Thirty years of military life had come to an end. The lonely sentinel presented arms as I slipped out of the headquarters gate. The street lights reflected on the polished bayonet affixed to his rifle.

Good-bye army life, good-bye comrades.

This was the beginning of an underground trek that spanned three countries and 7,500 miles. The path was to lead through hell, with countless deadly barriers along the way.

The first mile-post was the small ossuary for the remains of Japanese erected in the compounds of Ryab Temple, mercilessly destroyed by bombings. I got out of the car at the rear gate and peeped through the hedge, but saw no one. I wondered for a moment whether I had made a mistake. Then one of the disciples who had moved the night before woke up and opened the half door for me. He was tired and more asleep than awake as, rubbing his eyes, he said, "Good morning, master."

Nonetheless, his greeting was cheerful.

The disciples, suddenly raised by their master, were frantically folding up their bedding. I met the guardian of the ossuary, the old priest Chino.

"I am Aoki. I hope you will be kind enough to teach me."

The ossuary was composed of two towers, thirty-six feet high and sixteen-feet-square at the base. It contained the remains of Japanese who had died in Bangkok over the past fifty years and the votive tablets of 120 war heroes who had died in Thailand and in French Indochina.

Before taking up my chopsticks for the first meal of my new life, I had to chant three times; "*Homage to the Sutra of the Lotus of Good Law.*" I felt awkward. I told myself that this would not do, I would have to learn to become a priest completely.

After the meal, the old priest Chino poured hot water into his bowl, stuck his fingers in, and washed the clinging rice from the sides. Then he placed the bowl to his lips and drank. Somehow I could not bring myself to follow his example and picked loose the remaining rice with my chopsticks and then drank the hot water.

As soon as the morning meal was over, we lined up in front of the ossuary and, with young Kubo leading us, began chanting sutras. While we repeated the sutras together, with wooden and metal gongs keeping time, I found myself being captivated by the rhythm, learning much more rapidly than I had expected.

I realized the truth of the old saying, "Children near the temple chant unstudied sutras." In one week's time, I had learned the entire Prajna Paramita Sutra. I felt that I would find salvation here for my wounded soul. To chant sutras before this image morning and night seemed to me more a comfort than any regimen or strict training.

There was no light or water in the ossuary. Our only drinking water was rain caught from the roof through a trough into a large vat. In the backyard was a twelve-foot-square pond. It had not been cleaned out for years and was covered with greenish growth and smelled. However, after a day's training, it was our custom to strip to the skin and bathe in this pond. Our greatest pleasure was to surround a lone candle after supper for two or three hours until bedtime and talk together on the future of Japan.

For breakfast, we had *miso* soup and pickles; for lunch and supper, cooked dehydrated vegetables, with perhaps a piece of salted fish. Fresh fish bought in town was a rare luxury. Five yen worth of bananas were first offered before Buddha and then became dessert. Laundry was done by each man. I realized fully how extravagant and spoiled my past twenty years had been—twenty years during which orderlies had waited on me hand and foot. After a week's time I was able to put on the priestly robes of Thailand by myself.

At first we relied upon frequent tropical squalls for our water. Then, as the monsoon season gradually drew to a close, we began to suffer a lack of water. Next, mosquito larvae began hatching in our drinking water. The time had come for us to buy our water from the old Chinese who came daily, at one yen for two pails of water carried on a yoke. The water smelled odd, so I followed the water seller. To my surprise I found he was getting the water from a puddle formed in a bomb crater. A dead dog was floating in the pond.

In the face of the approach of the British forces, resident Japanese had problems in obtaining their identification certificates. Thai government and police officers must have felt that their turn to boast had now arrived. There were long queues of Japanese in front of Thai government offices. When their turns came I saw these Japanese, bereft of the backing of their country, rubbing their hands in pitiful pleas before Thai officials.

Finally our turn came. We were asked birthplace, age and occupation, then we had to sign our names to our affidavits. I took from my Dhuta bag the ink horn and brush that I had carried with me always, either on battlefields or in a quieter life. But I was handed a pen and told to sign my name in Romanized Japanese. I did not know what to do, until Kubo said he would sign in my stead.

"A Buddhist monk does not know English," he said, and I was able to pass the first barrier.

I noticed a Japanese, wearing dark glasses, standing by looking at me. He came close to me and prodded me in my ribs with his finger. It was Ishida, a classmate of mine in the military academy. He had come to Thailand several years previously as a member of a Japanese firm and engaged in underground activity. He was a specialist in gathering information. We spoke to each other with our eyes, putting heart and soul into them. I realized that he also sought to remain in Thailand and work underground.

We were then taken to the room of the Chief of the Religious Education Bureau to be interviewed personally. Beads of perspiration formed in my armpits and wet my robe. As the supposed head of a group of student priests recently arrived from Burma, I was first to be questioned. In the center of the room sat the Bureau Chief, like a judge at a trial. On both sides were seated members of the bureau. All eyes were turned upon me as I entered the room; I felt that they could see through my disguise. If caught, there was nothing I could do. I calmed myself.

"What sect do you belong to?"

"The Shinshu Sect."

"How many years have you been a priest?"

"Twenty years in Japan and roughly two years in Burma. I have only recently arrived in Thailand and am not as yet used to the Thai robes."

"Do you also beat drums?"

"No, it is only the Nichiren Sect that beats drums."

"What is the significance behind the beating of drums?"

"Oh" (and I felt cold sweat suddenly flow down my sides), "that is to chase away enemies of Buddha."

"For what purpose and for how long do you desire to study in Thailand?"

"I would like to stay for about ten years and become a link in bringing about eternal friendship between Japan and Thailand through Buddhism. If you will only allow me to stay in your country – –"

"Good. Please study hard and strive for the friendship of Thailand and Japan."

This one sentence was like gospel from heaven. I had passed my first test. They had watched with suspicious eyes the clumsy way I wore my robe. Yet in this way I passed safely.

The remaining seven pupils who were next on the inquisition stand succeeded in passing their tests, thanks to the impression left by my answers. I was more fatigued than I had ever felt on any battlefield. I slept soundly for the first time since taking off my army uniform. The snoring of my seven disciples was also loud. How great must have been the anxiety of these young men over the examination. Undoubtedly, they could not have encountered in all the examinations in the past one that worried them as much. I wrote:

ominous the clouds that darkly whelm the eastern skies
a hundred devils daily trod our homeland hills
gallons the searing tears that wet this yellow robe
but awhile must I sit within this crucible, steeling my soul

At the beginning of October, the Free Thai cabinet changed the name of Thailand to Siam and began suppressing the Japanese. I could feel the stealthy approach of danger. Kubo came frantically to me, his face sallow with fear. "A terrible thing has happened. This morning, when the Chief Abbot got into contact secretly with the Chief of the Thai Bureau of Religion, he was told all Japanese priests would be arrested without notice on October twenty-ninth."

I felt my heart thump. The Chinese vernacular press had for some time reported rumors that Japanese army officers had gone underground in disguise. British authorities had changed their tolerant early attitude and had decided all Japanese priests were to be detained and questioned until their true identities were established.

I knew, if placed in a concentration camp, I'd soon be recognized by some Japanese. There was too strict a surveillance for any possibility of my escaping the country. I felt that the end had come. However, it was by heaven's grace that I had been able to learn one week in advance when the British planned a surprise raid on us.

That evening a group of uniformed Japanese officers and non-coms appeared at the ossuary. "The senior aide-de-camp has ordered us to take home all the remains of Japanese officers and men deposited here."

It was evident that they were afraid of being involved in my affairs. I went to where two of the men were getting the remains ready to take home and asked, "What has happened? Why do you have to take away all of the remains so suddenly?"

"Something quite unexpected has taken place. Last night the British headquarters sent over an urgent order demanding Staff

Officer Tsuji's immediate appearance. The Japanese Chief of Staff told the British that Staff Officer Tsuji left a note and disappeared on August 16, and that Tsuji, judging from his character, had probably committed suicide. We are taking back these remains for the purpose of making a clean cut between the army and this temple."

Everything was now clear to me. The worst had come. There had not been a single letter either from my commanders or from my colleagues. If I had not taken the initiative to ask, I would have remained completely at a loss to explain this new development. It was certain that everybody was afraid of having anything to do with me.

"All right," I thought, "such being the case, I won't rely on anybody. Nor must I cause anybody trouble. If the British only knew that, disguised as a priest, I am living right next to their headquarters they'd come to get me. I'll fight to the last with my sword, until the rivets holding the blade to the haft break."

And I steeled myself to meet my doom.

Never since my desertion had I felt as oppressed and as stifled as I did now, but my indomitable will to fight flared up within me. In the bloody fighting in North Burma, the units defending the fortifications at La Meng had fought even after they had lost arms and legs and not a single man surrendered: it was a fight to the end. I resolved to stay underground in spite of all dangers. I thought the Imperial Rescript terminating the war undoubtedly a true Rescript, but so was the Imperial Rescript declaring war. If one Rescript is obeyed then the other is automatically disobeyed. In such an age as this the only thing to do, I felt, was to throw away all thoughts of self and to choose, according to one's own initiative, the path one believed right for the eternal future of Japan. From the standpoint of the British army, it was natural to scour the corners of the earth for me.

Churchill had said, "Undaunted in defeat, magnanimous in victory, liberal in peace, and resolute in war." Were Churchill in my place, he would undoubtedly have done what I did.

When the time came to see off the remains of the 150-odd war dead I had faced in my morning and evening prayers each day for more than two months, I was filled with sadness and a sense of impending tragedy. As long as they had rested in the ossuary, I felt the spirits of the dead, for whom I prayed, watched over me. But now I had lost my last support. I was completely alone in a hostile world. The tragic determination that filled my heart seemed to freeze the blood in my veins. How easy life had been in the great organization of the army, with supports both above and below, to right and left of me. Even when I stood at the head of my troops with the gold braid of a staff officer slung over my shoulder, a hail of bullets falling all about me, life was easier than this utter sense of aloneness that now oppressed me.

All the strength I had I poured into the performance of the religious rites that evening.

I felt as if I were a fish caught in a far-flung net that was slowly being drawn in—in toward the enemy. The net seemed too high for me to jump over and too strong for me to attempt a bodily breakthrough. I am ashamed to admit it, but I couldn't sleep a wink that night. I even felt a sense of uneasiness at the sound of Lao Tai's walking stick as he went his nightly round of inspection. At the same time, the sound reassured me; it was good to know that some one was watching. I often mistook the light of passing automobiles for the flashlights of men come to arrest me.

The morning sun of October 28 shone red through my window. It seemed to bless and encourage me.

I left the temple alone, filling my heart with prayer. I picked up a *samlor* and hurried toward Surion Avenue. I passed through a number of checkpoints as a Thai priest. I entered the Chungking headquarters.

The youth who had received me the other day greeted me with a smile and led me into a waiting room. After a short while, a difficult-looking youth swept into the room. In written exchanges, I learned that he was Section Chief Kuo. A little later Chief Secretary Cheng turned up for work. He was no more than thirty years of age. Thin and rather pale, he was nonetheless handsome. Who would have imagined such a youth as being the representative of Lieutenant General Hsieh, who was responsible for the 1,500,000 Chinese in Thailand.

With these big paws of a coarse country monk, I gripped the delicate hands of this youth in a grasp of steel. I could not help noticing the slight blush that colored his face. For perhaps an hour—no, more—we conversed by written exchanges of ideographs common to both our languages. He, being a native of Canton, could not understand my broken attempts to speak Mandarin, the official dialect of Peking.

My real name, my career, my part in the East Asia Federation Movement, the memorial service for Generalissimo Chiang Kai-shek's mother and my relations with Tai Li – – I wrote down every thing that I could.

"I want to go to Chungking, meet General Tai Li and Generalissimo Chiang Kai-shek, open the way for Japanese collaboration with China. If this is impossible, please arrest me immediately and hand me over to the British authorities. I am not a man to fear for my life and run away."

The two youths nodded as they read and I noticed their faces gradually color with excitement. Their eyes were shining. When I had finished, Cheng then wrote, "Please wait. We want to confer," and then left the room.

I wondered whether it would be good news or bad. I waited for thirty minutes, and when the two came back both were smiling. I shouted silently to myself: You've made it.

Cheng wrote with delicate fingers just two words: "Very good."

He told me then to arrange everything with Section Chief Kuo. To think of these youths, still not quite thirty, negotiating on more than an equal basis with both Thai and British high authorities filled me with envy. At their age, I was still a lieutenant in the War University. If they had been Japanese bureaucrats, just what measures would they have been able to take? In all probability the best they could answer would have been, "We'll ask Tokyo. Just wait a while!"

Filled with emotion and excitement, but putting on a serene exterior, I returned in a *samlor* to the temple. With my arrest scheduled for the next day, I had succeeded in planning an escape less than twenty-four hours before the action could be carried out.

British sentinels were stationed at night a short distance from the front gate of our temple. Inside the temple gate, plainclothes Thai police began to appear constantly. It was not an easy job to get through this barrier. On the afternoon of October 28, I hurriedly cleared up all my personal matters. I felt that neither the British nor the Thai authorities (except ex-Prime Minister Apaiyon) knew as yet that the priest Norinobu Aoki was in actuality Staff Officer Tsuji. The best thing to do was to make out that Aoki had committed suicide. Then Chino, Kobiki and the seven youths would not be held responsible or be grilled. I shut myself into my own room and wrote my last letters.

In a wooden box, inscribed, *Articles belonging to the late Colonel Masanobu Tsuji of the Japanese army*, I placed my sword and my blood-stained binoculars. Then I wrapped the box in a yellow robe and handed it to my disciples to be placed in the custody of the Chief Abbot of Mahatat Temple. I saw my yellow-robed disciples off with clasped hands until the dusk swallowed them from sight, and rolled back to cover me.

I slung a carpet bag over my shoulder, the bag in front and the blankets behind; then, dressed in the white shirt and trousers of a typical Chinese, I slipped from my room into the dark. I stopped for a moment in front of the main temple and offered a silent prayer. Then, like a thief, I walked silently toward the main gate.

It was exactly nine o'clock, October 28, 1945.

The main gate, to describe it more accurately, was the front approach to the adjoining Ryab Temple. Left half-destroyed by bombing, it was now overgrown with grass and weeds. Because of but infrequent worshipers, it had become the nightly gathering place of thieves. In one corner of the approach was an old poplar tree. It was a suitable spot to hide. Cowering behind the tree trunk, I waited for the promised car, but only machine-gun carriers came and went.

Every thirty minutes, punctually, patrols passed by and every hour the helmeted and armed sentinels were relieved. The muzzles of their guns were always pointed toward the Japanese temple. The watch that I had bought for my escape showed one o'clock and the street outside emptied itself of passers-by. I could hear drunken British soldiers shouting with loud voices as they chased slim Thai girls.

Two o'clock passed. Three o'clock. The streets became completely lifeless. Only the sentinels were alive and awake. Four o'clock came. My arms and face had become a swollen mass of pain from the countless mosquito bites. I thought that all would end when daybreak came. I wondered if my luck had all run out.

Wait, I told myself. The defense detachment at La Meng did not surrender. I decided to say my final prayers. Turning toward the northeast, I bowed my head in deep prayer. With the rosary given to me by my mother in my hand, I said in a small voice the *introibo*, the praise of Buddha and the Prajna Paramita Sutra. When I finished and looked up toward the gate, a miracle had taken place. Both of the sentinels were seated on the sidewalk, wrapped in deep sleep. The gods and Buddha had not failed me. Hot tears rolled down my cold face.

The eastern skies began to lighten almost imperceptibly. Early rising Chinese passed by in threes and fours, carrying bundles of vegetables, headed in the direction of the market. I adjusted the carpet bag and the blankets slung over my shoulders and started walking unhurriedly. I passed the gate. The two sentinels still slept, their heads supported by their rifles.

I coughed as if to clear my throat and stamped more firmly on the ground to make steps heard. I leisurely passed the sentinels. The sentinels, wakened by my footsteps, glanced upward a second, then went back again to sleep as if satisfied at seeing a Chinese. I felt a big burden roll off my shoulders.

I mixed with the hurrying Chinese vendors and reached an intersection where a Thai policeman stood on duty. I put my luggage down beside the police officer and waited for a *samlor*. Before the Thai policeman could suspect anything, a rickshaw approached. It was clearly a rickshaw reserved for Chinese. "Surion Avenue. Ten bahts, hurry, hurry," I said in Thai.

The rickshaw man, who had been on the lookout for a passenger, pushed down the shafts of the rickshaw. My Thai language studies had been justified. The rickshaw man must have been pleased to find such a good passenger. The regular fare to Surion Avenue was five bahts. I promised him ten. He sped on, overtaking several *samlor*. When told to stop by several British and Thai police along the way, he shouted back in an energetic voice, "This passenger Chinaman," and sped on.

There was little traffic along the streets and the rickshaw man outdid himself for speed. At 5:45 A.M., I entered the headquarters of the Chinese underground movement. The hunted bird had finally found refuge in the bosom of a fellow Oriental. The sun rose in the East, as if to brighten my future path. The Chinese headquarters showed no unpleasantness at the arrival of such an early guest, and I was shown into the waiting room. Ten young men were sleeping on the office desks and the sofa. They made room for me on this communal sofa. I had intended to stay awake, but before I knew it I was dead asleep on the divan.

I had passed through my first death barrier.

(Later, after 7,500 miles—20,000 Chinese *ri* or leagues—of travel and three years in disguise—part of this period as a military advisor to Chiang Kai-shek while still a wanted man by the British—Tsuji began the last leg homeward.)

One of my daily worries was how my fatherless children were faring. I often wondered how my wife could keep the home fires burning in a home that did not exist. I did not know even where my family was or how they had managed to live through the past several years. They did not have a single sen in savings and had not a single yen of income. I often thought that perhaps they had already starved to death. The whole family might have ended their lives in mass suicide. I was able to forget my family and sacrifice thirty years for the sake of my Emperor and my country, lulled by the sense of security of the guarantees given me by the state. Time and time again I had chided myself for the lack of will power shown by lack of attachment to my family. However, this was a human failing, a human weakness, a human sadness.

In August of the previous year, the Chungking government had guaranteed me contact with my family in Japan. Since then I had not heard anything further. Yet, as I had not had any bad dreams, I tried to comfort myself with the thought that my family must still be alive somewhere in Japan.

I had no idea when I would be able to return to Japan. I was a criminal who knew not when or where he might be called upon to give up his life. I decided to write down the actions I had performed in my forty years and leave this record to my children so that they would not repeat the same mistakes. I began with my childhood memories, and completed five volumes by the end of January, 1947: "My First Aspirations," "My First Taste of War," "Bitter Battles," "Good Battles" and "Evil Battles." I spent seventy-odd days on this autobiography of more than 400,000 words. It was a book of confessions and at the same time a book of precepts for my offspring. I wrapped and sealed the document and sent it to my family in the care of Staff Officer Chao, who was leaving for Tokyo in the company of Major General Wang. In the 400,000 words were the spirit of martyrdom for my country and my concept of humanity. I read over this document written in blood and tears and prayed, "My children, may you proceed with courage and with justice."

My whole heart went with this document.

At the beginning of March, I was lying in my semi-dark room that had once belonged to the maid, sick with a high fever from overwork and fatigue. Unannounced, Staff Officer Liu called on me saying: "Congratulations. A letter has come for you from your home."

I thought that I was having a hallucination as I stared at the letter, which had, of course, already been opened and censored. It was written in pencil in childish characters, but I immediately recognized my eldest son's handwriting. "Please forgive these long years of unfilial neglect. We are all healthy and well. Eiko is going to Shimizutani. I have quit school and through the kind efforts of Mr. Kawamichi am working in the Kimura Food Store. Mother is doing dressmaking ...."

My wife and children were alive! The gods and Buddha had protected the children of this sinful father and the wife of a sinful husband. My wife and children had suffered and persevered through desperate effort. My wife was working during the day in a clothing factory, treading a sewing machine, at nights attending dressmaking school. She had gritted her teeth, had suffered all manner of shame, but had brought up my five children.

My son had quit high school midway and had found work in a bakery. My heart went out to my eldest son, who was helping his younger sisters through school. I wonder how my eldest daughter felt as she studied at the alma mater of her own mother—a girls school that had welcomed her with warm sympathy. My wife, it seemed, had not written a letter, being absent at the mill. However my father-in-law's letter hinted at the difficult life my family was leading.

Whatever the case, they were all alive. They had all been allowed to live. I was the husband of an innocent wife and the father of innocent children—at whom people pointed their fingers and whispered in contempt. I could only thank the gods and apologize to my wife. I wanted to say, "Please bear a little while longer." Yet I did not know whether I would be able to meet them again. In the first half of my life, during which I had forgotten my family and my children, I had taken too great an interest in affairs of state, I had been too conceited in my own position. I now forgot my 102-degree temperature, raised my body and prayed toward the East. Hot tears dropped unchecked upon the letter from my child.

As Manchuria greeted its second winter of Nationalist control, the Chief of Staff, General Chen Cheng, was transferred there to take over the command of the Chinese Nationalist forces. He boasted that he would occupy and maintain by armed force the whole of Manchuria. However, the war with the Communists turned daily in his disfavor.

Studying the general situation, I advised boldly and bluntly the policy of a northern and southern "dynasty" in opposition, saying, "Abandon Manchuria, hold on for a time to North China, but withdraw all the rest of the Nationalist forces to the south bank of the Yangtze and consolidate your position there." However, this advice was greeted with resentment.

Men in positions of responsibility, from the Second Section Chief down, did not even try to transmit my suggestions to the Generalissimo, fearful of the gravity of the situation. They were endlessly absorbed in the disgraceful scene of discussing the local withdrawal from Kirin (Kweilin) and Changchun in Manchuria, without ever reaching a decision. I felt deeply the lack of capable men in the Defense Department. I realized that there was no way left to save the Chinese Nationalist government. There was no longer any reason the Defense Department should continue to feed me.

After awaiting the completion of "An Evaluation of the Material War Potential of the Soviet Union" in February I formally presented my resignation, only to be told, "The British are still looking for you. If you go home, you will surely be caught and sent to the gallows. Bear for a while and wait."

"I am very grateful for your thoughtful consideration of my future," I told the Department. "Since I was appointed to serve in the Defense Department, I have with sincerity produced material and data only to see these, time and time again, put aside unused. Even if I were not wanted in Japan as a war criminal, I could bear this and stay. I cannot remain a day longer in China if my purpose is only to escape capture. Whether I am arrested or not, I leave to fate. In my native home I have an old mother close to eighty years of age, sick in bed. If just because I am afraid for my own life I am unable to be at my mother's side at her death, knowing beforehand as I do now that she no longer knows whether she will live through each day, how can I continue my life knowing I have failed to carry out these filial duties? If I should be arrested upon my return home, I shall make no pleas in my own defense but shall go to the gallows with a smile on my lips. This is the only natural way in which I can atone for the sin of defeat."

This was the gist of an appeal I made directly to the Chinese Chief of Staff. Finally, at the end of April, permission came for me to return home. "You will be allowed a two-month vacation. We would like you to come back once again and help us out."

I doubted whether they really desired the return of an old and tough colonel of a defeated army.

Already aboard the ship were some three hundred Japanese compatriots from Taiwan. A motley crowd of ex-army war-crime suspects, professors from Taipei University, detained technicians, artisans and merchants. They were returning to Japan, having lost all hope in the face of the worsening plight of the Chinese Nationalists. The whole group was filled with pessimism over the future of the Kuomintang.

General Chen I, who had been appointed Governor of Taiwan immediately after the war to take over from the Japanese occupying army, was unable to restrain or control his officials and soldiers from wrong-doing. The smoldering resentment of the Taiwanese natives festered until it could no longer be held down, and it exploded in the "February 28 Incident" of 1948 of mass demonstrations by the disenfranchized Taiwanese against the mainlander Nationalists whom they considered more an army of occuppation than compatriots, followed by the massacre of Taiwanese and Japanese by the Nationalists in retaliation. The blood of these tens of thousands who were shot filled the hearts of Taiwanese with lasting hatred for the Kuomintang. There even appeared among the population a desire to shake off the rule of the Chinese Nationalist government and link hands and fate with Japan, even defeated as we were.

On the departure of the group from Taiwan, Taiwanese police, hiding from the sharp eyes of their Chinese Nationalist officers, afforded every convenience to the Japanese and showed toward them a protective attitude. After the end of the war, the Taiwanese had dreamed of the arrival of a magnificent army from their homeland to take the place of the Japanese forces. They experienced bitter disappointment on greeting a pack of starving wolves, carrying earthen pots and wearing straw sandals. Then came a wave of rapacious government officials who deprived them of their homes, looted their belongings, and brazenly accepted bribes. Paper currency, *Fapi*, unbacked by gold or silver bullion, flooded the country. Resentment developed into opposition and eventually a bloody struggle. Here, too, the Kuomintang revealed itself to be a tottering and corrupt regime heading for oblivion.

Our ship left Shanghai on the evening of May 16. I watched from the deck the fading skyline of Shanghai, doomed once again to be wrapped in the flames of war. Those who stood on the pier waving good-by, and those who waved back from the decks, were all filled with an indescribable feeling. When the ship passed the entrance to Woosung Harbor, I recalled to mind the old battlefield of the First Shanghai Incident, sixteen years before, on which I had lost sixteen subordinates.

My quarters were situated deep in the ship's hold near the stern of the vessel. We were packed in like so much freight, allowed only one square meter of space per person. I could not even stretch out my legs. The person next to me was a young fellow by the name of Nagai. A student of the Tungwen University of Shanghai, he claimed to be the nephew of the novelist Nagai Sanjin (Kafu). He himself was of the literary type. Yasuda, corespondent of the Domei News Agency, was also aboard, on his way home with a baby, not yet weaned, whose mother was a Russian girl he had since divorced. The child, whose name was Shepherd, soon became the darling of the ship. The hold, packed indiscriminately with men and women, was filled with nauseating odors and ruled over by selfishness. I wondered if this ship's hold were not just defeated Japan in microcosm.

A group of Japanese soldiers, among those who had been detained as war crimes suspects, were known as the Kiangwan Unit. Among these men was Major General Fukuyama, who had been a classmate of mine in the army university. He played Go from morning to night, all the while rubbing his bald head. He did not even guess that this pseudo-university professor could be his former classmate. Of course my disguise was meant not to allow him to recognize me, although we met face to face on several occasions. After this experience I gained confidence and felt that at this rate I would not be discovered. Then there was Kadoya Hiroshi, by dint of his rank, commander of our entire group of repatriates. I had known him several years earlier while at Supreme Headquarters in Nanking but he, too, failed to recognize me. My work clothes were black with the coal tar painted over the ship's bottom. No matter how one could have looked at me they would not but think me a university professor.

After two or three days' journey northward, the boat touched at Tsingtao. Here again, a customs inspection was held, even stricter than at Shanghai. Looting by the Chinese military police were even worse than at Shanghai. The Tsingtao group of Japanese repatriates, mostly women and girls, did not have the strength to repack their luggage which had been ripped apart mercilessly. Somebody suggested that we help the women. Some twenty of the strongest volunteered and, in a cloud of dust blown up by a strong wind, we helped these pitiful compatriots. Our mountain of luggage was immediately reloaded aboard ship and, dog-tired though we all were, we experienced the pleasure of having been able to help our neighbors.

Leaving the pier, we heard a voice in Japanese rise from among the crowd of Chinese police standing on the wharf. "Please take good care of yourselves. Do write, won't you? There isn't a single decent person among the Chinese dogs. Japanese are really good people."

What a surprise this was! The mystery soon cleared up, the voice had come from a Taiwanese police officer. This youth had been employed by the Japanese navy and had crossed over to Tsingtao. After the war he had become a Chinese Nationalist police officer.

From the pier, packages of cigarettes were thrown aboard ship. One Chinese watched with sour face this exchange of friendly gestures between Japanese and Taiwanese. He was obviously the officer in command, but he could do nothing.

After ten days our vessel finally entered the harbor of Sasebo. Our quarantine ended, instructions concerning our processing after landing were shouted through megaphones by repatriation officials and former army officers. I was impatient with the innumerable delays. I was seized with the desire to step on the soil of Japan as soon as possible. Every second seemed an eternity.

On the morning of May 26, we finally landed.

As I took my first step ashore, I quietly picked up a handful of earth and smelled its sweetness. It was the first smell of my motherland in six years. Could my longing for and love of the soil of my motherland be this strong?

Though the country was defeated, the hills and the streams were still left, together with the emperor.

Impoverished as this soil may be, it was our earth, it was our land.

By no means was it Stalin's land.

Withered and dried though these hills and streams might be, they were our mountains and they were our rivers.

By no means were they Truman's.

We must make this land green once again, with our blood, our sweat and our love.

If fertilizer is needed, then I felt I would not hesitate to grind to powder these old bones.

BANSHU PLAIN

by *Miyamoto Yuriko*

NUIKO WAS OUT by the gate. The instant she saw Hiroko coming, she beckoned to her urgently.

"What – – ?"

"Hurry up!"

Hiroko entered the house, wondering. Nuiko put her arm around Hiroko's shoulders as if to hurry her up the stoop. Inside a newspaper lay on the tatami floor mat. Nuiko opened it and pointed out an article: "What do you think of that?"

Hiroko, with obvious but uncommitted emotion, read that the Public Peace Law of Japan would be abolished in a few days in accordance with the Potsdam Declaration and that all political prisoners held under this law were to be set free in the near future.

"Then, Jukichi will be back sooner than expected. Oh, how wonderful!" said Hiroko's aunt cheerfully, coming out of the kitchen wiping her hands. "By now, they should have received the newspaper at the station in Iwakuni and your mother must be glad, too."

Hiroko, however, found herself incapable of acknowledging her aunt's open expressions of joy, not even with a smile. "We cannot say anything until we see more how things go." Hiroko sounded so tormented that Nuiko, her cousin, took a second look at her in surprise. Hiroko, still standing, stared intensely into the newspaper. "In such a place as a prison . . . well, things are very different from what we imagine. Jukichi has been punished not only by the Public Peace Law. . . He has been tortured in many ways . . . ."

Hiroko's heart was wrenched by the news that the political offenders of the Public Peace Law would soon be released.

Jukichi had been arrested after exposure by the spies whom the Secret Police had infiltrated into the Communist Party. It just so happened that one of the suspected spies had a physical defect, and in some way due to it met an unnatural but accidental death. Since the case involved the Secret Police personally against the Communist Party, the trial seemed to be a vendetta pure and simple. When Hiroko learned of the charges and followed the proceedings at the court for the first time, it appeared to her eyes and ears that the state had used its power in too wily a manner to care about the justice or dignity expected of it. Justice here was not judged by common sense, but by a quite opposite spirit of arbitrariness. Jukichi was treated most cruelly. He alone, among the several defendants, was sentenced to life imprisonment, though the charges against all, the responsibility placed on them, were the same; he differed only in having been in the party a shorter time. Next to one name were written as many charges as seemingly could be enumerated. Hiroko felt painfully that each charge was an iron link in the chain which resounded heavily at Jukichi's every step, every movement. She looked upon the incident as a natural event of social history. She did not find anything wrong in what Jukichi and his comrades had done. It was the spies, the actions of authorities who maintained their positions by the intrigues of spies—that was a criminal way to conduct a political struggle and showed moral decadence. Hiroko could not understand: Why was it that those who were young and unselfishly absorbed in improving society in accordance with the natural process of history, why should they be penalized?

To be found guilty even under such transparently unreasonable law, was for those like Jukichi's mother something bad and fearful. How many times had Hiroko during these past ten or more years had to soothe her and struggle to make her keep faith in her son.

Right there, reading that the political prisoners punished under the Public Peace Law would be set free, Hiroko knew in her heart that here was for her the last and most unendurable torture. Immediately after the acceptance of the Potsdam Declaration, Hiroko had been struck with sheer joy. Quivering with anticipation, she tried to picture the inner thoughts with which Jukichi received the news. Constantly running through her head were such thoughts as "When is he coming? I wonder when he is coming. How wonderful it would be to go up to the far north to meet him in Abashiri, and come home together by sea.

Time passed. After a month or so, she began to doubt the Declaration would ever be put into practice with such a questionable government in power. Could the Public Peace Law be abrogated, really? When? How? All the progressive people in Japan, who had been tortured for so long, had the same doubt as she. By the tens of millions they looked to the future, suspiciously, dry-eyed.

The instant it became known which door would be opened in that wall that was the Public Peace Law, Hiroko felt like a mother calling for her child, not yet rescued and about to be left in a flaming house. "Jukichi? . . . Jukichi? . . . Others are coming out . . . . What about Jukichi?"

Hiroko, however, had no one to whom she could unburden her anxiety. The flame, which in her mind was driving her beloved husband into intolerable danger, did not show itself to anyone else.

Hiroko, the newspaper still in her hand, went listlessly back to her room and sat down at her favorite place. First her aunt and then Nuiko, not knowing what to say, quietly slipped away.

After an hour or so, Hiroko called from where she was still sitting. "Nuiko, are you in?"

"Yes, I am. Is there something you want?"

"Could you please go to the post office for me?" Hiroko handed Nuiko two letters marked with red ink for registry and special delivery. "Anyway, I think the best way is to ask Mr. Tsukamoto and Mr. Nagata. Depending on developments, I might even have Mr. Nagata go to Hokkaido to prevent any injustice being slipped over on us. You agree with me, don't you?" Hiroko asked.

All the family were familiar with Mr. Tsukamoto, Jukichi's close friend since childhood. Mr. Nagata, a lawyer, had steadily dealt with the troublesome paperwork for many years. Hiroko had written them about the news, asking them to investigate how Jukichi was actually going to be treated. She told Mr. Nagata to draw money for the trip from Mr. Tsukamoto, if he felt it necessary for her to go to Abashiri. For her absence from Tokyo, she had managed to put aside some money for any emergency that might arise while she was away.

Nuiko went right out. Hiroko thought over what else should be done now. For the several years Jukichi had been on trial, Hiroko, knowing little about the law, had judged and acted according to common sense, relying on her insight and imagination. Jukichi perhaps never realized how many of the inconveniences he had to suffer were brought about by her frequent oversights and errors,

Hiroko slept in an eight-mat room[1] by herself. Though it was a few days short of October, she still had to use a mosquito net in her room. The late moon rose. The *daimyo* bamboo cast shadows on the paper *shoji* panels through the outer windows of the verandah.

In Tabata there used to be a small restaurant called "House of the Spontaneous Smile." On a wall panel opening on the inner courtyard was a sumi-ink painting of bamboo said to have been drawn by the famous Taikan while intoxicated.

Every year, a meeting of haiku poets was held there to reminisce upon Akutagawa Ryunosuke. Jukichi, as his first major academic research, had brought to light the change in the thinking of Japanese intellectuals as shown by the literature and, most particularly, the suicide death of Akutagawa.

Hiroko had read that treatise of Jukichi's in a magazine she found on a table in a small hotel in a foreign country. What was the Hiroko of those days doing then? Did she ever imagine that Jukichi —whom she has thus come to know—would become so thoroughly entangled in her life as this? Who can say that Jukichi, then throwing the entire energy of his youth into his research and writing, himself imagined that in another three years he would be cast into prison sentenced to life.

Then again, Jukichi might have known that something like this would happen and had resolutely prepared himself and had gone ahead and married her anyway.

Watching the shadow-play pictures cast by the *daimyo* bamboo leaves stirred faintly by every wisp of breeze, reminded Hiroko, lying in bed with her eyes wide open, calling up memories of the dusty trial court shining in that late April sunlight. At 10 A.M. of the very day the appeal was to have been judged, Tokyo had been alarmed by a formation of small planes. Hiroko had gotten a call from Mr. Nagata, who had been in the court since before the appointed time.

He said on the phone that the trial would be postponed. She'd taken off the steel helmet which had been lying heavy on her shoul-

---

[1] Japanese rooms have floors covered in inch-thick packed-rush mats, or *tatami*, each measuring a standardized three by six feet.

ders and gotten out of her new *mompei* coveralls. By and by, the air-raid alarm was downgraded to standby. Then a second call told her that the court had suddenly decided to open and that she should come immediately.

"How spiteful they are! Surely they know the family can't make it in time," said Hiroko.

"Anyhow, please come as soon as possible. I'll try hard to delay the opening," Mr. Nagata answered.

It took Hiroko an hour to get from her house to the court. She had to walk a way, take a street car and walk again. There was no shorter way. She was out of breath when she rushed into the third-floor courtroom.

The hearing had already been opened and the slender-faced chief judge of the triumvirate was reading aloud in a formal drone from some paper. Jukichi was sitting in the first row of seats. Two guards had usually sat apart from him, now were close by on either side on the same bench. Hiroko sat behind Mr. Nagata, the sole audience in the otherwise deserted court.

The paper the chief judge was reading was the summary of the review and the sentence. Hiroko felt strange about the whole thing. For what purpose had there been the preliminary examinations or the trials? She found that the analysis and description of the event Jukichi and his comrades had been trying to clarify with their reasoning and an objective examination of the situation, differed very little from the one-sided presentation of the prosecution that had been written twelve years before. A slight difference could be noted, though, in less use of vilification and in the fact that the event was now judged a simple accident, not premeditated as it had been considered before. Whatever efforts Jukichi made, however reasonable his statements might be, the court had decided before-hand. The sentence was a manifestation of judicial obstinacy.

Hiroko's amazement was renewed, though she knew she made it out too simple, at the fact that a fifty-year-old husband and father, an educated man, could stand there without the slightest hesitation, reading out the most unreasonable judgment.

The chief judge finished reading. Then pausing a minute and raising his voice, he read that Jukichi would be sentenced to life imprisonment. He continued and rattled on in a most business-like way that Jukichi could further appeal within a week if he were dis-satisfied with the judgment. All the members of the court stood up at once. So did Jukichi. Hiroko, unconsciously standing up, caught sight of Mr. Nagata's honest white face, now turned an unusually deep red.

All of them followed at the chief judge's heels into the anteroom. Jukichi, leaving, turned to Hiroko and smiled. It was his usual smile. He widened his mouth to knit the edges of it in a hint of cynicism. It was the smile she knew so well. It drew from her a smile. But hers was only a momentary one. Weaving between the benches, she headed straight for him. The guards on either side kept walking, as if to separate them, urging him on. All of Hiroko's movements and her facial expression revealed her concern. Jukichi accepted and understood this; he smiled another smile—one to soothe her. Then turning around and speaking so that either Hiroko or the lawyer could take it, "Well, then, see you the day after tomorrow, again." With his manacled hands, he put on a braided hat and went out. That was a Saturday.

Hiroko could not picture how she herself had looked then, though for the rest of her life she would never forget how Mr. Nagata's face had turned so violently red, or how Jukichi, face smooth and pale from years of illness and being cut off from sunlight, with his gentle but indomitable black eyes, smiled almost humorously.

Those eyes and that smile of Jukichi were formed in the play of *daimyo* bamboo shadows upon the autumn mosquito net—as they were on the small pillow covered in white, and across the palms of Hiroko's hands. Jukichi's hair, which had not yet been cut short, fell long and disheveled over his forehead and gave her a delightful feeling when she ran fingers of memory through it. How many years have passed since her fingers actually touched it?

There is the word "cruelty," so is there the fact of cruelty. If Jukichi and his comrades were not released from prison, while others are set free with the abolition of the Public Peace Law . . . this is cruel . . . too cruel. . . .

I wonder if cruelty itself is not but power used in such a way that harsh treatment cannot be considered to be impossible.

She sat up in her burning bed, passion billowing forth from her longing for Jukichi, swelled by resistance to the cruelty of power.

In none of the few-minute meetings over the past twelve years had Jukichi shown confusion or suffering on his face. Seeing that face, Hiroko would be refreshed, forget her agony. One summer when he met her in the reception room he had been suffering from dysentery and didn't even have enough strength left to sit up properly on his chair. He came in his nightgown and sank in a heap on the chair. From across the table, his hair, which had fallen out almost completely was but a thin suggestive wraith of a hairline and random wisps, exactly as an artist would draw a ghost. Hiroko, blinking, stared with wide-open eyes. Even then when he was perhaps dying, he still had that smile, which was her salvation. When she looked at that smile, Hiroko spontaneously returned it, and her round face reflected the ripple of excitement which stirred within.

Hiroko, however, knew that night must come for her. She knew too that night undifferentiated from the interminable night-like day, also was Jukichi's plight. Enduring the variety of days and nights, she began to feel that she and Jukichi had become a mysterious ship. Night and day meant to her, not an aimless lapping of waves against their ship asea, but a tidal flow of time which would never ebb, a transition of history.

After leaving Himeji, Hiroko spent a day getting on and off trucks, walking hurriedly along leaning on some cart or other. Now she is on a wagon, her tired feet dangling down like a child's.

To both sides of the highway spreads the broad Banshu Plain illuminated by the diaphanous setting sun of autumn. Mountains are seen in the westward distance where Mt. Rokko would be rising behind Kobe City. Beautiful light white clouds floating across the sky sooth Hiroko as she gazes at them from the cart.

On such an autumn afternoon Hiroko is unexpectedly on an old wagon on her way east through the Banshu Plain. She is going forward to Jukichi . . . . This expectation makes the slowness of the old-fashioned cart seem very comforting. Banshu Plain has a unique undulation, different from that of Tokyo's Kanto Plain or that around Nasuno along the far northern Tohoku Line where Hiroko used to live. These fertile fields are plowed lightly to blend with the remote mountains of Hanshin, which though high and steep, rise calmly in the evening sky. Here and there are dazzling pools like shallow lakes.

Their baggage on the cart with Hiroko, two young men follow along the highway. Once accustomed to walking, they put their suit jackets over their arms and begin to whistle.

Both are cheerful youths with beautiful teeth, which almost seems a Korean characteristic as much as crooked teeth are a Japanese. They often joke and smile. They speak in Korean. All the other Koreans Hiroko has seen on her trip were moving west, in the direction of the channel and home; only these two are going toward the east to Osaka or perhaps even Tokyo.

They seem to have something good waiting for them at their destination; they jest and run after each other like frolicking puppies; they sing songs at intervals. Still, they never wander far from the cart.

The autumnal sun, combed by the breeze, melts Banshu mountains, fields, small village and trees into one golden glow. The wagon moves very slowly along the solitary highway toward their destination. The clatter of the wheels, "*katori, katori* ..." unexpectedly harmonizes with the gaiety of the young men. All is in harmony with Hiroko's heart, filled as it is with various memories. Such would never happen to her again, to be carried so along the highway like this. Hedges of a small town, rusty remains of large factories standing beyond the pine wood of Akashi—Hiroko stares at them.

She feels in all sincerity that the whole of Japan is surging forward like her slow cart.

DAMOI—HOMEWARD BOUND

by *Yamamoto Tomomi*

THE STATION was a turmoil of prisoners. They arrived from camps scattered all over the environs of Karaganda. Flying red and white placards and flags, with pictures of Stalin held high, the repatriates seemed in high spirits even though everyone seemed to be seriously ill. I could see some walking toward the station supported by their comrades. The biggest group was from Camp Number 6.

On the grassy space by the railway station a podium had been erected. The democrats from each camp would get up on the podium and swear to "work for the reconstruction of a democratic Japan" and to "overthrow the reactionary Ashida Government." In the background, Soviet political officers egged the democrats on, and a prisoner's band played the "Internationale" and "Red Flag."

It was already dark when we got on our car, the sixteenth in the long train. We were thankful that our group of internees was able to be together. Major Egin personally came to the car to bid us farewell. I felt my heart go out to him and, for a moment, the bitter memories of Karaganda days dimmed. On August 8 our train finally began its homeward journey.

Our *damoi* (Russian for "going-home") train consisted of fifty-odd cars. White and red placards were nailed to outer walls and pictures of Stalin, and bunting, giving our train a festive look. Inside each car were placed large, medium and small buckets—one of each. They were for storing and carrying drinking water and food.

97

For utensils we were each provided with a tin can and one tin mug. One of the cars was devoted to the headquarters of the "Democratic Committee." It housed the democratic leaders and an orchestra composed of young and ardent prisoners. We were given copies of the *Short History of the Communist Party* and were told to elect a leader for our car. The idea was to put finishing touches to our political education before our embarkation for Japan.

With the heat of summer past, and we could feel autumn in the air. As we traveled north, even the days were cool, the nights quite cold. With the exception of those placed in the several cars reserved for the seriously ill, we were not provided with mattresses or blankets, and there were two or three nights we could not sleep for the cold.

Our *damoi* train sped eastward, carrying its miserable freight of 1,300-odd sick and crippled prisoners of war, the slag from the Soviet Union's vast crucible of prison labor. Though our bodies were worn, our limbs torn and our flesh weakened, our hearts burned with hope and joy. The train's wheels sang a jubilant song as we told ourselves we were returning – – returning home after a long exile.. How different it was from our westward trip three years before. The train whistle had sounded so devastatingly lonely then.

Three years of hard labor had had flattened our cheeks and deepened our eye sockets. Our faces were tanned ebony black from the fierce sun of Kazakhstan. I stared at my callused hands and read a story of toil and suffering. in their deep, dirt-engrained lines,.

Just as we had changed, Siberia had also been transformed in the three years. The attire of the Soviet people had greatly improved. There were few now who went about barefooted. New buildings had been built by the tracks, new coal mines opened up. The railroad bed had been improved, the tracks properly ballasted and made firm. Perhaps for this reason, our train swayed less and traveled at a greater speed than three years previously.

All along the tracks we saw Japanese prison camps. Japanese soldiers waved at us and placards bearing "democratic" slogans decorated the entrances to these compounds. I realized that these Japanese prisoner of war had contributed the greater part of the improvements I saw on all sides.

Hours on end I watched the countryside speed by—past Irkutsk—Lake Baikal, shimmering beauty of deep blue with large steamers plying its surface—Ulan Ude, the hillsides dotted with army camps and masses of tanks parked side by side.

Everywhere I saw signs of the eternal fear that hovers over the Soviet Union. Tunnels and bridges were guarded by soldiers with machine guns. Each line of the doubled-tracked Trans-Siberian Railway crossed bridges that were set miles apart—obviously to minimize damage from possible bombing. If the spans had been set side by side. they could be blown up by one lucky shot. Spaced as they were, two hits would be necessary. These reminders of the evil of the Soviet *vlast* dampened my enjoyment of the beauty of the countryside. The glory of the stretching *taiga*, the rolling meadows in the river valleys, and the pastoral patches of farmland scattered here and there seemed tainted by tyranny, and I would turn away my eyes in sorrow.

Traffic on the Trans-Siberian Railway had greatly increased. Trains were traveling westward at ten- or fifteen-minute intervals. At first the hellish screech of passing trains woke me from my sleep; after the third or fourth day I became used to the sound. The majority of the trains were composed of boxcars or flatcars piled high with coal, ores, lumber and limestone. There were also oil tankers and refrigerators. Once or twice we saw large cannons being transported west. Often we came across Russian prison trains, with their miserable load of human freight. Once we stopped in a siding just opposite one of these. From a barred window peered a beautiful young girl. She asked for a smoke. I tossed her one *papiros* from the twenty-day ration that had been given us on our departure. She told me she had been a clerk in a Moscow department store and had been arrested for having stolen a blouse from the counter. Now she was being sent to some place in Siberia to serve out a seven-year prison term. She envied our freedom and wished us good luck. Even today the memory of that face haunts my mind.

Just west of Chita we came across a gang of Japanese prisoners working on the railway track, packing gravel under the ties. They told us that they had gone as far as Nakhodka, on the Sea of Japan, for repatriation but had been sent back as "reactionaries," not ready to be returned to Japan. They warned us that we should throw away our homemade mahjong sets and our chessboards. Otherwise, they said, we too would be regarded as "reactionaries" and be detained in Russia. As soon as our train started to move, we threw away all baubles that might mark us as still "bourgeois" in the tastes of our captors. At the junction of the Molotov Line, running to Manchouli on the Manchurian-Soviet border, and the Trans-Siberian Railway, we were taken to a public delousing station for our bath. There we met a group of Japanese "democrats" on their way home from some district conference of "democratic leaders." They came aboard our train and, to our surprise, showered us with invectives. They did not like the way we went around in our undershirts during the day.

They did not like our use of the post-position -*san* (Mr.) in addressing our friends. They called us "reactionary" and lacking in "democratic training," even criticized the way we sang the "Internationale." To them we were lukewarm prisoners, not fully converted to their own brand of militant Communism.

I was completely shocked by the fanatic zeal of these youngsters, each man hardly out of his teens. I realized that the indoctrination of prisoners in eastern Siberia had been carried out with an intensity that I had not dreamed possible. It was evident that unless we were careful we would be marked as "reactionaries" and possibly detained at Nakhodka. I resolved to be on guard.

We reached Nakhodka on the afternoon of August 26, eighteen days after our departure from Karaganda. I saw the sea and breathed deep of the salt air. With deep emotion I told myself that just beyond the ocean lay Japan and home. At last I was being sent home. I had traveled safely five thousand miles across Siberia. My heart swelled with joy and relief.

Upon alighting from the train, we were formed into ranks of five abreast and led to Camp Number 1. This, I learned, was the receiving center for prisoners arriving in Nakhodka from the interior. To my surprise I found Japanese prisoners guarding the compound, not a single Soviet soldier in evidence. In fact, the whole camp was run and managed by Japanese. Leaders of the "Democratic Committee" welcomed us from the platform of an open-air theater. We were then allotted our quarters.

The camp was a village of tents set up on a sandy beach; inside, two-tiered platforms served as our bunks; our latrine was a wooden pier built out into the sea. The food served to us was plentiful and nourishing, although it was the same *kasha* and black bread that we had eaten during our stay in the Soviet Union. I realized that the Soviet Union was making a last-minute effort to fatten us up for delivery to the Japanese government.

No regular work was required of us. However, we would at times be called out to carry rocks from a nearby quarry to build up a sea wall against high waves blown shoreward during storms. We were required to sing the "Internationale" and other Communist songs as we marched to the quarry and back. Discipline, Communist discipline, was a *must*, and we had to close ranks and keep in step as we marched. Our only guards were Japanese members of the camp staff.

On our way we met other groups of prisoners, singing in the same lusty manner. They belonged to Camp Number 2, next step in our processing. Here the prisoner had his clothing checked. Here also was he given his last bath before his return to Japan. The next and last step was Camp No. 3, where each prisoner was put through a rigid "customs" inspection. In short, stripped of whatever money he had and all printed matter, written notes. I also learned there was a Camp No. 4, where the seriously sick were interned. Prisoners in this camp awaited the arrival of hospital ships from Japan.

I will always remember the thrill I got when I first saw a Japanese ship enter the harbor. It loomed in a distant haze, gradually approached land, then stayed four hours before leaving for Japan. I told myself that I, too, would be on a ship within a week or so.

Soon it did come our turn to move to Camp Number 2. Here the barracks were made of lumber and seemed more substantial than Camp Number 1, but we found ourselves troubled by fleas, bedbugs and clouds of black flies that hung thick on the ceilings during the day and tormented us at night. The finishing touches to our political indoctrination were continued—lectures, discussion meetings, *Nihon Shimbun* reading circles where we read aloud this Communist Japanese-language newspaper, song practices, demonstrations, plays and motion pictures. We hardly had any time for rest.

The leaders of the "democratic movement" told us that the Japanese government was not interested in seeing Japanese prisoners returned. Since repatriation began in May of that year, only twelve or thirteen ships had been sent to Nakhodka. In addition, although the ships could carry five thousand men on one trip, the Japanese government was limiting prisoners to two thousand. Thus, only 25,000 could be repatriated monthly. In June so many prisoners had piled up in Nakhodka that many had to sleep outside on the cold ground. Some, we were further told, had been transferred, as a result, back to interior camps to await their turn. The reason for this unwillingness of the Japanese government to accept prisoners for repatriation was blamed by our captors on the critical food shortage in Japan, the problem of unemployment and the lack of preparations to greet repatriates.

This explanation aroused us to anger and added fuel to the fire of anti-Ashida sentiment, which the "Democratic Committee" sought to instill in the prisoners of war. Until we finally boarded our repatriation ship, we believed these lies and cursed the Japanese Government.

One day, I was present at a discussion meeting sponsored by the "actives" of Camp Number 2. The talk drifted to the plans each of the prisoners had for his return to Japan. With the best of intention, I told the group that I wanted to go to the United States to see what "democracy" was like there. One of the leaders of the group asked me whether I believed America to be democratic.

"Of course, I do," I replied. "America was an ally of the Soviet Union and fought in the democratic camp against the Nazis and the Japanese militarists. Now that I have seen 'democracy' in the Soviet Union, I hope to see 'democracy' in the United States."

A hush fell over the group. The leader looked at me and said, "Comrade Yamamoto, are you in your right senses? You seem to harbor dangerous bourgeois thoughts. Only the Soviet Union is a true democratic country. The United States is a country of imperialistic aggression."

I answered, with more heat than I had intended, "Democracy is equality. I believe that we should hear both sides of the story and see both sides of the world. I do not believe that the Soviet Union has a monopoly on democracy."

White with anger, the leader warned, "Comrade Yamamoto, you are a reactionary. You are not ready to go home. You still need to be taught discipline and Communist theory."

I shrugged my shoulders and left the group. By next morning I had forgotten the incident. Two days later our group was called out for transfer to Camp Number 3, the next step in our processing for repatriation. At the gate the names of the men in our group were read out. I eagerly waited for my name. The last man left the gate, but my name had not been mentioned. I became frantic and went to the Japanese reading the list. He checked and told me that I had not been included. I felt as if struck by a huge hammer.

Like lightning I went to the headquarters of the "democratic movement." The man who had warned me the previous day was sitting in a corner, looking at me triumphantly. I told the committee chairman I had been left off the list of men for Camp Number 3.

"We know," he answered, You need to study a little longer in the Soviet Union. You are reactionary and will have to have some of those bourgeois thoughts pounded out of you. Tomorrow morning you will be taken to Camp Number 5 with a few other people and there set to work."

I spent a sleepless night, gigantic waves of misery rolling into my heart. I had come this far and now I was going back to a labor camp. I dared not venture a guess as to how long I would be kept.

The next morning, I was called out to the front gate. There were four other men beside me. We were all "reactionaries," unfit to be sent home. Led by one of the Japanese members of the camp management, we headed for the hills behind Nakhodka. Time and time again, I looked toward the sea and cried in my heart at missing my chance to go home.

Camp Number 5 turned out to be a neat compound of wooden barracks, painted a clean white. I was handed over to the Japanese camp authorities with the explanation that I needed "correction for mistaken thinking." To my surprise, I ran into friends that I had known back in Camp No.3 in Alma Ata. To my greater surprise, I learned that the bulk of the 1,300 men, left in that camp when we departed for Karaganda, were still in Nakhodka. The group had arrived here in Nakhodka early in June and only the seriously sick had been sent home. I saw Nagayama, who had been in my platoon. "Nagayama-san," I called. Like a slap in the face came his answer: "Comrade Yamamoto! Only reactionaries use the word -san."

I was surprised at the change that had come over him. The affable youngster I had known in Alma Alta was now a rabid Communist. I found this true of all the others. I felt alone in my misery.

For one whole year I was to live in an atmosphere of intense suspicion and fear. It was for me an amazing, though trying, lesson in the formation and the workings of a police-state psychology. A man was first driven into desperation. This was a simple task. Any prisoner living for months within sight of men returning home, would gradually lose all hope. It was agony for me to still be able to watch the repatriation ships steam into the harbor and leave with their load of happy prisoners. It was agony also to think that just beyond the blue barrier of the sea lay Japan and home. When something is held too long just beyond a man's reach, he loses all hope of ever grasping it. This was how it was with the prisoners in Camp Number 5.

Then we were set to work, harder than ever before. The bad heart I had developed early in my imprisonment, now for some reason or other had become completely normal. My pulse no longer acted up. Perhaps this was because I was now at sea level. Whatever the case, I was sent out to work on neighboring farms and on the port facilities of a planned gigantic harbor, named in honor of Zhdanov, Deputy Prime Minister of the Soviet Union. Upon completion, the port was to outrival nearby Vladivostok.

The work we had done in Alma Ata or Karaganda was nothing compared to that forced on us at Nakhodka. Pay, food, fear of punishment were no longer incentives. The prize at stake was our return to Japan. If we wanted to go home, we had to be good "democrats." To be good "democrats" meant that we had to show a frenzied anxiety to work to our bones in building up the Soviet Union. The fear of being branded as "reactionaries" and of being transported back to Karaganda was the lash that whipped us to superhuman efforts. The norms accomplished were fantastic, but the Japanese camp leaders never seemed satisfied.

At the same time our political indoctrination was stepped up. On our way to and from work, a man read articles from the *Nihon Shimbun* to us as we marched. During intermissions, we sat around in circles and had more Communist doctrine pounded into us. During the actual working hours, we dared not rest nor talk with others. Even a slight letup was interpreted as shirking and a demonstration of a reactionary trend. We were afraid even to voice our utterly human longing to go home to Japan.

Upon our return to the camp, we underwent further indoctrination, attending lectures and plays. The theme was always hatred. Everything was a "struggle," a "fight." We were always combating imagined "enemies of Communism" in our midst, in our own hearts, and in Japan.

"You are the vanguards of a revolutionary army. You are training to land in the face of the enemy when you return to Japan, you must overthrow the present government, abolish the emperor system, throw out the American tyrants, and establish a people's republic"— day in day out, the same theme of hatred was pounded into us. We were preparing for a "struggle to reconstruct Japan into a democratic nation." We were preparing for a showdown battle with the "new Fascist ruling class of Japan and their puppet police." We were training to become reinforcements for the Japanese Communist Party in its "fight to liberate the Japanese people from foreign domination." Thus, a new fascism arose in our own camp. We were required to be militant in our bearing and attitude. We marched to work as if we were on a parade ground. Our language became terse and military. A completely new idiom was concocted as vehicles for the new chauvinism burgeoning in our midst.

We had to show conformity and agreement with the slogans mouthed at political meetings. By the fervor of our *shikari* (so it is) and *soda* (that's so), which we shouted at our speakers, was measured our political loyalty to Communism.

The plays that were shown us, put on by the "actives," harped on this same hate motif. They were well-acted, with a passion rare even on the legitimate stage. They moved the spectator strangely, planting rancor deep within his heart.

I, too, found myself influenced by the atmosphere in which I lived. I knew that I had to be regarded as an "active" if ever I was to see Japan again. I realized too that I had to try doubly hard; for there was already a black mark against me. I took part in the plays, the discussion meetings and the kangaroo courts that periodically took place to denounce our erstwhile leaders. Such kangaroo courts, called "popular trials," illustrated most aptly the underlying mob psychology that makes Communism a danger. Any laxity on the part of our camp leaders was asignal for a "popular trial." We would haul a leader before a mass meeting, criticize him for staying in the camp while others went out to work. This, we charged, was "anti-democratic." A true active showed his fervor for Communism by his deeds. We would strip leaders of their powers, brand them as "reactionaries," and relegate them to the ranks of common prisoner.

In this way there were several changes in the Japanese camp *vlast.* In time I came to be recognized as one of the leaders. However, I well knew the temper of the mob. I absolutely declined to take any position of authority and continued until the last as a common worker, though a recognized "active." As a result, I saved myself the ignominy of being hauled before a "people's court" and being taken down by the mob.

When winter came to Nakhodka, the ships from Japan stopped coming. It was a dreary and bitter time. Although heavy snows blanketed the roads and covered our work site day in day out, our work continued. When spring arrived, I once again picked up hope as reports of the resumption of repatriation filtered into our camp. Then the ships came and, from our work sites along the harbor, we watched column after column of prisoners from the interior of Soviet Russia march the two and a half miles from the cluster of repatriation camps to the embarkation point.

Summer came and passed. With each passing month, my hopes of ever returning to Japan became dimmer and dimmer. The first signs of autumn were on us when we heard the news that the repatriation camps in Nakhodka would be closed. I knew then that I would never see Japan again. Everything seemed to darken before my eyes. I resigned myself to a lifetime in the Soviet Union. With my knowledge of the Russian language, I told myself, I would be able to make out somehow. Perhaps they would free me after a time. Perhaps, in due course, I could settle down and marry some Russian woman. These thoughts ran daily through my mind.

One day, in the second week in September, we were suddenly ordered to prepare for our departure. It was then that the great news was given to us. We were at last going home. It was a happy moment when we moved to Camp Number 1, part of which was being dismantled. We were told that we were among the last leaving; the camp management would also leave on the next ship or so. Our ordinary work clothes were exchanged for fresh ones in Camp Number 2. Then we were sent to the last barrier, Camp Number 3. This, too, was safely passed.

The *Takasago Maru* lay docked at the pier that we had helped build. As we lined up on the wharf, our leaders called on us to sing our Communist songs. As the Soviet officers counted us aboard, we marched up the gangplank singing at the top of our voices. Nurses waited on deck to greet us. Their kind words brought tears to my eyes, but I wiped them away. The evil spell of the Soviet Union was still upon me—I could not show any human feeling.

For three hours our ship waited at the dock, although every prisoner had come aboard. We were waiting for a truckload of lepers, Japanese prisoners of war who had caught the dread disease in Siberia. They finally arrived. The sailors swabbed with disinfectant the decks where the lepers had passed on their way to the infirmary. Then, with a shrill whistle, the *Takasago Maru* began moving. I was on my way home after three full years and eight months of captivity. The ship pulled away. I was free.

LOVE IN THE ANNAM JUNGLE

by *Oka Masamichi*

THE SKY over Saigon was clear as it always is, and the streets sizzled in the shadeless 95-degree heat. I felt dizzy in this heat, but I picked my way along under the tall acacia trees, feeling unusually conscious of the heavy sword and bayonet at my side. Roy, who walked with me, did not say much. The heat was too much even for him, I guess. Roy was Vietnamese, a member of a secret organization whose aim was the independence of Vietnam from France. He spoke some English, but his Japanese was more fluent. He and I were on our way to his headquarters.

I'd had little interest in the independence movement in Vietnam, but Roy had urged that, as a memento of my last days in Saigon, I meet its leader. I had allowed his urging to get the better of me.

He took me through a small store and stopped before a room in the back. "Here it is," he said and led me inside. In the room were more than ten Vietnamese, on the four walls maps of all sorts. Roy spoke in Vietnamese to the one who sat at the center. I could not understand, but I perceived that he was talking about me. I could see right away that this man was the leader. He got up slowly from the chair, then extended his hand to me. "Glad you came," it sounded to me, with the expressive gestures of the French. We talked about this and that for a while. He seemed to know a great deal about me.

Then, suddenly, he asked, "What is your opinion of our independence movement."

107

The leader's question baffled me. I was merely a passer-by, and naturally enough could not answer such a question put to me in all seriousness. When the leader saw that I could not answer, he began to explain to me about the movement. He said that the French rule of Vietnam had now come to its end, that "the people of Vietnam are ready to revolt against the French exploitations." He spoke these words with heated eagerness, pounding the table with his fist. "In order to win this independence, we must have the cooperation and help of the Japanese. I presume you are willing to give us that cooperation."

There was no room for yes nor no. I saw for the first time that I had been deceived by Roy. I noticed that the others, who hadn't said a single word, had surrounded me. If I refused, I knew what to expect. I looked at Roy; he evaded my eyes, and kept his lowered, but presently he bowed his head and murmured, "Please, help us."

I was a lieutenant of dentistry in the Japanese army. Roy was a native of Saigon. He and I were friends, but there was a certain limitation to our friendship. I had never expected him to deceive me like this.

With the termination of the war, I had received orders to head for Phnom Penh whence I was to board a ship for Japan. I had intended to go to an airport in Saigon to fly to Phnom Penh. On the day before, Roy had given a farewell party for me, at which time he urged me to see his leader. I accepted the offer, merely thinking that he wanted to show off to me his wide circle of acquaintances. And this was the result.

The leader and his aides looked somewhat menacing, and yet I saw that there was a feeling of entreaty, too. But I, on my part, faced the moment of deciding the course of my entire future. There was only one way to stay alive, and that was to cooperate with them, to take part in their independence movement. There ensued a heavy silence, at the end of which I opened my mouth and sighed, "All right. I will cooperate."

My answer loosened the tension immediately, and I said inwardly, "All right I'll show them what I can do. I'm young and strong. It may not prove insignificant for me to take part in this revolution."

The time was the end of August in the year the war ended. Saigon at that time was tense, on the eve of revolution. By day there were demonstrations big and small, and at night shots were heard everywhere in the streets. All the young people were concerned with this independence movement, either directly, or indirectly, or so it seemed. But this promising situation did not last long. The Allies who had ability and power arrived, replacing the Japanese army who had neither. The leaders of the independence movement and their comrades gradually left Saigon and took cover in the jungle. I had been under close watch while in Saigon, and finally left the city with the leader. After many days we reached the jungle in Tay Ninh district, and here my days as a soldier in Ho Chi Min's army and my war against the jungle started.

In the jungle I met a girl, or rather re-encountered her. Many had run to the jungle with their families; there were many women and children. There were also young women who had come into the Ho army on their own. Nyun was one of these. She spoke excellent Japanese, having worked during the war for a Japanese firm in Saigon, where I had seen her once or twice. The unexpected reappearance of Nyun threw a bright light into the life in the jungle which was naturally dark and oppressive. She looked lovelier than when I had seen her in Saigon and her nineteen-year-old body was full of energy. I found myself drawn to her. Her duties were interpreter and KP. I suppose she too had a special feeling for me from before. We met alone, often, and these rendezvous increased as time went on.

By this time we Japanese became busy. Our duties were public relations with the Japanese army, to go to them and ask for the arms and ammunition for which they had no further use. I left the jungle once with this mission to go near Saigon to see battalion and company commanders and negotiate with them for the release of their arms and ammunition. Of course they had no more use for them, but that did not mean they should give them to the Ho army. The mission was not an easy one. Some of them sympathized with me, but refused. Some of them bawled me out, told me to go back to Japan, while others wanted to know why I chose such a hard task. My mission was not a success.

Then the communists gave me still harder orders. They told me to take some poison with me to the Japanese and rob them of their arms. I, a Japanese, could not take this order—that must have been obvious. I perceived an underlying motive behind this order It came from Hee, the commander of a company. He was in love with Nyun, and wanted to do away with me by impressing upon me an order I could not possibly take.

He was raving mad and threatened me with the point of his bayonet. "Why refuse my order?" he demanded.

"I can't deceive and kill fellow Japanese," I said flatly.

"I did not say for you to kill them," he lied. "I merely wanted you to bring back their arms."

"But I still don't want to deceive them." I was adamant.

He put me in confinement for noncompliance. "I'll give you two days to think it over," Hee said before he closed the door on me. "In two days you choose either obedience or death."

I was locked up in a hut built in the jungle. I did not sleep that night. Hee might really kill me on the pretense that I had disrupted military law and order. But I had one hope: Nyun.

Nyun did not betray me. She and some Vietminh soldiers whom I did not know freed me after a short skirmish with the guards. When she first found out that there was little chance for me to come out alive, she went to the neighboring company, met a company commander by the name of Tom, and begged him for help. I was deeply touched when I learned that she had gone in the dead of night through the jungle to save my life. I took her hand and wept on it. Commander Tom, who had given her the soldiers who helped release me, welcomed me into his company. Nyun, of course, went with me. She and I were married shortly after that. In the communist camp, marriages are free.

Among the Vietnamese there is a religious organization called Kao Dai. It has a membership of some two million and, besides being a religious group, is a political and ideological organization. The Kao Dai had an army of about five thousand men which immediately after the war sided with the Vietminh, waving the flag of independence, but shortly afterward it succumbed to French propaganda and went over to their camp.

By the time the rumor spread that Kao Dai was acting suspicious, the gap between Kao Dai and Vietminh was too deep and wide to be mended. We Japanese faced a predicament, for my company and Kao Dai were closely situated and naturally the Japanese in their group were friendly with the Japanese in our company. We hated to see the gap grow between us.

Just at this crucial time Captain Okada of our company was killed while on a scouting mission. He was a typical old samurai and we—that is, the fifteen Japanese in our company—were deeply attached to this man. His death shocked us profoundly, for it was rumored that he was killed by the Vietminh and not by Kao Dai, as the Vietminh would have us believe. We Japanese knew how he was loved and respected by the Kao Dai themselves. The Kao Dai liked us Japanese and we could see no reason for their killing the captain. The rumor was further strengthened by the suspicious character of the Vietminh, who looked with deep skepticism on the continued friendship that existed between the Japanese of the Kao Dai group and Japanese in the Vietminh. The Vietminh had thought Captain Okada was the leader of this alliance.

We Japanese began to wonder if we might not follow in Captain Okada's footsteps. We had often overheard the Vietminh whisper that "the Japanese are only to be used." The Vietminh, a people long oppressed by a foreign power and naturally distrustful of any foreigners, including the Japanese from whom they sought help, could not, we felt, be relied on.

Japanese, one by one, not long after the Okada incident began escaping from the Vietminh. Some said that from this jungle in the Tay Ninh district one could cut across Cambodia and get into Thailand; others suggested the northern route to Hanoi, saying once there, one could find some kind of hideout; still others thought to run into China proper through Indo-China. Not one said he would surrender to the French. We all believed the rumor that, having come from a communist camp, we would never be allowed to live if we returned to the French side.

I did not join these Japanese in their escape. For one thing, I had Nyun; for another, I knew there were French armies in the north and felt sure that it was impossible to enter Hanoi or China proper.

One by one, all the Japanese left except me. About this time there was a reorganization in our army and the company I belonged to came to be called the 11th Branch Company. I was the sole Japanese soldier in it. Later, rumors seeped through to us that most of the Japanese who had tried to escape had been killed by the French or had died of jungle diseases, while those fortunate enough to escape disease, death or French capture were forced to return to the company. They were all emaciated, and easily fell prey to desperation, for there was little hope for them in the jungle and they could not surrender themselves to the French. I was at the time bedridden with malaria, but I kept telling the returnees not to lose hope, that we would all find some way to live. But my encouragement brought little result, for one day all of them took a group of Vietminh and attacked a company of French trucks, meeting wholesale destruction. It was a suicidal act.

From this time on I made up my mind to forget that I was a Japanese. I even changed my name to a Vietminh name, An Torun, and decided to live the life of a Vietminh in every respect. My wife agreed with me wholeheartedly, saying "You are no longer a Japanese who once occupied the French Indies. But please don't forget that you are a soldier of a defeated nation." She often repeated these words, urging me not to look for promotion. There is no rank in the communist army, so there are no officers or non-coms. She urged me not to want to become a company or a battalion commander with responsibilities. "I know how you feel, but please cooperate," she pleaded. "It is foolish to be ostracized by them because of trivial matters."

So I joined the Vietminh in their morning ceremony of the raising of the independence flag.

A year or two of the life in the jungle passed peacefully and uneventfully. To escape French attacks the communists penetrated deep into the jungle. Other than occasional contacts with French reconnaissance planes and scouting parties, there was hardly any fighting in the area.

The communist Vietminh worked their own vegetable gardens, planted rice, hunted. The staple food was rice, and most of it came from the south, but the shipments were disrupted often, and often we suffered its scarcity. There were many days when we lived on yams and tapioca. Our shelter was a leaky hut and we were soaked to the bone when it rained. When out of food, we lay around on empty stomachs.

Our baby was born in a hut built of grass and bamboo. We were overjoyed at the sound of the baby's cry, on a bed made of bamboo shoots, for it seemed to us a miracle that a strong, healthy baby could be born to a woman who lived on rice and salt and hardly any other nourishment. The baby was a girl, our girl.

We named her Kon Choku. In this district it was a custom not to formally name a baby until it was a year or so old, but to call it by a pet name of some animal. Kon Choku meant "little mouse."

The Germans in the company loved her, and sang "Schön" to her. These Germans had been prisoners of the French in Africa during World War II and had been brought to the French Indies to fight against communists. They then became the prisoners of the communists. In this jungle army there were, besides these Germans, some French who had surrendered to the communists; Spanish, Belgians, and Poles who had fought under the German flag during the war and who had been French prisoners and followed the German prisoners' fate. These Europeans had no resistance against malaria and many of them died. The Germans had an innate hatred for the French and fought against them bravely.

Kon Choku brought forth that thing called human, so love long forgotten in the hearts of these men who had become despondent in the jungle. Some days she was never returned to us, going from one hand to the next. The Vietminh fought over her.

Nyun and I were beside ourselves with joy in having Kon Choku, but we were in the depths of poverty, the kind of poverty neither of us had ever experienced before. As for our clothing, I had only one black suit rationed to me by the communists. Nyun had two, one of which was tattered beyond mending. Of course when I had first come into the jungle I had had some Japanese army clothes, but these had long since been exchanged for food.

Kon Choku never knew a real toy. She only had a stick to hold in her tiny hand. My wife got an empty medicine box from the dispensary and put a coin in it for Choku to rattle. She liked the sound it made, and shook it for all it was worth, clucking happily. It was the only toy Nyun and I were able to give her, she who was the only source of joy and happiness in our otherwise grim lives.

One morning when she was about ten months old I was awakened early by an unusual cry. I jumped out of bed and took her in my arms, but she would not stop crying. She looked frightened by something, her pulse was fast, her breathing hard. Soon she began to have spasms. I ran to the dispensary, and got the chief. He was a chief, all right, but with very little medical knowledge. He looked at Choku, and merely shook his head.

"Anyway, we'll give her a shot of camphor," he said. It seemed to take some effect, for her spasms stopped, but there was still no life in her face. I was seized with a strong premonition that she would die. Her pulse became faint, her breathing weakened.

"Choku, Choku, don't die," my wife hugged her, her face wet with tears. She kept repeating Choku's name, but Choku never opened her eyes again. It all happened so quickly. Who took her life away? What in the name of fate snuffed out the life of so small a creature with no resistance?

Choku had had acute meningitis. She was buried in the jungle. I asked to let Choku take with her to heaven the only toy she ever had. The teeth marks of Choku on the box stayed in my mind a long time.

We had not been attacked by the French in a long time. Except when the communists sent out guerrillas, there was hardly any fighting between us and the Franco-Vietnamese Armies. For one thing our base was too deep in the jungle; for another our defense too well organized. Every road, no matter how narrow, was studded with land mines and any road wide enough to pass on was barred with huge trees placed crisscross. The entrances of these roads into the jungle were heavily guarded and, even if the French tried to attack, they would have been no match for the communists who knew the jungle inside and out.

But the long lull did not mean that the French had forgotten us. They sometimes sent native scouts or dropped incendiaries from the sky. One day, after these aerial bombings had continued an unusually long number of days, we heard an explosion quite distant from our barracks. It sounded like one of our land mines.

"Enemy?"

It was the enemy. After four long years they had finally caught up with us. Without knowing how big a force we faced, or what their intentions were, the fighting began. Whether it was because they were surprised by our land mines, or that they found our guards, we did not know, but they kept up the machine guns for a long time. There was a certain amount of disorder on our part because we hadn't seen any fighting in a long time, but considering it all, and due mostly to the training we had kept up, the soldiers took to their stations very quickly, while the non-combat groups took to shelter.

The sound of the machine guns came closer. We could hear our rifle shots mingle with those of the machine guns. Perhaps our soldiers had met the enemy. Fighting continued through the night. If we held on to our position we knew from experience that the French would never come closer than absolutely necessary. And we also knew that they left with the dawn.

It was not due entirely to this French attack, but our company was forced to leave the jungle where we had lived nearly five years. We headed south. The most immediate reason was the lack of food. Our first plan to raise our own food did not work and we could not fight starvation and malnutrition as forcefully as we fought our human enemy. We had come to the limit of our physical endurance. The soldiers were actually living corpses—cheeks sunken, eyes bulging, legs like rakes, with flat torsos topping them. It was unanimously agreed that we should quit the jungle.

On July 19, 1951, we left the jungle of Tay Ninh for the district of Tan An, about one hundred kilometers northwest of Saigon and the biggest rice area in the district. The way was long and a march with women and children would be difficult. If we could manage to cover six to seven kilos a day, it would still take us a good half month to reach our destination.

The march started with the combat groups in the front and the non-combatants following. The entire group was barefooted; we carried enough food to last twenty days. From the third day we started on night marches, which were far more difficult. We could not even talk loud, for we were passing through enemy territory. The jungle is dark even in the daytime and at night it was pitch dark. Poison snakes and poison ants were everywhere. Then there were those horrible ticks that lived on the leaves. If bit by one, even an adult ran a temperature the next day. Leeches are grotesque things. The ones in this area were about an inch long and lived in wet ground. If one stood on one spot any length of time, leeches crawled up, fastened to a leg, and sucked blood.

My rice rotted. Wet from the rain and steamed by the jungle heat, it mildewed. Then it turned yellow and rotted from inside. There is nothing you can do with it when it gets to that stage.

After we had marched about twenty days, the jungle thinned out and our vista brightened; before us was a river, one of the branch streams of the great Mekong. It was a deep river and the stream was fast. On the bank were many cutters that our comrades in the south had prepared for us.

"Boats!"

Everyone suddenly came to life. Boats epitomized civilization for us at the time, for we could go forward without the painful use of our legs. There were some children who now saw boats for the first time.

Beyond this river was the Dang Kup Moy district. Once across, Nyun came down with dengue fever. The march had to be continued; I took her by the hand and carried our meager belongings hanging on both ends of a pole, resting on my shoulder. On the second day after we had entered Dang Kup Moy, it rained all day. It was still raining when we started our march next night. I didn't mind getting wet so much as the slipperiness of the road. Nyun was half dazed with high fever and every time one of us fell the other did, too. Getting up was hard enough for me, but I had to pick her up with me. Her breathing was hard and only the sound of it, heard through the rain, assured me that she was still alive. The water became deeper and deeper and soon it came up to our knees.

After a while, we finally reached a high plateau. We took a much-needed rest. The rain stopped, the moon came out, but we could still hear the water gushing all around the lower sections that surrounded the enemy's fortified aircraft emplacements.

Nyun rested on my lap, still as death. I could feel her high fever through her clothes onto my flesh. She would not answer me. After some rest, we resumed our march. Where we stayed was too high, we made too easy targets for the enemy.

We finally reached our destination after such hardships as we had never before experienced, and there we took up a sort of colonial troops' life. Food rations became much better, and both Nyun and I improved in health rapidly.

There was a woman by the name of Min who lived near us. She told us that she had made a number of trips to Saigon, going through some very vigilant French guards. We did not know why she took such risks to go to Saigon, but we decided to ask her to contact Nyun's parents, which had been impossible when we were in the jungle.

On her first trip Min could not find Nyun's parents, but on her second we gave her the address of some rich relatives of Nyun's. She found them and brought back with her presents from Nyun's parents: materials for Nyun, a hat for the baby—we now had our second child—and a shirt for me.

When we found that Nyun's parents were well in Saigon, I decided to send Nyun to them. I could not leave the communist army, but Nyun was a woman, and she had a baby. The communists were fair to women and children. When I spoke to Nyun about my thought, she was at first against it. But after I talked to her, explaining that to continue as we were the three of us might die, but separated one of us should be able to stay alive, she finally consented to go.

"After about a month, I'll come back," she said, explaining that she intended to leave the baby with her parents and come back to me. I was vigorously against this idea. I felt strongly that mother and child should not be separated. She said then that she would just try to visit me in about a month.

So Nyun left. I thought back to those six years we had spent together, never separated for even a day. I gave her little comfort, we spoke different languages, and yet, in spite of it all, she loved me deeply. The memories of our six years were filled with sadness, rather than the sweetness of love.

A month after she left I went to the Munitions Headquarters in Cholon to wait for her. But unluckily I came down with malaria and had to be hospitalized. I begged them to let me stay until Nyun came, but they brought me back to Dang Kup Moy and put me in the hospital. About ten days later a letter came from Nyun with six hundred piastres in cash, some clothes, sweets and razor blades. The presents were not much, but her deep love expressed in them was almost painful. Her love for me, involving the risk, danger and hardships of walking all the way from Saigon to this hidden jungle retreat, cut into my heart.

"My loving Nyun," I wept while bedridden with malaria, reading, "I left the baby and came here but missed you. The money— six hundred piastres—is not very much, but please take it. I am sorry I was late as I could not get the passport in time. It is very difficult to obtain a passport from French army territory into the free territory and the French sentinels are very difficult to deal with. Please take care of yourself. I will wait for you for any number of years."

The letter had evidently been written from Cholon. It also said that when she parted with Min, she had sent by her the sum of one thousand piastres, a blanket and a mosquito net. I had not received them; I showed the letter to Min, saying that I would like at least to have the mosquito net. Min said she knew nothing about any of these things. Naturally I believed my wife. Filled with hatred for this woman, I filed suit against her with our command committee and with all the evidence against her, I won the suit.

Shortly after this I received another letter, saying that Nyun in tended to come to Cholon again. I applied for a leave and went there. Again I missed her. But I wanted to see her so much this time, that thinking she was only late, I continued to wait for her even though my leave was up. I sat around doing nothing for over a month. My company kept sending for me to come back. One day a dispensary chief of my company saw me at Cholon and bawled me out. "Why can't you obey military regulations," he demanded.

I had missed Nyun twice, but I reluctantly went back to my company in Dang Kup Moy. Then a letter came from Nyun. She was in Cholon, where I had waited for her over a month. Such is the irony of fate!

Not long after this I was released from the Vietminh communist army. It was not an order, but more or less permission, for I had applied for the release myself. The idea had been Nyun's. Her second letter advised me to apply for the release, to put in an application that since I was not well I could not be of much service, and therefore should be let out of the army, so as not be a burden to the communists. Nyun had always been my guide and adviser in all the things dealing with the communists.

This time, too, I followed her advice. I received the notice of release much quicker than I had expected. While in Cholon waiting for Nyun, I had become friendly with an officer of the Cholon unit. When I became a civilian, I immediately went to this man, Lee, and he introduced me to a big farmer, who owned three water buffaloes. I obtained a job as a farm hand—in a mixed territory of both French and Vietminh forces. Lee often came to see me. One time he confessed that he wanted to surrender to the French and wanted me to go with him. He wanted to go to Cambodia.

But it takes some preparations to surrender to the French. Besides, who knows but what we might be killed for once having belonged to the communists. We were thus discussing surrendering to the French on our way from a hospital where I was being treated for beriberi when we were caught in the midst of the biggest aerial attack we had ever experienced. We saw paratroopers pour out of the planes and land less than a mile from where we crouched on the ground. The sight of countless white parachutes raining down from the blue sky was impressive. The big air attack signified the beginning of the long awaited French offensive.

One day in May, 1953, not very long after this big attack, I sat in the sugar plant in Hippoa talking to a battalion commander of Vietnam government forces. Lee and I had finally surrendered to the French, or rather we had sneaked into French territory in the dark of the night.

We got into a boat, rowed by the daughter of Haai house, crossed the river and entered Hippoa. Lee was afraid of being caught as a revolutionist, and ran away. I immediately reported to the police. The feelings toward the Japanese were unexpectedly good in the police office as well as in the town. The battalion officer of the government forces welcomed me with open arms.

"We have no intention of hurting the Japanese at all. If you like, you can stay with us," he said. "I have a deep concern and respect for the Japanese spirit. If you know kendo and jujitsu, we would like to have you teach us."

Before me were bottles of a beer I had not seen in years, American cigarettes which I saw for the first time. The battalion officer further said he would help me find Nyun and my baby and repeatedly urged me to stay with the government forces. "Please understand that it is not our desire to fight against our own brothers. The sadness of killing our own people is beyond your imagination. The source of this tragedy is that we are a weak people," he explained. "This weakness allowed the independence group to seek help from the communists, while we stand with the U.S.A. We fight our own people—it's like eating our own flesh. The underlying motive of the two camps is one and the same, a strong independent government."

There sounded through all this the pathos of a weak nation. The commander begged me to stay, but I left him and went on to Saigon. It had been eight years since I had left this town, where I had been persuaded to join the Vietminh at the point of a gun. Of course I was under the watch of the government army. I was questioned on my enlistment in the communist army, my activities since, my plans for the future.

I had nothing to hide. The group that questioned me belonged to the French army and was called 2-o Company. It was a sort of gendarme unit, if not a secret police. They seemed not to know what to do with me because I was a foreigner of a non-friendly nation. Presently they moved me up to Supreme Headquarters. I was questioned again, but the French officer who questioned me, a lieutenant, asked "Where do you want to go from here?"

I told him that I wanted to look for my wife and he consented, saying he would look for my wife with me. He put me in a jeep and took me to MacMahon Street immediately. But I did not know Nyun's house. All I knew was that it was on that endless street. In the first place I never dreamed that I would be looking for it like this, and I was unprepared for any real search; naturally we did not find it. The lieutenant's kindness was in vain.

As I had no one who claimed me, I was allowed to stay in the French army barracks. But I was not allowed to go out. I stayed in the barracks every day, having nothing to do. Vietnam noncoms and their wives felt sorry for me, tried to look for Nyun themselves, but also in vain. What worried me most was that, being a foreigner with no one to claim me, I might be sent back to Japan. Thus I spent about one month in despondency. I was treated well, but I lost weight daily.

One day I was given two days' leave. I had a feeling that this was my last chance. If I could not find Nyun this time, I felt sure I would be sent back to Japan. With a white suit that was given to me by a Vietnamese and a pair of shoes such as I had not worn for years and which almost killed me, I went back and forth on MacMahon Street. Whenever I saw a woman about Nyun's age, I ran after her, or turned back and followed her, scrutinizing her face to make sure she was not Nyun.

Whenever I found a group of people together, I went up to them and asked them about Nyun, but they all shook their heads. My feet began to bleed, and I took off my shoes and went barefooted. Is it possible that I shall never see her again? I asked myself. I regretted having surrendered to the French indiscreetly. Had I stayed in Cholon I might have had a better chance of finding her again.

The next day I wandered out into the streets of Saigon again. The town of Saigon was the same as it had been eight years before. On both sides of the well-paved streets, under the green trees, walked men in white open-collar shirts, women in Annamese costumes, with not-a-care-in-the-world looks. A woman peddler passed by, calling out whatever it was she was selling in a high voice. Foreign cars, Renaults and Citroens dashed by.

I started to go to MacMahon Street again, then changed my mind. I headed for Buniyan Market. I remembered suddenly that Nyun had written that she was in a textile business, selling materials. Buniyan Market is in the most crowded part of the town and Malays, French, Annamese, Chinese and Indians walked its alleys. I almost passed out from fatigue. I, a foreigner, was looking for one woman among the 150,000 people of Saigon.

"Where are you going?" I was suddenly called from behind, and I turned. A woman stood smiling at me. Who was she? "Where are you going, An Torun?" she asked using my Annamese name.

Then I remembered. Right after we went into the jungle and before we married, this woman had been staying with Nyun. She was the first acquaintance I met since coming to Saigon.

"Nyun—I'm looking for Nyun. Do you know?" I stuttered.

She probably thought I looked queer, for she looked at me for some minutes, before she spoke again. "Your wife is in the market," she said. "Come with me," and she started to walk before me. I was so excited I could not say anything. Presently the woman stopped. Before me was a small dress material shop, and a woman stood in front of it. It was Nyun!

We faced each other without uttering a word. She stood there wide-eyed. Then an expression something like fright ran through her eyes for a fraction of a second, but immediately her poised, cool, assured look that I had been used to seeing for so long was back, and she gave me a loving glance.

"You are back," she said and smiled.

REVENGE

by Mishima Yukio

IN WALKING THROUGH, say, a bright, sunny seaside resort, one passes at times a house that exudes a strangely dark quality. The sensation is inexplicable, but somehow it creeps up on you. The house itself may be in perfect condition, nothing dilapidated about it or the least bit out of place—it may even be bright-looking, but the darkness is there, emanating every moment from within.

The Kondo place is such. There is not a thing broken or neglected about the house. All the locks are new and shiny. A well-kept lawn, with a neat white fence encircling it, and yet there hovers about it a lonely, ominous aura of some sinister secret locked within.

Two name plates hang on the gate. One says *Kondo Torao*, and on the other *Natsu Masaki* is written in small, quivering ideographs, as if to hide behind the first.

The household consists of five. These are Kondo Torao, the master of the house, and his wife Ritsuko. They have no children. Torao's mother, Yae, lives with them on a small inheritance left by her husband. Then there are Natsu Masaki, Yae's late husband's widowed sister, and her daughter Haruko. The last two had kept a separate household until recently—a small apartment—but since they had almost used up what little money Natsu's husband had left, they had to depend on what Haruko brought home by teaching kindergarten in a nearby Catholic Church. They have come to live with the Kondos to save room rent.

122

Torao himself commutes to work in Tokyo from this seaside resort. He comes home at exactly the same time every evening. Then the family gathers in the dining room for supper.

They are sitting around their late supper table. The dead calm that comes every evening is particularly bad tonight, the air humid and close. The dining room is not lit very bright. The entire house is dark for that matter. They are saving on their electricity bills. Broiled fish and salad served individually are on the table.

"Mother bought this fish from the fishermen directly," says Ritsuko. She is always the first to open the nightly conversation.

"Bargained! Bought them very cheap," the old lady says proudly. "If you know how, you can always buy things cheap."

Torao hardly ever joins in the conversation of the women. A former lieutenant in the army, he is very well built, but his face is pale and his rimless glasses add coldness to his features.

Natsu, too, eats in silence. She and her daughter look exactly alike, even to their anemic complexions. Natsu's care-worn lines add sharpness to her thin face.

The conversation lags. The sound of evening waves reaches their ears. The family has a queer habit. Whenever conversation lags, all stop eating and listen. They cock their ears as though expecting to hear something. This doesn't happen too often in the day time, but is particularly noticeable at night.

And this is one of those times. As they listen, they suddenly hear a noise in the kitchen. They all turn their heads that way, their faces slightly pale.

"It's only a rat," says Yae.

"Yes, it's a rat—it must be," adds Natsu, and laughs all by herself, artificially and too long.

Suddenly Ritsu puts her chopsticks down, and starts to speak determined to get something off her chest. "I've got to say it. I thought I'd wait until supper was over," she says, without looking at anyone in particular, holding the edge of the table. "I went swimming today. Alone. And I saw him – –. Genbu. He was standing quite close, glaring at me."

The four of them stare at Ritsuko.

"But that's impossible, how could he be here in this town?"

"You don't know what he looks like in the first place."

"But I did see him," Ritsuko insists. "He was about sixty, strongly built, about five feet seven in height, not clean shaven. He had on an open-collared shirt, and khaki trousers. I think he had on a pair of *geta* ."

"Oh! I know," says Yae, calmed. "That is the description of Genbu that Yamaguchi-san gave in his letter. You just happened to see a man who fits that description. If Genbu leaves his hometown, Yamaguchi-san will send us a telegram." She looks around, she pauses. "The more I think about it, the more I am grateful that we happened to know Yamaguchi-san, living in the same town as Genbu."

The entire family is dependent upon this Yamaguchi for their peace of mind. Yamaguchi is obligated to Yae's husband, who had been an official in the Ministry of Internal Affairs before he died. Yamaguchi is an old man, now retired to his hometown, the same as Genbu's. Yae wrote to him, asked him to write back a detailed report on Genbu. Yae used Natsu Masaki's name because she did not want the name of Kondo to be known in connection with this affair. To keep Yamaguchi's goodwill, Yae often sends money and presents out of her meager funds. Yamaguchi, to break the monotony of his retired life, writes back long letters. He also promised that as soon as there is a sign of Genbu leaving town, he will notify the Kondos by telegram.

"It's only your imagination," Yae says, meaning to comfort Ritsu.

"But I still think it was Genbu. I felt it in my bones." Ritsu is stubborn. "We'd better be very careful tonight."

"Yes, we'd better, whether it was Genbu or not." Yae looks at Torao. "You see that everything is locked. Make sure of the garden and all." Then she falls into a half monologue. "But we are in some fix, aren't we? We can't go to the police. If we do, and tell everything—terribly embarrassing for Torao. Might even affect his future."

Torao continues to keep silent, sullen. He is the only one eating now, but he is doing so mechanically, merely putting his food into his mouth. He too is highly upset. His forehead is covered with perspiration, but he doesn't even wipe it. His wife takes a handkerchief and daubs it for him.

Dinner over, they move to the porch to cool off. A whiff of a breeze comes in from an open window.

"How nice and cool," Yae exclaims, a bit exaggeratedly.

"By the way, I remember now that I had a similar experience not long after we had that first letter from Genbu," Natsu starts again, returning to the topic. "I saw him in my dream. The face of Genbu whom I've never met—it was so vivid. I remember it very well."

"It was your imagination, too," Yae answers her, not altogether unhappy that Natsu has returned to the topic everyone fears. "I do the same thing, every night, almost. Even now. It must be the same with you, Torao. Especially as you knew Genbu's son."

"We should have our ground covered with small pebbles," Ritsuko exclaims brightly, thinking her idea excellent. "Then we can hear the slightest footsteps. With the sand we can hardly hear anything."

"And where do we get the money for such a thing," Yae says. "Luckily, we can trust Yamaguchi. But even now I often wake up in the middle of the night, suddenly. It's been eight years. Eight long years have we been living in this same state. Not a day of peace."

Yae and Ritsu exchange glances, and those glances reflect the years of continuous worry and fear. Still, after these eight long years, when nighttime comes the family gathers into one room, locks up everything, shuts out the outside world. Every night a nightmare attacks some member of the family; a huge Genbu standing at his or her head, holding an ax up ready to bring down . . .

"I suppose it will have to come someday," Yae sighs.

"What would have to come?" someone asks.

"I said, Genbu will come someday. Torao might just as well be prepared. I am. Of course, I am not young. I have only a short life left. But poor Ritsu and Haruko, they are so young yet."

Ritsu and Haruko are in the kitchen, washing dishes. In the silence, the rustle of the paper in Torao's hand is a roar.

The doorbell suddenly peals.

The three look at each other quickly. The two in the kitchen rush to where the three sit. The five of them stand around the table. None speaks a word. No one has ever called at this late hour before.

Torao turns his body, wondering whether to go to the door or not. Yae stops him, and whispers to him low, "It's best not to resist. I'll go to the door."

Yae turns on the light in the guest room, then at the front door. In the dining room, the three women surround Torao. Torao's face shows deathly pallor. Natsu holds her daughter's hand tight.

The tension heightens when they hear the voice at the front door.

"Masaki-san, telegram," the interloper calls.

"To me, why, who – – ." Natsu starts to the door.

"Auntie, it must be from Yamaguchi," Ritsu says. "He can't use the name Kondo, you know."

The four hear Yae walk from the front door, through the guest room into the dining room. The expression of high joy on her face is in odd contrast to that of fear on the rest of them as they rush to her side.

"*Kuratani Genbu died—Yamaguchi ,* " she reads aloud, and falls to a chair. She closes her eyes, leaving the four to their joy. She seems infinitely tired.

"I am so glad," she says at last. "Now, I can burn those letters I kept for the police, in case . . ." She gets up, opens a box on a chest of drawers, takes out a bundle of envelopes. Out of one of them she draws a letter, brown with age. She reads aloud:

To Kondo Torao:
   You have come back to Japan, after putting the blame for a war crime on your subordinate—my loving son. How could you do it? I, his father, will avenge him. My hate for you will not stop until I kill you and your whole family.

Signed in blood.
Kuratani Genbu

Yae, after reading, puts the letter with the rest. She stands up, places a pan over a hot plate and puts the bundle into it. Long before the letters' brown papers catch fire, all can smell the evil odor of the burning blood on the paper, turning darker brown.

The papers catch fire fast. As the last flames die down and the pan holds only gray ashes, the family is thrown into new, fresh fear.

"You can't put too much store in that telegram," Haruko says. "Maybe Genbu himself sent it to make us drop our guard!"

THE SAD SAMURAI

by John Fujii

HIS NAME is Watanabe.

He was the admiral of a dry-land fleet in the final stages of the Burma retreat who is now making a living selling soap.

Or he was a lieutenant who spent the first half of the war in a Manila hospital with malaria and the last half on Peleliu Island in the Palau chain, a virtual prisoner of war, his island surrounded by US-occupied isles within view.

Or he was a Domei war correspondent, attached to the army, who spent the war years following one division from one theater to another only to miss the final battle. He eventually heard his first shot of the war six months after the surrender when Vietminh guerrillas exchanged small-arms fire with a French patrol just outside his Saigon internment camp.

These are the ex-samurai who meet by chance at Shinjuku station between trains, jostle each other on the crowded Ginza, or sit on adjoining stools at a cheap sake shop.

These are the sad samurai who have surrendered their swords. These are the modern "Ronin" looking for a cause. These are the bewildered souls who try to forget prison camp to *pachinko*'s pinball jangle and a shochu-gin jag.

You meet them everywhere in Japan.

There is the general who asks you to write a letter in English to a business firm in Bombay. He has a nominal desk job in a concern managed by a former subordinate. The last time you remember him was as a tired old man sitting disconsolately in the bleak prison yard at Singapore's Changi and before that with the epaulets of a staff officer attached to Field Marshal Terauchi's Southern Army headquarters. Another 'PR' officer with the Southern Army, Malay-speaking, evaporated into the native population to evade British counter-intelligence, then was warned by friends the British were pulling 'short-arm' inspections in their hunt for non-Muslims. So, being short and swarthy, he threw away his clothing, donned a G-string and took up bow and arrow and headed for the jungle. He took Stone Age life as long as he could then decided it better to be in jail in Japan so walked into a British camp, went up to the commandant, saluted smartly and offered his bow and arrow with, "Lieutenant X, Imperial Japanese Army, surrendering." He now runs a documentary film company.

There is the Nisei interpreter from Hawaii who served eight years of his twenty-year sentence as a war criminal and is now selling advertisements for an English-language newspaper. Another Nisei interpreter assigned to monitor Allied radio for the staff of the Manchurian army, scolded by superiors for warning them they were about to lose the war and that the Russians were coming, appropriated non-com's ID and uniform and a shoe-box full of gems from the bribe-safe and went AWOL. Expecting to be rounded up by the Russians, he befriended a US Army major on observer duty and sent the shoe-box home with him to his mother in Japan as "personal effects." He got back home from Siberia some years later. the box was there, unopened, and he used it to finance a magazine publishing house.

The army lieutenant who never heard a shot fired in anger—who spent the war in a hospital and on a by-passed Pacific atoll—makes a visit to the capital just once a year to pay his respects to his fallen comrades at Yasukuni Shrine and then retires to his Shizuoka farm because Tokyo is too foreign.

These are the men who appear out of nowhere and then drift back into the crowd at Shinjuku or Asakusa.

Many of the former professional soldiers have made their read-justments to peacetime living. A former admiral is president of a thriving export-import firm; one former staff officer is managing director of an amusement company; while a former Air Force major represents his industrial concern in the New York office; a former *kamikaze* suicide pilot returned to his ancestral position as Grand Tea Master and is promulgating this most sophisticated and peaceful traditional art overseas; while still another staff officer, noted for his spectacular underground escape[1] from arrest as a war crimes suspect, has been elected to the National Diet from his home province.

Others have found their niche in postwar society, holding down positions commensurate with their experience and ability. In Japan nearly every man is an ex-samurai since universal conscription marshaled every able-bodied Japanese into uniform at one time or another.

Some have drifted into the twilight of society: the men who make a living on the edge of human decency and legalized rackets. But these are the handful who refuse to cope with the changed times. There are others who brood in their native village, futilely awaiting a day of retribution.

Perhaps the most unfortunate are the "men in white," the war cripples who solicit contributions in the trains and trolleys and who line the approaches to Yasukuni Shrine and even local shrines in small towns. They are the human pariahs of modern Japan, the men who are unable to make a living due to their wounds and are forced to swallow pride and dignity to ask for alms from their more fortunate comrades.

Their pensions are meager in inflationary Japan, and hospital space inadequate, so that they are spewed out into a society that tries to forget them. But the conscience of a mother who has lost her son in battle, of a former soldier who remembers how he was spared from injury, and of a general public who sympathizes—keep these "sad samurai" from starvation.

---

[1] See in this volume, preceding, 'Underground Escape."

BLACKOUT

by *Koyama Itoko*

TERUYO saw the clouds breaking as she finished breakfast, and now the sun shone brightly. Its welcome warmth reminded her that spring was just around the corner. She heard someone shake the front door roughly and shout "Hello." She got up and went to the door. As she opened it, a man quickly thrust a ball of rubber bands under her nose.

"Don't want any," she said, just as quickly, and locked the door without giving him a chance to open his mouth. He walked away and she heard him muttering to himself. On a nice day like this after rain for four or five days at a stretch, there were usually many peddlers and junk men.

"Look, plum blossoms! They're in bloom. One, two . . . there's another." She heard Ichiro's young voice as he played with the little girl next door.

Teruyo sat on the porch where the sun beamed in, and brushed her husband's everyday clothes. Thinking a slight stoop gives one a refined look, she brushed and straightened the wrinkles caused by it rather reluctantly, she smiled when she found a soiled handkerchief, a stub of rubber off a pencil, and two steel *pachinko* pinballs. When she opened the handkerchief, she smelled the faint odor of her husband. She looked around quickly and brought it close to her face. She liked her husband's smell. It had an odor quite indescribable, both sweet and sour, slightly "greenish," but with a vigor of life, with a faint sweetness of chestnut flower. She could smell her husband's body from his handkerchief. As she pressed it against her face and slowly drew in a deep breath, a deep feeling of happiness enwrapped her whole being. Her eyes half closed, her head cocked slightly to one side, she immersed herself in her husband's odor.

"*Gomen kudasai.*"

She came to with a start, and turned crimson to her neck. She remembered suddenly that she was busy today. She had a pile of washing, umbrellas to dry, and rain shoes to wash. She quickly rolled up the handkerchief and pushed it under the trousers as if to hide it from someone, before she stood up.

A man over thirty, dressed in an old-style dark suit, was standing there. She didn't know him. He had a bundle in one hand, and she muttered to herself, "Another peddler?"

"Is this the house of Yamada?"

"Yes."

The man's deeply tanned face relaxed a bit. Then he started to search his pockets for something.

"Who is it, please?"

"My name's Sato, and I'm from Sanshu."

Never heard of him, she thought—"Sanshu?"

"No, you don't know me. I was only asked to – – " The man brought out an envelope of good quality, but which was all wrinkled.

"Oh! "

"I was asked to deliver this to the master of this house. The man who asked me, his name is Yoshida, was with me on the boat," he said. "I repatriated from Java—Yes, a late repatriate . . . Yoshida, he said he was from Sumatra. The master here, I heard, was on Sumatra, too."

"Yes, that's right."

As he talked, Teruyo became a little cautious. About half a year ago, she remembered . . . there was a man who had said he had repatriated from the south, and she had been swindled in a big way. His talk had sounded straight enough to convince her, had given her the impression that her husband was obligated to him, that he had been taken care of by him on the boat. So, she had fed him a good lunch, and had given him train fare home. She had been highly reprimanded when her husband came home that night. But this man, he didn't look the kind . . . he looked too naive. She thought hard and quickly.

"I am only related to the family here. I was asked to mind the house today. I—er—I don't know anything—."

What if Ichiro should run in, yelling "Mommie," but he was safely outside the fence. The man believed her and, nodding, said "I went to his office first, but they said he was away for a few days and gave me this address. It happened to be quite close to where I am staying, so I came here.

"I am going back home on the next train. I don't come to Tokyo often, so I didn't want to take it back with me."

His talk lacked the smoothness of a swindler. His eyes were simple, didn't look as though the head behind them were capable of any false design. Teruyo relaxed her guard a little.

"That's very nice of you."

"I should've sent it earlier, but it was way in the bottom of my trunk and I forgot all about it. Well then, I am leaving it with you."

Teruyo dropped her eyes to the envelope awkwardly. Something made her hesitate.

"I don't know—I don't know whether I should keep a thing like this or not."

"Of course, I know how you feel. But neither can I afford to keep it forever, and I can't very well throw it away, you know. It's only a letter. Just give it to the master, and I'm sure it will be all right. Good by, then."

The man picked up his bundle and turned to go. "He is not a bad man," she thought. "He brought this thing purely out of kindness." She glanced absently at the name in Roman letters in faded ink. Then she noticed. "Oh! But look. The name of the company is right, but this name is not. How is this read? It begins with J."

"What!" he exclaimed, turning back.

Then he said simply, "The name is Yamada Yaichi, isn't it? Then that's how they spell it. In Malaya, the 'Y' sound is spelled with J. They write 'Jamada Jaichi.'"

Teruyo turned the envelope over. She read "Rahima" in 'Roman' letters. "Is 'Rahima' a person's name?"

"I think so."

Teruyo's curiosity was suddenly aroused. "Is it a man's name . . . or . . . ?"

"I think it's more common in women," he answered.

"From a woman—to my, uh,—I, I mean, to the master here. From a woman in Sumatra? On what business, I wonder, at this late date?"

"Oh, there are plenty of them like that. I don't know much about Sumatra but in Java—I had three letters to deliver, all from women. The ones who don't forget and write at this late date usually have children. They usually send photographs of their children."

"Children?"

"Women there are lighthearted. I had one myself, but as soon as I left I forgot her. You can make them easy, but forget them easy, too. But when they have children, then they are different. The memories become deeper, I guess. The letters I brought were all to my friends, so I know well. The two of them had a child each. Both of them looked very much Japanese—they were nice kids."

"Then the master here also had someone like that too?"

"Don't know about that. Yoshida said something, but I don't remember."

"And where is he now?"

"Yoshida? You got me there. He and I parted at Shimizu Port. "Well, I must go. I guess you better not say anything to the madame here. Once some awful trouble broke out—of course I only heard about it afterwards. To tell you the truth, I don't enjoy this kind of errand myself. But can't very well throw the darn thing away, you know. Sometimes they enclose a tiny precious stone. But really, it was a good thing it was you today, and not his wife. I must hurry now. Good-by."

And he was gone. Teruyo, as though in a trance, heard him open the door, step out, and shut it but did nothing. Even after his footsteps were heard no more, she stood there dumbfounded.

When she came to, she realized she was holding the letter in her hand. She felt something like a sting on the tips of her fingers, and threw the letter to the floor. But she picked it up again like a child commanded to do so, and returned to the porch with it.

The sun was still shining, but it did not look the same to her. How it could change so in a matter of five or seven minutes, she didn't know. Was the sky blue or black? The sunshine stung her eyes. She started to pick up the things she'd left; his clothes, rubber stub, pinballs, and all. They felt different, surfaces rough, or cold or crude. They all felt bad to her hands. She pulled out the handkerchief from under the trousers. She put it to her face absentmindedly

—it was a habit with her. The odor was still there, sweet and sour, the odor of chestnut blossoms. She swallowed bitter saliva. She swallowed again and again, but something stuck in her throat and wouldn't go down. She felt nauseous. She leaned over the edge of the porch, but nothing came up. She felt a chill in the pit of her stomach.

Teruyo never once doubted her husband. He was a quiet man, an introvert, extremely kind. Their premarital private detective check showed that he had never had any relations with women. Just as Teruyo's parents feared, he was awkward and was at a loss at their nuptial bed. That's the kind of man he was. It was during the war that they were married, and like everyone else they didn't have much of a honeymoon. He soon got used to married life, and he had learned to love well enough to satisfy Teruyo. The half year together before he was called to duty was spent without even noticing the scarcity of everyday necessities, or the severity of life in wartime, so happy and content they were with each other. To this day she couldn't remember without blushing the last night she had with him before he left—neither of them slept a wink. She was sure she conceived Ichiro that night.

He wrote to her even from the boat, and many times after he got to the front line. Even as the war became more severe, and mail had a hard time getting through, she continued to hear from him. She wrote to him when Ichiro came, and he sent a pair of rubber-soled shoes by return mail. When the war ended, he was on the first boat back. To get back that soon, he must have gone to considerable trouble. So, all told, he was away only about two years.

After he returned, there seemed no outward change in him except that he loved her more deeply, and was kinder. He often talked about boats that were sunk, and automobiles that were overturned and burned.

"Sure thankful that I am back alive. After all, Japan is best."

She once heard him talk thus in his sleep. He seemed genuinely happy when tending to their little garden. "He needn't become so domestic, so young," she even thought to herself.

And this Yaichi of all persons. Teruyo could not possibly make herself imagine the other woman. How, when, could a thing like that happen? She had kept all the letters Yaichi wrote to her. She didn't have to get them out. She remembered them all, each and every one of them by heart. How could he write letters like that to his wife with one hand, and hold Rahima with the other. No, no, not Yaichi! She didn't know about other men, but not her Yaichi.

Try as she might, she could not picture her husband holding another woman in his arms.

Then what is this letter left by a man in dark, ominous clothes. The letter which gave her such a feeling of apprehension. It was sealed tight– Why? He said it happens quite often. He said when a woman writes at this late date, she often has a child. Teruyo put the letter against the light. The letter papers, folded, filled the entire envelope, but half of it felt hard and was darker.

"Is it a picture?" she wondered. "Feels like it. But why should I believe that man whom I've never met before, a man who appeared suddenly, and disappeared just as suddenly as the peddlers and the swindler. I am the one that knows Yaichi better than anyone else. That man never even saw Yaichi once. Yes, everything will be clear if I open this letter." Teruyo brought out a pair of scissors, and started to put them to one corner of the envelope, and stopped. Until now she had never opened anything addressed to her husband, no matter how trivial it may have seemed. But that was not what made her stop.

She suddenly had the premonition that if she opened it some dark, ominous thing would jump out of it, and would spread its wings throughout this house. After all, was not everything happy and peaceful until that dark messenger came? Teruyo threw the scissors to the floor.

Ichiro came in and started to chatter something, but she answered him absentmindedly. She couldn't remember, afterward, just how she spent that day. She ate lunch with Ichiro mechanically, and just sat all day by the pile of washing she'd got out in the morning to do.

She hardly slept that night. She dreamed often of being chased by someone, woke up many times. Sometimes she heard someone at the door, that husky voice saying "*gomen nasai*," and then she would really wake up. Then, remembering it was the middle of the night, she would say to herself that no one would come at this time of night, and try to go back to sleep.

And then it was morning, and Ichiro was sleeping by her side as usual. Teruyo sat up, fluffing her hair, listened absently to the distant rumble of the train. When she came to fully, she realized that her nightgown was soaking wet and stuck to her skin, and she felt as if she had taken a bath with her clothes on. The face of the dark-clothed messenger and the letter flashed in her mind. It was then she realized who it was that had chased her all night in her dream. An instant later she felt that she had had dreams like this many times before, that this sort of thing happened quite often, and that really was nothing, nothing at all to worry about. Teruyo got up, and still in her nightgown, went into her husband's study. She opened his drawer. The white envelope was still there. "Then it really did happen."

The letter was there, where she had placed it the day before. Then the memories of what happened yesterday welled in her mind, clearly and definitely, with great impact She wondered if she were going to spend today as miserably as she had spent yesterday. Each day would increase her mistrust and jealousy of her husband, increase her own unhappiness. Would the days continue like this until her husband came home? What would she do when he did come home? She started to drop her thin nightgown off her shoulders, then leaned against the desk, as if falling.

The next day, she could not stay in the house any longer. She felt like crying aloud. She feared she would go crazy. She took Ichiro, nonchalant and happy, oblivious of his mother's inner turmoil and called on her sister. Her sister lived beyond Omori. It took them almost an hour to get there by train and bus. Teruyo's sister was nine years her senior, but having had no children, did not show it. Her chief worry was in her husband, a doctor, who was forever chasing women.

She was sitting in a room littered with magazines, reading. She wore a sober expression. Ichiro went out to play on the lawn with their country girl nurse.

"You know those question and answer columns in the news-papers? Their advice is sometimes impossible. Just because it's other people's affairs, their answers are quite irresponsible. Private detectives are much more dependable."

"Are you having trouble again?" Teruyo interjected.

"Oh yes, same as ever. Your Yaichi-san is different, I know, but most men you can't trust them one minute. Once they are out of the house, they let go of themselves like birds out of a cage. By the way, you don't look your usual gay self, what's the matter?"

"I don't know. I just haven't been able to eat anything these last few days."

"Maybe you're going to have your next one. It's about time, isn't it?"

"No, it's not that."

"Then let my hubby give you a check."

"Is he out on a call?"

"So he said last night, but it turned out to be some 'urgently' sick woman. I gave him a pretty bad time last night, so I think he will come home all right tonight."

"What do you do at times like that?"

"What do I do? You mean when he is up to something? I go after him thoroughly, check everything, and leave no stone unturned"

"And when you do find out everything, doesn't it make you feel worse?"

"Yes, but if I don't, that would be worse yet. I show him all the proof how he slept with a certain woman on such and such a night, at such and such a place. With a two-faced husband like mine, that's the only way to deal with him."

"But I rather feel that even if there were something, I'd feel happier not to know anything. You know, innocence is bliss!"

"Not with me. I've got to know everything once I get suspicious, or I'd never feel rested—it would get on my nerves!"

"Yes, it does doesn't it" Teruyo mumbled inaudibly.

"You, who always brag about your Yaichi-san, what's wrong with you? It couldn't be that he is up to something, is it?"

"That's what I can't be sure of."

"If something is wrong I'll look into it for you. I know a real good private snoop. He is a bit expensive, but real good. If it's someone at the office it won't take more than two or three days."

The more eager her sister became the more reluctant Teruyo was to confide in her, and she found herself holding rigidly, like a soldier defending a fort, to her belief in Yaichi—denying everything, everything. Some mistake it must be. It couldn't be—I know."

But, once back home she couldn't help going directly to the desk drawer. She felt herself spinning round and round in a circle.

When Yaichi finally returned, it was after nightfall.

"*Okaeri nasai*" she greeted as she met him at the door. then she saw his lively self with his usual half smile on his right cheek, her mind was suddenly made up. After all these days of indecision . . . she had tried to remain calm till then, but found her hands shaking in voluntarily, from time to time.

The lights went out just as he finished changing into his at-home kimono.

"Are we still having blackouts in Tokyo? They say we don't have enough water in the power dams, but what we really lack is brains in our statesmen, not water."

Teruyo emptied a kettle of hot water into the wash basin. Yaichi, after he washed up, took the candle into Ichiro's room to have a look at his son's sleeping face. Teruyo, sitting in the dark in the dining room, heard him murmur something to the child.

"What's the matter. Did something happen?" he asked as he came back in. "Why so quiet?"

He was out of the bedroom and had put the candle and a stick of sweet cake on the table.

"Got a knife?" he asked.

"Yes, here . . . "

Teruyo gave it to him, and poured some tea into his cup. Her throat was dry, but she could not bring herself to drink with him. Not just now. Her husband looked inquiringly at her over the flickering flame of the candle.

"There's a letter for you from Sumatra," she whispered, half hoping he wouldn't hear and it could be forgotten.

"Yes?"

Just then the light came back on.

There was only an expression of simple curiosity on his face. Teruyo took out the white envelope. Yaichi looked close at the addressed side, cocked his head, and turned it over to the other side. His brows pricked and his face turned pale. His cheek muscles pulled crookedly to one side and tightened. These, Teruyo did not miss.

The candlelight dimmed. Her husband's fingers went to one corner of the envelope, then stopped an instant. Teruyo reached out, grabbed the other corner and pulled. She felt a slight resistance, but not much. Taking the letter in her right hand, she put it over the candle flame. Yaichi started to say something, but without turning she put up her free hand to stop him, holding it up as if to ward off something. Dainty whiffs of smoke hugged the envelope. The candlelight dwarfed to a tiny speck, almost went out . . . then at the next instant, the envelope burst into flame, illuminating the entire room.

"Teruyo – – !"

Teruyo, tightened her lips, hung on to the envelope until it almost burned her finger tips. She inhaled deeply then blew out the flame.

As if that were the signal, the light went out again.

No one lit the candle.

"I thought this was the best way. I couldn't think of any other way," Teruyo murmured low in the dark.

There was no sound, not even of any movement. The room was as if empty.

After a while, Teruyo noticed that her hand was being held. She felt the hold tighten slowly to a firm, warm grip.

THE AFFAIR OF THE ARABESQUE INLAY

by Ishikawa Tatsuzo

Dear Sir:

Reference is made to your latest inquiry after our investigation into the present whereabouts and recent activities of one Mr. Wu Kao-chih.

We hereby take great pleasure to inform you of the results of our inquiries to date.

It is also sincerely requested that you would kindly understand that our report as yet includes certain insufficiencies primarily due to the difficulty in establishing the present whereabouts of the person involved.

Yours Sincerely,
(signed:) T. Torii
Chief of Torii Detective Agency

Encl: Report to date. T.T.

Mr. Wu Kao-chih, of Chinese nationality; born Nanking, 1918. Father alleged to have been a noted trader by the name of Wu Hsiung-ta.

Mr. Wu Kao-chih studied Economics in a university in Shanghai. Later he was brought to Japan by his father. Here he studied economics at Waseda University, as evidenced by student enrollment records of said university.

In 1937, the Lukowkiao Incident set off the Sino-Japanese War. However, Mr. Wu did not return home until 1938, upon his formal graduation from Waseda University.

After the war, early in 1946, he again came to Japan, allegedly making a quick fortune at smuggling and such activities by taking full advantage of his nationality.

In June, 1951, upon the signing of the San Francisco peace treaty, and resumption of Japanese authority over the affairs of Third Nationals and the subsequent decline in his business, he returned to China.

His subsequent whereabouts are unknown, except for August, 1953, when Yumiko Ueda, with whom he had maintained a special relationship while he was in Japan, received by mail an expensive English-made jewelry box. The parcel noted the origin as Nanking.

To our regret, further details are not available.

Judging from several old photos he left in Japan, he would seem to be five feet five inches or so in height, tending toward plumpness, of a jovial disposition, and of Southern Chinese racial type.

According to information gathered from his acquaintances in Japan, we have drawn up an outline of his life and character as follows: During his entire three years in Japan as a student of the Economics Department of Waseda University, he rented a room in the home of Mr. Arai Yasuhiro, then a director of the Japan Formosa Spinning Company. Regarding him, widow Arai recalls, "Mr. Wu Kao-chih was a very steady student and pro-Japanese." She also said, "My husband was a good friend of senior Mr. Wu. We invited young Wu to our house. Brought up in a good family, he was very polite and modest. But he also had progressive ideas—thinking that China should throw off her old ways and rebuild a new China that could cope with progress and the rest of the world."

Mrs. Arai's impression coincides with those of Wu's classmates. He remained a bachelor, and was strictly against the Chinese custom of early marriage.

In spring of 1938, upon his graduation from Waseda University, he returned to a China under Japanese military occupation. Further records of him from that date until 1946, when he revisited Japan, are unavailable due to lack of means of investigation from here. However, consolidating data from testimonials of Ueda Yumiko and other people, the history we have reconstructed for him during the period in question is an extremely tragic one.

In December, 1937, the Japanese Army was pressing close to Nanking city from the east. Mr. Wu Kao-chih, then in Tokyo, had received no word from his family since November. After the fierce fighting on December 12 and 13, Nanking surrendered. The Japanese Army issued the formal declaration of the occupation of Nanking on December 17. Mr. Wu desperately wanted to know of his father, mother and sisters. He did all he could to find some means of returning home, but the severe restrictions which then prevailed allowed him no chance of exit from Japan—legal or illegal.

Late in March, 1938, he somehow managed to return to his homeland. In Nanking, he found only ashes and rubble where his father's office had been. His father's house was demolished. All possessions had been looted. No trace of his parents or sisters was found. He was told that tens of thousand of Nanking citizens had been massacred by the Japanese Army; then the corpses were buried in mass graves outside the city walls.

For almost half a year, Mr. Wu wandered around trying to locate —or at least to learn the whereabouts of the bodies of—his family. During that fruitless search, Mr. Wu's attitude toward life seems to have undergone a complete change. So, too, did his personal character.

From that time until his return to Japan in 1946, his activities are unknown. He is believed to have availed himself of the opportunities offered by the confusion of the war and to have established his financial position solidly. In 1946 Mr. Wu came to Japan, alone. First, settling himself in the so-called Nanking Street of China-town, Yokohama, he started trading. Soon he moved to Tokyo, pocketing large profits through the importation of American luxury goods, Taiwan sugar and bananas. Black-marketing gasoline seems to have brought considerable money into his pockets.

He bought a fine house in Denen Chofu, hired secretaries, maids, drove a Cadillac—himself, no chauffeur. At night he frequented cabarets in the Ginza with his friends.

It was about February of 1950 that Ueda Yumiko got to know Mr. Wu. Yumiko was then 32, had been working at Cabaret Tokyo from January of the same year.

Ueda Yumiko was born on a farm in Kumagaya, Saitama Prefecture, near Tokyo as second daughter. Her father, Ueda Harukichi, died of illness in 1944. After finishing girls' high school in Kumagaya, she came to Tokyo to be a student nurse at the Central Red Cross Hospital. Later she became a nurse in the First National Hospital, where she worked for three years.

The relationship between Mr. Wu Kao-chih and Ueda Yumiko became regularized in 1950. Mr. Wu bought a house in Takabancho for Yumiko and her child, providing a maid. But this relationship was brought to its conclusion as described in the following.

Our investigator interviewed Ueda Yumiko, who is now living at her brother's farm in Kumagaya. She told our investigator, "I first met him in the cabaret where I worked. He always brought a few friends with him. His speech and manner were so natural that I could hardly believe he was a foreigner. He was a fine, clean-cut gentleman, generous with his money. He was perhaps at his most prosperous at that time. I overheard it said that he could make several hundred thousand yen selling an imported car to a local.

One night one or two months after they first met, Wu was drinking sake at the cabaret. He looked at his watch, and murmured that he didn't realize it was so late. Yumiko unconsciously looked at her wrist watch and said, "Oh, it's just nine-sixteen."

Wu looked at her wrist—then stared at the watch as if to check its movement.

"What are you gazing at?" Yumiko says she asked.

"It's very beautiful. May I see it closer?" he said and took her hand.

"No, it's only a cheap one. I'm ashamed," she reportedly answered.

"No, it's not at all cheap. It's a rather rare watch. Do you mind if I see its back?" He was unusually insistent, she recalls.

Yumiko took the watch off her wrist and handed it to Wu. He turned it over, closely examining the inlaid arabesque design of a little red flower. Then he returned it to her without a word.

Half an hour later, just before they left, Mr. Wu whispered into Yumiko's ear, "Yumiko-san, couldn't you sell me that watch for five thousand yen?"

Surprised, Yumiko hesitated.

"Maybe five thousand yen is too cheap? Will seven or eight thousand yen do? I must have that watch," he insisted.

"Why? It's just an old watch. You can buy any brand-new one you see," Yumiko said.

"Please think it over. I don't mind paying even ten thousand yen for it." And he left.

The next day, he came to the cabaret alone—which was unusual He asked her about the watch. She sold it to him, agreeing to eight thousand yen—but when later she opened the envelope he had given her she found ten one-thousand-yen notes.

Placing the watch in his vest pocket, Mr. Wu asked her: "Where did you buy this, Yumiko-san?"

"I was given it."

"Is that so? Well, may I ask who gave it to you?"

"It's a keepsake of my dead parents."

"A keep-sake? Was your mother wearing this?"

"It was from my father."

"That's not true. This is a woman's watch."

"Yes, that's right."

"Let me guess. It must be your lover who bought this for you."

"Oh, it's such a trifle, let's forget it." She tried to change the subject, but Wu turned serious and started to tell her a story. He had a very intimate friend—a crazy collector of timepieces—whose collection included more than fourteen or fifteen hundred old and new, Western and Oriental, watches and clocks. Wu had allegedly picked up some slight knowledge of watches from his friend. Wu told her that the watch was an extremely novel piece—not made in Switzerland, England or America. Nor did it look Japanese. The design on the back side seemed Chinese, but the face was in the European style.

He wanted to know where it came from. Otherwise, he said, he could provide no clue to his friend's research—that was the general outline of Mr. Wu's story. Yumiko was taken in by it. She confessed, "In fact, I don't know the details of its origin. I got it from a relative of mine who had been a soldier. It often goes out of order—It isn't a good watch—"

"Is that so? . . . a soldier gave it to you . . . I wish . . . well, if I could see him sometime . . . That soldier couldn't have been to, say . . . well, Korea? . . . Manchuria? . . . Singapore? Perhaps China? . . . I wonder . . ."

"Yes, he's been to China. During the war. And he returned - - wounded in battle."

"Ah, I see . . . China!" He raised his voice a little. He smiled. His eyes glistened strangely.

After this Wu came to Yumiko's cabaret as often as twice a week. In addition to the usual tips, he began leaving special pocket money in her hands. Yumiko was naturally impressed by the fact that Mr. Wu was a bachelor, living alone in a big mansion.

Not long after, she was invited to accompany him on a business trip to the Osaka-Kobe area. It was a five-day trip with stopovers at the Takarazuka Hot-Spring and Kyoto hotels. At this time they entered into their special relationship. Yumiko confessed to him that she had a child. Mr. Wu bought clothing material and other presents for the child. According to Yumiko, Mr. Wu Kao-chih was not of a demanding nature, never trying to monopolize her.

About a month after that trip Mr. Wu bought a new, though small, modern house in Takabancho. Yumiko moved from her shabby room in Asakusa-Tabaramachi, with her child, and hired a maid. In short, she became a mistress to Mr. Wu Kao-chih, a Chinese living in Japan.

Every month, she received fifty thousand yen as living expenses (equal to three months salary for a white-collar male), plus occasional presents and extra money he gave her whenever he visited the house. Yumiko's life became comfortable. She quit the cabaret, but was still able to save more than twenty thousand yen a month. Then one night Mr. Wu Kao-chih resumed the long-forgotten talk about her watch. It came as a surprise to Yumiko, who had believed that Wu was interested in the watch for his collector friend.

It was a lie—a pious means to an end.

It seems that that watch had, without any doubt, belonged to Wu's mother. His father had bought it for her on their twentieth wedding anniversary. The design, specially ordered by his father, precluded there being another like it in the world. Wu wanted to locate the person who had had the watch previously. Whoever gave it to Yumiko might know something about his parents and sisters, missing since the occupation of Nanking.

Mr. Wu also told Yumiko that he had to see the soldier who had given the watch to her. His real purpose in revisiting post-war Japan was not to make money but to find Japanese who knew the fate of his parents and sisters. He "had a hunch that some Japanese should know," he said, his face suddenly gone white.

Yumiko had no reason to refuse to cooperate with him, particularly as she was being provided for so generously, but a chill went down her back when she thought back later of how Wu had, as the ancient saying puts it, "attained the goal by sure steps."

She was thankful for all he had done for her and her child, whatever his real intention might have been. Yet she could not disclose the truth. What would happen if that soldier was the very person who had killed Wu's family? The soldier was none other than the father of her own child.

Yumiko confessed to our investigator that she had "only hatred and no obligation at all toward that soldier," but still she was unwilling to disclose his identity to Wu. Nevertheless, her past finally yielded to the power of her present. He was the father of her daughter; still, he was never her formal husband. On the other hand though only a mistress, Yumiko felt a love and obligation toward Wu, sentiment that finally made her confess the name of her former lover.

Haneda Otojiro, registered domicile Odawara City, Kanagawa Prefecture. After finishing middle school, worked for Hakone Tozan Railway and at other jobs. In 1935, entered army as a Private Second Class. In August, 1937, at the outbreak of the Sino-Japanese incident, went to China. By the time of the fall of Nanking, was a corporal. In July, 1938, Cpl. Haneda received a wound in a guerrilla mop-up—bone fractures of left thigh and knee joint. Hospitalized in army's Nanking Hospital, later re turned to Japan. In First Army Hospital met Ueda Yumiko, then assigned there as a nurse.

After about a year, he was released from the hospital with a slightly crippled leg. Soon after, rented a room in Tokyo, where both lived together. In spring 1941, Yumiko gave birth to a girl.

Not long after the daughter's birth, Haneda left Tokyo for Odawara—with the excuse that he could find a better job there. Six months passed without a word. In the spring of 1942 Yumiko received a letter telling her that he had to marry another girl as the inevitable result of certain circumstances. In the letter was enclosed a check for three-hundred-yen (then about US$300). Yumiko tried every way to locate Haneda, but failed.

As to the watch, Yumiko told Mr. Wu that she had received it while she was nursing Haneda in the First Army Hospital. He said that he bought it in a curio shop in Shanghai. Mr. Wu did not believe the story told by Haneda. Rather he suspected that former Corporal Haneda had been among the troops occupying Nanking. It might be said to be the instinct of a son whose parents had been killed.

No sooner had Mr Wu obtained the name of Haneda from Yumiko than he went straight to Odawara city not long after the Okada incident. In five days he succeeded in locating Haneda. He seems to have spent a considerable amount of money in checking over the whole town through five Chinese residents of that city.

Haneda Otojiro was not living in Odawara. But Mr. Wu did locate Haneda's brother, who revealed Haneda's whereabouts as near Okachimachi, back in Tokyo. Haneda was dealing in black-market goods of the American occupation forces. He was living in a four-room house near Ueno, with wife and employees—but no children.

Mr. Wu was not so hasty as to call on Haneda at his house. He went to the shop Haneda was operating. First approaching as a customer, Mr. Wu was soon selling him imported articles—at prices considerably below market. Haneda was delighted. Haneda soon began to treat Mr. Wu as a trusted friend. Haneda did not see through Mr. Wu, who passed himself off as a Japanese called Iwamoto Yoshizo.

They were soon on quite familiar terms. One night at a sake party Mr. Wu, alias Iwamoto, asked Haneda, "By the way, this may sound odd, but, don't you by any chance know a girl named Ueda Yumiko?"

Haneda was startled. "Anything happened to Yumiko?" he asked.

"No, nothing. But is she your wife?"

"No. Not my wife. But I lived with her for a while."

"Did you?—and, uh, you had a child, didn't you?"

"Yes, I did. Is . . . my child is all right?"

"Seems so. Seven or eight now, isn't she?"

"Maybe, eight or nine, by now. How on earth do you come to know them?"

"No, no, I don't really know them. Only, well, one of my friends is taking care of them. A few days ago—I was in his house—we talked about the Okachimachi Market. This woman suddenly asked me if I knew a man in the market called Haneda. I was surprised. She seems to have been working in the Cabaret Tokyo in the Ginza district. But then I think she had already quit the place," said Wu, alias Iwamoto.

Soon after Haneda Otojiro went to the Cabaret Tokyo to find Yumiko. He was directed to her new home. Luckily, Mr. Wu was not there.

The moment Yumiko faced Haneda, an old, almost forgotten, burning rancor welled up in her heart. She kept him standing on the stone floor of the entrance hall, never asking him to doff his shoes and step inside.

"Halloo, Yumiko. It's been long time—"

"What brought you here? I really wonder how you could even dare to come," she sputtered in rage.

"Of course, I have no face to come to you like this, but—I just wanted to see my child."

"Your child? Huh! You wouldn't really like to face the child you deserted, would you? You'd better leave."

"Don't talk like that. That time, well, I was in a really tight squeeze. I, er—I apologize—" Haneda tried all the excuses and explanations he could muster. "You see," he said. "Well, as a matter of fact, I have given you so much trouble in bringing up the child—but, if you agree, I would like to send her to the university—with my money. I mean, I am getting along fairly well now." He also added that he had no child with his present wife, who was willing to adopt his child by the former affair.

Yumiko was furious at his selfishness. She threatened him with a pair of geta clogs she grabbed from the stone floor. He left without further argument. Yumiko did not say anything to Mr. Wu, as she feared giving him the wrong notion that she was continuing her old affair.

She received an anonymous parcel, obviously from Haneda, though it had no return address—there was one hundred thousand yen inside. Unable to return it, she kept the money in the drawer of her wardrobe. A few days later a messenger brought a basket of fruit. She refused the basket and returned the money with it.

Haneda Otojiro tried to get his child back through various means —money, presents—all of which failed. In consequence he apparently began to consider some drastic action to achieve his end. But it took another month before he could finally carry it out.

In the meantime, Mr. Wu was handling Haneda in his way. Practically all of Haneda's business now depended on "Iwamoto Yoshizo." It was precisely the way Mr. Wu had approached Yumiko, made her his own, and explored the secret of the watch—the way only a persistent Chinese could pursue.

One night "Iwamoto" took Haneda down to Atami Spa and got him drunk. Making sure that he was tight enough, Iwamoto—alias Mr. Wu Kao-chih—asked, "You always wear khaki pants. You've been in the army?"

"Of course.—Who's asking me? I am a corporal—decorated—Order of the Golden Kite—" Haneda said in drunken pride.

"Well then—you were crippled in the leg—an honorable wound?"

"That's right—mortar shell got me. Almost lost a leg—"

"Where did you go? South?"

"Central China. From there as far as Nanking. Had a real rough time ..."

"Central China? Then you were there early in the war?"

"Sure, just after it broke out. I went there in August. First, Shanghai, then to Changshu, Wusieh...."

"Nanking?"

"Yeah, Nanking. I climbed up that front wall . . . must have been twenty feet high . . . straight up."

"No, it must be higher than that?"

"Do you know Nanking, Iwamoto-san?"

"Sure, been there many times. You see, I was an interpreter. I'm pretty good at Chinese," Wu said.

"Really?"

"True. It was terrible, Nanking. We killed, oh . . . fifty, sixty thousand . . . "

"Ah, far more than that. We just couldn't figure out how to dispose of all those corpses. I myself must have got ten, maybe fifteen," Haneda confessed.

"Yeah? Even I got five or six," Wu lied, pouring sake into Haneda's glass. ". . . You been near the old Military Academy?"

"Sure. That building was turned into a headquarters—later."

"Back of that building, there was hill commanding a good view, remember?"

"The big mansions, I remember, I remember. Our unit cleared that area."   "There were some people left behind, I think."

"Just old men and women. They begged and begged—mercy—it was really funny."

"Get any loot?"

"Sure, loads. We couldn't carry it around, though we could take anything. We threw it all away. And then, anyway, I was sent back, wounded around then."

"Then you didn't bring back anything?"

"Nothing—except a little watch I took—"

"A watch? That'd be a good souvenir. Where'd you get it?"

"Let me see—an old woman. She had a good watch . . . from an old woman. I tried to take it . . . she wouldn't let me have it. Then an old man told her to let it go. He spoke some Japanese . . ."

"Yes . . . and then you . . ."

"I guess so . . . anyway, they're dead. We were busy mopping up, you see, so I locked 'em up in a room and threw in a grenade . . . I went away, busy . . . I don't know what happened . . . besides, who cares? Just some old Chinese . . ." Haneda was so tight that he probably didn't even remember his words the next day.

Wu finally knew the murderer of his parents. Yet, that night he slept in the same room with Haneda as if nothing had happened.

Mr. Wu Kao-chih began scheming to kill Haneda. Yumiko tried to persuade him to hold his hand, but Wu did not listen. He cold-bloodedly checked every possibility of murdering Haneda—or in his words, avenging his parents. Take him mountain climbing and push him off a cliff; drugs; fake auto-accident; push him from an express train. Every possible murder-method Wu thought over and re-checked, and rejected. On the other hand, he kept Haneda in a good mood, still supplying him with goods at cheap prices.

Then, a tragedy took place. On October 3, 1950, Yachiyo, the daughter of Yumiko, mysteriously disappeared on her way home from school. That evening Yumiko reported her daughter presumably kidnapped to the police and a search was begun.

The police went to Haneda's house only to find no trace of the girl. Haneda set up a firm alibi and was quickly cleared. Three days passed without news of the missing girl

Yumiko lost her composure. Mr. Wu seemed to have been of help, at least in public, as her friends report. But he did not try to deal directly with Haneda. "Mr. Wu Kao-chih, protector of the missing girl" knew such action would spoil his hopes of revenge Yumiko was no longer normal—sleepless nights, days of worry. On the third night, when Mr. Wu was away, she dashed out of the house. How she got there she could not remember, but later that night she was standing in front of Haneda's house in Ueno.

She knocked at the door. Haneda came out. She pounced on him, screaming, "Give me back Yachiyo. Give her back!"

Haneda called the nearby police box. The police officer came, listened to the trouble. but hesitated to get involved in some family squabble between a man and woman who had once lived together, someplace else. It was out of his jurisdiction, he claimed, and put Yumiko into a taxi, telling her to go home.

She didn't. She came back to Haneda's again, went inside the garden. She set fire to several places around and under the house.

Flames spread; the fire enoyee of Haneda's shop came to the Ueno police station to give himselveloped the whole four-room house.

Neighbors were alarmed. Yumiko was seen crazily jumping around the flaming house, shouting, again and again, "Give me balk my Yachiyo." She was easily caught by the police.

Haneda's wife narrowly escaped. But Haneda himself was found the next morning, a burned body among the ashes and rubble.

In the afternoon an emplf up, bringing Yachiyo with him. He had been ordered by Haneda to kidnap the girl and take her to Odawara. Hiding there for several days, he had read of the tragedy in the newspaper.

In February, 1951, Ueda Yumiko was sentenced to serve five years in Toyotama Penitentiary. Mr. Wu arranged to send Yachiyo to Yuriko's brother in the country.

In May, 1951, Mr. Wu Kao-chih disposed of all his business affairs and his properties. In June, he left Japan. A few days and before taking a Taiwanese Civil Air Transport plane for Hong Kong he paid a visit to Yumiko in the Penitentiary. "I guess, I owe you so much," he said. "You did the thing in my behalf. Because of you, I did not become a murderer. Yet my parents have been avenged."

He handed her a one-million-yen time-deposit certificate and an ivory signature seal with which to claim it, and said, "I am leaving Japan for good. When you are released, please use this money for yourself and Yachiyo-san. I'll be wishing for your happiness, from a faraway land."

Then he left.

In February, 1953, her lawyer arranged her release on bond using part of the money Mr. Wu had left. Yumiko went back to her brother's where Yachiyo was staying. In August of that year, a beautiful London-made jewelry box was delivered from Mr. Wu. There was no sender's address, just the postmark "Nanking." No further news has come from Mr. Wu, since then. But Ueda Yumiko is living peacefully, helping out on her brother's farm.

In that jewelry box lies the seal Mr. Wu had specially made for Yumiko—an ivory seal, with the arabesque design of a little red flower inlaid in the top.

EDITOR'S NOTE: In 1992 this Nanking Massacre was still being vehemently denied by leading Japanese who should know better, including such as Ishihara Shintaro, author of *The Japan That Can Say No.*

PLEASE NOT A WORD TO ANYBODY

by Mizuki Yoko

I DON'T REMEMBER when Mrs. Komori first came into to our neighborhood or when she moved away, but I do remember how I was attracted by her native manners. We never once passed on the street with just a casual nod of the head. We always exchanged gossip, oh, twenty and thirty minutes at times, sometimes much longer, talking about this and that, mostly that . . . .

I began to see less and less of her and when I did see her I noticed that she had lost some of her erect posture and immaculateness.

Just before I saw her last, I noticed she spent more and more time in the vacant lot in front of the local shrine, playing absent-mindedly with her two small children, or pushing the carriage to and fro intently.

"The old lady Yano died recently," she said one day.

"What? When?"

"About ten days ago," she said in a low voice. "But, please, not a word to anybody. It's sort of a secret."

"But why?" I asked, curious.

"Well, you remember she never joined any of the customary neighborhood donations. But, well, we thought it best just not to bother anybody."

The old lady Yano was Mrs. Komori's landlady. She was a notoriously mean woman, not just stingy, but really downright mean. There is always one like her in every community. She never once put money into any neighborhood collection for sick donations or

152

bereavements, saying she needed special consideration herself although everyone knew she had quite a bit of money hoarded away. She had let the Komoris have the room, called Western-style because it had a wooden floor instead of one of tatami, with the understanding that they move out when the baby came. But when the baby did come, and it took to the old lady, she became friendly and said they could postpone moving until the baby entered primary school.

Once, quite some time ago, when I first came back from the country, to which I had evacuated from the threats of airraids, I went to get old lady Yano's bag and money for the rice ration. She was sitting in her dark three-mat room in the center of the house the only room she kept for herself since renting out all of her rooms. An old velvet scarf, in vogue many years ago, was wrapped tightly around her head; she sat before a chest of drawers, the like of which can only now be found in some antique shop—you know the kind, black lacquer, inlaid sparingly with mother-of-pearl.

What aroused my curiosity further was the money bag she had—a black leather thing, the kind my mother used to call an "opera bag," and that I used to see only in old pictures that were carried by grand old dames of the Meiji or Taisho eras. This bag and the graceful *biwa*-lute that stood against the inlaid chest impressed me and stayed in my mind a long time.

"Who was she before?" I asked myself many times. I knew nothing of her background, for she had moved to our neighborhood while I was away in the country.

What I heard about her later was that her husband was at one time a fairly well-known journalist and had owned a small paper in the country, but her married life had not been very happy as her husband had a woman on the side. They never had any children. After her husband died, the girl she adopted from a distant relative and raised, ran away with a lover. Old lady Yano later adopted a grown-up youth, and the neighbors remember how happily she took this adopted son's new bride around to introduce her to them; they felt sorry for her when the young couple felt the old lady was a burden, left her alone in the big old house, and went away to live in the country where he got a job as a teacher in a small college.

But the sympathy was short-lived. Old lady Yano rented out all of her rooms. Everyone knew she had more money than she could spend, yet she was never friendly with neighbors.

She had died of cerebral hemorrhage. Mrs. Komori sent a telegram to the adopted son and did everything she could to help. She was appalled, however, when the son came with his wife and had no sooner arrived than he put the old lady into a coffin and took her away to be cremated. They didn't even see to it that her body was bathed, let alone change her clothes into the customary white pilgrim's kimono, traveling hat and straw-sandaled costume to prepare her for the long journey to the other world. The kimono for the dead is always sewn by three people, so Mrs. Komori would have known had a third person been called on to help.

"The young people nowadays." The tenants all shook their heads.

The young couple announced that the house was now theirs and they were going to move in; they wanted all the tenants to move out as soon as possible. The tenants protested that it was next to impossible to find another place with only a few days' notice. The couple moved in anyway, and immediately started to complain that their children quarrelled with the Komoris' and that the Komoris made too much noise.

"So, the only thing to do about it is to spend the daytime like this, to keep the children separated," Mrs. Komori smiled faintly. "But I don't mind this nearly so much as I do their suspicious nature."

The couple were sure that the old lady had some money put away somewhere and they had started to search. They lifted the *tatami*, they took down the ceiling and wall panels, but no money was ever found.

"The way they look at us, I'm sure they suspect us." Mrs. Komori put on an expression of sheer perplexity.

"It is funny, isn't it, that there is not a yen anywhere?" I put in, equally perplexed.

"But you see," Mrs. Komori came close to me and said almost in a whisper, "I saw her get the money out one time from a money bag she kept inside her kimono, between herself and the broad *obi*-sash. She kept it there all the time, day and night. There was a lot of money in it. They should have at least changed her clothes when they put her into the coffin. Well, I must find some place to move to." She smiled again faintly. "Come to think of it, she wasn't such a bad woman."

I never saw Mrs. Komori after that.

BLACK MARKET BLUES

by Koh Haruto

OHIZUMI met Jack Kurosawa in front of Shimbashi Station and the two walked toward Tamura-cho. The streets were full of Christmas decorations; there were many show windows that had big and small Santas. It was only three days until Christmas.

"Don't worry. I've heard that there's never been a miss so far," Jack assured Ohizumi, looking at him from under his hunting cap.

"I don't know anything about this guy Buchanan we're about to see," Ohizumi said bluntly. "I put my trust in you, you know that."

Ohizumi had never had any previous dealings with Buchanan. He had not wanted to come to Tokyo with the dangerous dollars in his pocket. His wife Takako did not want him to either. Ohizumi did all his buying and selling of dollars at his hideout in Kamakura. Those who wanted to sell or buy came to him, and he did his business sitting down, but these last few days he was rushed with dollars. He'd gotten rid of most of them, but the five thousand he had taken yesterday gave him a big headache. Because of obligations from the past he could not refuse the money. He felt, when he bought the money, that he would have a hard time with it. Sure enough, he could not get rid of it in one day. It was too close to Christmas and, though everyone wanted dollars, no one had enough yen for them.

"It's such a big amount, you know," Jack said, keeping his voice down. "Buchanan is about the only person who can buy such an amount so close to Christmas."

Ohizumi felt that Jack was trying to make him feel obligated to him, which annoyed him. He intended to give Jack about fifty thousand commission if the deal went through. He knew, of course, that after Christmas there would be no sale of dollars. He nodded to Jack, looking sharply right and left from behind the gold-rimmed glasses that he wore for disguise. Outwardly his easy manner and big shoulders made him look like a boxer, but he was constantly conscious of the five thousand dollars in his pocket.

"I know it's the way with this business. When it comes in like this, I have a hard time getting rid of it," Ohizumi had to confess. "I've got to find more new outlets."

Ohizumi intended making this his last deal. After Christmas, through New Year's, he intended to take Takako to Osaka and hide there for a while. Jack didn't know this, so he answered him lightheartedly. "After we get there, if you feel it isn't safe, we can always leave without doing any business," he said. "There is NHK, the Radio Japan Building. It's not so far now."

Ohizumi could hardly hear Jack for the noise on the street. Ohizumi intended doing just that, leaving the office if he smelled anything. The money was not all his; a part of it belonged to Moriwaki, his partner in this business.

They turned the corner and entered a street that was like the bottom of a gorge, then stopped in front of a six-story building with granite stone steps. They walked up to the third floor—they did not use the elevator—and knocked on a door. Beside the door hung a small wooden plaque with Buchanan's name in Japanese. Ohizumi did not fail to note the position of the elevator before he reached that door.

Inside, they were shown to some chairs by a tall blonde girl who disappeared into the next room. "Let's sit down," Jack said and buried himself in a big chair.

Ohizumi followed suit, and asked, "What kind of a fellow is this Buchanan?" He said it rather as if wondering about it himself, and not as a question. "What does he do?" This time it was more like a question.

"I really don't know," Jack said.

Ohizumi had asked the same thing before on the way here and got the same answer. At that time Ohizumi had thought Jack wanted to keep his client's business a secret—not say too much about him—but Ohizumi understood now that Jack really did not know.

He made sure of the two exits—one that they had just used and the other through which the blonde had disappeared.

There are those who run away after getting the money, and those who point a gun, he thought. "Did you do your business in this room, too?" he asked Jack.

"Yes, I waited a long time then, too," Jack answered. "Not even a cup of tea. I don't even remember what Buchanan looks like. Come to think of it, I don't even know that it was him," he muttered between puffs on his cigarette.

The fact that Buchanan was willing to buy five thousand dollars told Ohizumi that he was not just an ordinary black market dollar dealer. Ohizumi looked at his watch. It was past three. If he was robbed of this money, he would be finished. He had never been robbed before, but he knew of many who had. One of them committed suicide. It was a distasteful business, but the takes were big. Even after dividing the share with Moriwaki, there should be one thousand yen in it for him.

Twenty minutes passed. He'd finished three cigarettes. "He makes us wait, doesn't he?" Ohizumi said quietly, but he was restless inside.

"What do you want to do?" Jack asked. Ohizumi knew he couldn't say much; they might be listening in the next room.

Ohizumi looked at his watch again. Thirty minutes had passed, but still no Buchanan. To Ohizumi, Buchanan was "first time," but to Buchanan too, Ohizumi was "first time." There was no reason for him not suspecting that Ohizumi might be a cop. Ohizumi was beginning to feel a choking sensation. "It's a bad business, this black market." He tried to think of Takako to calm his nerves.

He'd met Takako in one of the new cabarets. The mouth that dimpled when she smiled was terribly sexy. He had divorced his former wife who had two children by him because she would not come in with him on his black market dealings. Takako told him to quit as soon as he made enough money to start a bar. Most of what he'd made in the past was spent in divorcing his first wife, in marrying Takako, and in buying his hideout in Kamakura. He'd had to start all over again at the beginning of this year—but now, at the end of the year, he had made just about enough to start a bar. I'll quit this time for sure, he thought.

Wonder what she is doing now. She didn't want me to come to Tokyo today. I didn't either, for that matter. Ohizumi was thinking these things when the door to the next room suddenly opened. Ohizumi got up and took a few steps backward, eyes glued to the big man who had walked in with a package under his arm. From past experience Ohizumi felt that it was going to be all right, but it was best to be on guard.

"Did you bring the stuff?" Buchanan asked in broken Japanese, looking at Jack searchingly.

"This fellow has it," Jack answered. He had also gotten to his feet. "This is the one I told you about over the telephone a while ago."

Buchanan shifted his searching gaze from Jack to Ohizumi.

"I have it here," Ohizumi patted his breast pocket. Buchanan put the package on the table. Ohizumi saw at once that it was in thousand-yen notes, for the right package two million yen would be about one foot four inches square. As these calculations flashed through his mind, Ohizumi's nimble hand unbuttoned his coat and brought out the envelope containing the dollars. Jack stood by, watching.

Ohizumi put the dollars on the table. It was a breath-taking moment. Their glances imparted fire. Ohizumi did not think about anything, he only followed the other's motions. Everything, even his life, depended on this moment, but he did not even think of that.

The deal was over. Ohizumi divided the thousand-yen notes into two, put one into the envelope, and the other into his grip.

Buchanan did not say anything unnecessary. Ohizumi wondered if Buchanan was a German. He did not seem like an American, nor Australian. He imparted a heavy feeling. Ohizumi walked to the door, thinking, 'Best not to show my back to him.'

After getting out of the building, he hurried to the station. He felt the fears that he had not been aware of when he exchanged the money with Buchanan. It's best to return to Kamakura as quickly as possible, he thought. This is the last deal in dollars, the last business of the year for me.

He felt elated when he entered the second-class commuter car of the Yokosuka line. But when he reached home a foreigner was waiting for him. He had brought eight thousand dollars. Ohizumi took it against his better judgment. Maybe it was because the deal with Buchanan had gone off so smoothly, maybe because he had been at the business for years.

Takako was furious. "You said yesterday with that five thousand dollars that you were through."

Ohizumi could not answer back. He felt the error too keenly himself. "It was as much your fault, Nancy," he answered, using his pet name for her. "You should have sent him back and not let him wait for me."

"All the money we saved to open a bar," she said in tears. "The day after tomorrow is Christmas Eve. Tomorrow I wanted to go shopping with you on the Ginza."

He had invested more than two million yen in this deal. He remembered Jack's advice. But the price had been so cheap. If successful, the profit would be terrific.

"I'll get rid of it tomorrow. Think of it, we'll net five hundred thousand. We need all the money we can get to start a bar, you know that."

"I know, yes," Takako answered but not cheerfully. "I know the more, the better. But I'm worried."

"Don't worry, I'll get rid of it, all of it" he said, trying his best to make Takako feel at ease. "We'll clean up everything the day after tomorrow, celebrate the Eve in Ginza, and leave for Osaka. We'll start the preparations for the bar after we come back, if the coast is clear."

Next day, Ohizumi sat alone in his living room, thinking. The night before he had succeeded in making Takako believe that everything would be all right, but he himself did not really know where to turn to get rid of the eight thousand dollars. He couldn't ask Jack again. He thought of his co-worker in Yokosuka, but knew even he could not handle such a big amount. Then he remembered Peter Nemuro, a boxer by profession. Peter had once traded dollars, but although quick with his fists, he had not been so with his brain; he'd suffered one big loss after another and finally quit. But he might know of someone. Ohizumi called him in Tokyo by phone. Peter, after hearing that Ohizumi could not talk over the phone, agreed to come to Kamakura immediately.

When Peter came and listened to Ohizumi, he advised him to go to Jack. Ohizumi told him in detail about his deal with Buchanan. "I think Jack was right. There's only two days to Christmas, you know," he said, and folded his arms.

Then Peter thought out loud, "— Fukumoto, he was once a member of the boxing club I belong to."

"Can you contact him right away?" Ohizumi asked quickly, and added, "—can't lose any more time, you know."

Peter left after promising to contact Fukumoto immediately. Ohizumi gave him five thousand yen and assurance that there would be more after the deal went through.

The arrangement was made that day for Ohizumi to meet Fukumoto at the Milano, a tea shop just off the main Ginza Street. Ohizumi's was to identify himself by wearing a brown overcoat and gold-rimmed glasses, while Fukumoto, he was told, was a small, pale-faced fellow.

Ohizumi called Moriwaki, his partner, and told him he would call on him about noon the next day, and told him to wait for him. Moriwaki had invested five hundred thousand with him, and after this deal was over Ohizumi intended to clear the account with him, and wash his hands of the whole nasty business.

When Ohizumi went to the Milano the next day, a small, pale-faced fellow got up from the corner booth. Ohizumi walked up to him.

"Glad to meet you," said the pale-faced fellow and smiled. He was well-mannered, which gave Ohizumi the feeling he was not quite dependable. Then to his mind came the face of Takako who had said with a dark expression just before he left, "I have a bad feeling this morning. Somehow, I don't want you to go today."

He shook off his sense of foreboding and immediately started to talk business. "Is it you who wants to trade?" he asked.

"No, it's not me," Fukumoto answered quickly. "As soon as Peter called me last night, I contacted several others and came across a fellow named Seki who said he would buy."

"I see. Where is this fellow Seki?"

"I contacted him just before I came here," Fukumoto continued. "Made arrangements for you to make a deal at the place called Kagetsu in Tsukiji."

Ohizumi wondered why Fukumoto would not take him to Seki's house. He also wondered why he had to wait until three that afternoon. He would have to call Moriwaki and extend the hour of appointment with him.

"It's big money, you know," Fukumoto said. At present market prices what Ohizumi had was equivalent to three million yen. "I suppose Seki has to have some time to get that much money ready."

"All right then," Ohizumi said. "I'll meet you there with Seki at three. You sure he'll be there?"

"Oh, sure," Fukumoto said.

From there Ohizumi went to Moriwaki and told him to accompany him to Tsukiji that afternoon. Moriwaki was skeptical about the way Ohizumi did his business, and said for him to divide his money. Ohizumi replied he did not have time, that he had to get rid of it before Christmas. All the time he was talking to Moriwaki, he was thinking of Takako, and the prospective bar he was going to operate with her. With her looks it was a cinch men would flock to her bar like bees to flowers. What made him think so much about his new bar was probably his appointment in Tsukiji. About three years earlier, at the height of his business, he had frequented a place called Kiku-no-ya, House of Chrysanthemum in the red-light district. He had become chummy with a geisha called Kikuharu, Chrysanthemum Spring. That was before he met Takako. Fond memories of those days came back to him and he only half-heard what Moriwaki was trying to say to him. "Well then, let's meet this fellow Seki," Moriwaki said in the end. "If anything smells bad, all we have to say is we didn't bring the money. Where are we meeting him?"

"That's the funny thing. It's close to Kiku-no-ya."

"Really?" Moriwaki was also amused. "That's very interesting." Moriwaki and Ohizumi both laughed knowingly.

After a quick lunch they left Moriwaki's apartment early. They went straight to Tsukiji to have a look at the place first. Moriwaki carried the money, for they thought it best that Ohizumi should go to the meeting alone without anything on him. They first went to a small tea shop where there was a phone. Ohizumi took down the phone number and told Moriwaki to come to Kagetsu as soon as he called him here.

Ohizumi then went to Kagetsu. The house had a high, black fence on the street side, which shut out the street noise. Once inside, Ohizumi had the illusion that he had come far, far away from the Ginza. The girl who met him at the entrance hall took him to a room with an expensive-looking *tokonoma*, with all its usual hanging scrolls, flower arrangement and art objects. She asked him to wait. She sat on the *tatami* mat at the exit, her finger tips touching the *tatami* as she bowed, got up, slipped out, got down on her knees again to close the sliding partition. Her quiet graceful manners, typical of waitresses in a *machiai* or tea house and high-class Japanese restaurant, reminded him again of the time he used to come to these places often. Then he had been dealing in cigarettes and food stuffs, sending out his assistants with two or three truckloads every day. His biggest clients were these *machiai* places and high-class restaurants.

While Ohizumi sat thinking of these things, the partition opened and Fukumoto came in. "Seki was waiting for you, but he said you might be late and he went to the theater," he explained as he sat down. Ohizumi thought it odd. He knew he was not very late. He thought afterward that this was when he should have smelled something, when he should have quit the place.

"Did you bring the money with you this time?" Fukumoto asked.

"I don't have it with me now," Ohizumi said. "But my partner has it—he's waiting for my call in a nearby tea shop."

"Well then, please call him," Fukumoto said getting to his feet again. "I'll send for Seki at the theater." He left the room.

Ohizumi called Moriwaki, and told him to come. In the meantime, the waitress carried in cakes and fruit and put them on the table. Moriwaki came immediately, and Fukumoto joined them, saying Seki would come right away. Ohizumi thought it odd again; for he knew that though it takes a little time to call a person out from a theater, this was taking a little too long. Just then the partition at Ohizumi's back suddenly opened wide, and three big foreigners came in. Ohizumi and the others jumped to their feet. One of the three foreigners, a red-faced giant of a fellow, pointed a gun at them.

"C.I.D.," he barked. "Put up your hands."

Ohizumi was quiet. He slowly put his hands up, and scrutinized Fukumoto sharply. Fukumoto was pale. Ohizumi wondered if this was Fukumoto's doing.

"Why are you carrying dollars?" the red face continued. "We're going to question you."

Ohizumi thought then that they were phonies. The investigations were always carried out at headquarters, not at a place like this. He thought of all these things while watching one of the three men search Moriwaki, and take out the eight thousand dollars he had in his pocket. He gritted his teeth—Ohizumi would not have let him have it that easy; he would have jumped out of the window before he let these phonies have it.

"It's our business if we carry dollars," Ohizumi yelled. "We carry any amount for our business. If you want to investigate, take us to your headquarters."

"We'll take you to headquarters, all right," the big fellow said, with a mocking smile. "Walk," he said, and pointed the gun at the three Japanese.

Seki did not show up till the end.

After the Japanese were shoved into a car, the three foreigners stopped another taxi. This fact convinced Ohizumi that they were phonies; if they had been C.I.D., they would have been there with a jeep. Inside, alone in the car, Ohizumi put his big hands around Fukumoto's neck. "How dare you fool us like this?" Ohizumi said between his teeth.

"I don't know, I don't know anything," Fukumoto wailed and cried like a baby.

"Then it's Seki, Fukumoto was only a decoy," Ohizumi decided.

The car with the three foreigners was following their car, but the distance between the two got greater and greater, and finally it disappeared.

"Turn the car back to Kagetsu," Ohizumi ordered. But the people at Kagetsu did not know Seki, said he had never been there before.

Ohizumi turned again to Fukumoto, but he only sobbed, "I only did it so I might make some extra money for the New Year."

Fukumoto said he knew the apartment where Seki lived, but when they went there Seki had already moved out. They learned then that Seki was a Chinese by the name of Sai. Ohizumi, for the first time, ate dirt—and hard.

Just as he came out of the Ikuta Building, Ohizumi was stopped by a policeman.

"I want to ask you something," he said. Ohizumi did his best to suppress his fear and remain calm. Could Fukumoto, whom he had just left, have reported him? It couldn't be.

"What do you want," Ohizumi said slowly.

"Not here," said the policeman, "Please come to headquarters." The policeman was extremely polite, with a faint smile flickering around his mouth all the time. Ohizumi was glad he did not have any dollars on him. In his pocket were a few yen notes, and an I.O.U. he'd just had Fukumoto write out for the money he'd been robbed of by the phoney C.I.D.s. He wanted to report the robbery but to do that was to invite being arrested himself.

"I am not doing anything," he said, his eyes darting sharply right and left, remembering to keep a smile. "I don't know what you want, but ask me here, if you want."

"It won't take you long," said the young policeman, still polite. "I only want you to come with me for a little while."

The policeman was asking him, not ordering him. Perhaps it is nothing to worry about, Ohizumi told himself. Because of his past job during the war—he was once a private secretary of a cabinet minister—he had many friends everywhere. If anything went wrong, he could ask their help, though he wasn't quite sure about actually getting it.

"If you are not going to tell me why, I don't have to go," Ohizumi said firmly. "I am busy. Besides, if you want to arrest me, you'll have to take the proper procedure."

The policeman seemed to think it best not to rile him. He said gently, "Were you not robbed of some dollars by some phoney C.I.D. agents?"

So that's it, it was Fukumoto. He reported because he couldn't pay. The reason he was robbed was because Fukumoto was a fool and was now trying to get him this way—I'll kill him! He turned these things over in his mind quickly.

"Don't know anything about phoney C.I.D.s," he barked. "I'm busy, don't you see? I can't be bothered. I live in Kamakura, and come to Tokyo only to do business."

"We know you live in Kamakura," the policeman said. "Do you come to Tokyo every day these days?" The policeman's manner remained calm and polite. Cold sweat came over Ohizumi; so they were following him. "There were others who were robbed besides you," the policeman continued, unmindful of Ohizumi's fear. "One of them reported it and the phoney C.I.D.s were picked up. They confessed everything. We checked with the *machiai* house in Tsukiji about you."

Ohizumi thought for a moment about giving up to the police, and then changed his mind quickly. What's wrong with me these days? he thought. If I complain, I'm only confirming that I traded in dollars.

Conversation dragged on for a while but in the end the policeman gave up, and said, "I'll report to my chief that you would not come. That's all I can do for now," and they parted.

Clad in a dull, yolk-colored overcoat of good English material, Ohizumi looked the prosperous businessman, but in fact since the phoney C.I.D. incident, his money was all gone, and he was having a hard time figuring out how he was going to pay his bills. He walked into the Lilac tea shop, where he had once carried out million-yen deals.

"Has Akiyama been here?" he asked the head waiter.

"No," he answered without changing expression, and whispered something to a waitress.

She came up to Ohizumi and said in a low voice, "Mr. Akiyama called and said he would be here about four," and left to fill his order.

"Wonder what he wants." Ohizumi looked at his watch. Forty minutes more until four. He drank his coffee, and left the tea shop to kill time, leaving word that he would be back.

When he got back, Akiyama was waiting for him. "I've news for you," Akiyama said as soon as he saw Ohizumi. Akiyama was excited. "Kamioka is here in Tokyo. He's driving a big American car. One of only three such cars in Japan now, the latest model Chrysler sedan."

Kamioka was in the textile black market, but Ohizumi had lent him money a couple of times before. "He went to Kobe, didn't he?" Ohizumi asked. "I think of him once in a while. He was a quiet fellow," he added.

"Said he wanted to see you," Akiyama went on. "He'll be here at two tomorrow. I thought sure he was having a hard time," said Akiyama.

"Yeah, he was kind of slow, as I remember him," Ohizumi said. "Is he an auto broker?"

"No, I think he's in this—," Akiyama also made a gesture of giving a shot to his knee.

"Maybe I'll borrow some money from him," Ohizumi said, thinking back to the days when he was able to lend one or two million yen to his friends easily. Now his position had been reversed.

"Kamioka wants me to go down to Kobe with him, and I think maybe I will," Akiyama said. "He said he'd find me clients. I've got to deal with foreigners in my line of business, and that's where there are many traders. Why don't you go, too?"

"If I were young like you—" Ohizumi said. He didn't know what Takako would say.

Akiyama smiled at that. Ohizumi, who once couldn't be without a woman one night, had stopped going to bars and cabarets after he had married Takako. After the baby, Tamako, was born, he went home early every night

The next day Ohizumi met Kamioka at the Lilac. He looked quite dapper in his gray overcoat and soft hat. When he had gone home the night before, he'd told Takako about being stopped by the police and about Kamioka, and told her that he might borrow some money from him. Takako was pleased, and they both forgot about the nasty business of the police, talking for hours about opening the bar.

"Let's go out," Kamioka now said, after the greetings were over. "I've got my car outside."

The car they got into passed the front of the Piccadilly Theater with its gaudy movie announcements and crossed the bridge. Kamioka came close to Ohizumi, and said low, "Heard about your mishap at Tsukiji. It was a darn shame."

"Yeah, a rotten business," Ohizumi said. "The place made me a bit careless. And I got stopped by police yesterday, too. One bad thing after another. I want to quit this business and start a bar with my wife," he said in the end. "I want to help your work a few days, to make enough to start this bar."

Kamioka put his hand into his pocket and drew out a newspaper-wrapped bundle. "Please use this," he said. "I have lots of money now."

"I will borrow it then," Ohizumi said. He felt the money from outside, and thought it contained about a million yen. "I am going to use this money to help you, and make some capital for the bar. I have a hunch the police are after me, so I don't want to take too many chances, and also, I want to quit it in two or three days."

"Okay," Kamioka said cheerfully. "I'll make the contacts for you right away. My name's George Mizuki, remember."

Their business was risky. They made a lot at a time, but they lost big, too. Once Ohizumi was followed by the police and he had to throw into a gutter drugs worth five hundred thousand yen. At one time a loss of three million yen meant nothing to him. Now everything was different. It had become hard work to make fifty thousand.

When he got home, Takako met him with a letter from the policeman he'd met that day in Tokyo. It said that the police would not inconvenience him in any way, and therefore wished him to come to police headquarters.

In the course of the following few days, he was followed constantly by police. In three days he made enough money to start the bar and was busy getting things into shape.

One day after he had been to see Fukumoto to get the money the latter was paying him bit by bit, he was walking toward the Lilac to meet Sedo, his new partner in the bar business to whom Akiyama had introduced him. He was told that Sedo's wife had worked in a bar, and that Sedo was once a manager in a hotel in Atami. He neared Sukiyabashi Bridge, and looked back, from sheer habit, only to see the same old policeman, making no attempt at concealment. Cold sweat came over him.

"You did not come after all," the policeman said, smiling wanly. "We waited for you."

"But don't you see," Ohizumi had calmed by this time, "as I told you the last time, I had nothing to do with it."

"There are Japanese, Koreans, and Chinese who were robbed just like you," the young policeman said quietly. "The total money stolen was fifteen million yen. The phoney C.I.D. men were caught, but we need witnesses to confirm the crime. I'll see that no harm will come to you. Please come with me."

"But I am busy," Ohizumi answered bluntly.

"I know that, but the American court requires witnesses." The policeman was half pleading. "Those who were robbed all say the same thing you do."

"If you make it so that I was robbed of yen," Ohizumi said, "then I'll come with you."

"That's all right," the policeman was quick to agree. "All you have to say is that you were robbed by the men in Tsukiji."

"If you fool me, I'll never forgive you," Ohizumi threatened.

"Sure thing," the policeman assured. "I won't cause you any trouble."

Ohizumi got into a taxi with the policeman. When they arrived at headquarters and saw the officer in charge, Ohizumi was told that the man who reported the robbery was a Japanese, a former Navy Officer. He was robbed of eight hundred dollars, but when the phoney C.I.D.s got in the jeep, he took the number and reported it. They arrested a C.I.D. first lieutenant by the name of Burton and another C.I.D. sergeant by the name of Michael.

"Burton has confessed," the officer told Ohizumi. "The American authorities asked us to investigate the local victims, and your name came up."

"I thought it was kind of funny," Ohizumi admitted. "But I could do nothing at the point of a gun."

"They are going to have a trial next Thursday," the officer continued, "And we want you to appear as a witness."

"I am busy with my business," Ohizumi told the officer, somewhat exasperated.

"We know that, but according to the American procedures they cannot establish a crime unless supported by witnesses," the officer explained. "We had about three appearing, but they all backed down at the crucial time. We want you to please have courage and be a witness."

The officer pleaded with him. Ohizumi thought of Takako and the newborn baby. After all, the dollars robbed from him would not return, and he did not want any part of any trial. But at the same time he did not want to be labeled a coward. Then too, the police had been following him for the last few days and must know of his activities in dope peddling. It might be wiser to listen to their wish now.

"The policeman who brought me here said you would fix it so that I was robbed of yen and not dollars," Ohizumi said. "I'll be the witness with that agreement."

"Yes, that's all right. We'll do that," the officer said, an expression of relief coming over him.

"I have my wife and a now baby to think of, you know," Ohizumi whined. "I don't want to be pinched, on top of being robbed."

"I don't blame you a bit," the officer said, smiling. "The court-martial will be held not very far from here. You can go see the officer of the judicial affairs across the street from there and work it out with him."

Ohizumi knew that it was bad to deal in black market dollars. But it was not only men like him who dealt in them. There were many politicians who bought dollars in large amounts. If the military law officer would agree to Ohizumi's proposition, he had decided to be their witness, to prevent more Japanese being robbed by men like Burton and Michael.

He spent the rest of the day on the business of his new bar. He had doubled the money he borrowed from Kamioka in three days and had returned the million he borrowed. For the new bar, Sedo would put up two million yen, just twice Ohizumi's amount. The profit would be divided four to six. Ohizumi also agreed to the bar being registered under Sedo's wife's name, in order to be prepared for any unforeseen outcome of this military C.I.D. trial.

The next day he went to see the judiciary officer to get his legal agreement.

On the day of the trial he went to the place as directed. He got off the elevator on the fourth floor, and started to walk down the hall. He met a huge man—a face he had not forgotten. Seeing Ohizumi, the man growled to him in broken Japanese. "If you testify, I'll do this to you," and he drew his open hand across his throat. "And you'll be sent to Okinawa, maybe."

According to American law, until a crime is established against a person, that man can go about as a free man. No wonder no one was willing to testify.

Ohizumi only smiled. He had given up dealing on the dollar black market. He'd already got the money to start his own bar. He had returned the money to Kamioka, too. So, if anything should happen to him, Takako and his baby could live on the profit from the bar.

He entered the waiting room. There were two Chinese, a man and a woman, both young. They had dark expressions on their faces. Burton came in, this time with another tall fellow Ohizumi remembered. This must be Michael. They both threatened in their broken Japanese, while an MP looked on expressionless.

The time came and they all entered the courtroom. When he sat down in the witness chair, he forgot about Takako and his baby. He forgot about the new bar he was about to open. He only remembered the mortifying feeling he went through when he was robbed by the two men he was about to testify against.

"These are the men," he yelled. "These are the ones who robbed me of three million yen," he said, renewing the fear and remorse he felt when the money was taken from him.

About a month later, he heard Burton and Michael had been sent back to their country. He was paid for the four days he spent testifying in court.

His new bar was opened in a great location near Kyobashi. It was christened Pearl. But Sedo and his wife would not give him his share of the profit from the very start.

It was registered under Sedo's wife's name, so there was nothing Ohizumi could do about it.

Ohizumi gave it all up. He just wasn't cut out for the rackets. There was an honest job open in a lumber company and he made an appointment with the personnel manager.

THE ONLY ONE

by Nakamoto Takako

SEIKO ran into Sumiko's all excited, jabbering rapidly. It was about their mutual friend, one of the Tachikawa set, Rose. She had married a GI and was to leave for America soon.

"She's some sharp one, that Rose, ain't she?" finished Seiko, very much affected by the news about Rose. Sumiko didn't seem to care at all, though. Stretched out on her double bed, she just continued to smoke all through Seiko's tale and to look up at the sky through the open window. Merely "humphing" intermittently, she felt that Rose was taking a big gamble with her future.

"We are 'only ones' and that means having only one man, so that's just as good as being married," she offered.

"No, it's not," Seiko answered angrily, "Being married and being an 'only one' are two entirely different things." Crushing her cigarette with her manicured fingers, she continued, "Don't be a fool! Marriage is the only way to go; we can't just go on like this forever."

Sumiko, in her cool and contemptuous manner, felt that Seiko was being terribly stubborn and stupid about the whole thing.

"Gosh, how I wish John would marry me and take me to America. Wouldn't you like that too, Sumiko?"

Sumiko just stared at the ceiling. Seiko, seemingly ignored, paced the room impatiently. "This room depresses me," Seiko said, "Let's get out of here and go see that amateur play that' on in the village."

Sumiko, too, wanted to escape from this tension "Yes, let's. My Robert isn't coming tonight." She got up and dressed quickly.

It was a balmy spring night. They walked towards the village theater. The little village of Nishitama had almost completely covered all of the old scars of the war now six years past.

The theater was small and packed with people—its air was heavy. The first play of the usual multifeatured program had already started. It was "The Son" by Osanai Kaoru. On stage, under the dim lights, the story was approaching its climax. Father, a policeman, stood face to face with his own son, whom he sought in the name of the law. As a first attempt by an all-amateur cast, the play was effectively done.

The play ended and the lights went on. The audience was quick to notice the presence of Sumiko and Seiko. Whispers of *pon-pon* and *pon-suké* echoed around them, but they were used to this being called whores, and managed to ignore it with a studied callousness. There were a hundred and fifty more girls like them in the village, and nobody knew where they had come from.

The curtain went up for the second play. A young bride and her mother-in-law were arguing about some minor kitchen matters. "You're nothing but a daughter-in-law," the old matriarch screamed, "You mind your place."

Sumiko bit her lip. Memories flashed into her mind. She saw herself again as a young bride suffering those same agonies ten years before.

"Get out of here," she heard the old matriarch again. "How dare you answer me back!"

Sumiko bit her lip harder. She fought an urge to leap onto the stage and slap the mother-in-law in the face, as she had wanted to do so many times so long ago. Tears welled in her eyes and rolled down her cheeks. She let out a soft whimper. Crying at a cheap amateur show like this, she said to herself, but the tears kept coming, threatening to turn into sobs. Suddenly the curtain was down, the lights were on, and she was aware that the people around her were staring in amazement, and she heard them whisper, "Imagine! A *pon-pon* crying."

She paid no attention, but Seiko did. She pulled at Sumiko hard and insisted, "Let's get out of here."

Outside the heavy scent of flowers and new leaves filled the air, and the great change from the mustiness of the crowded theater left them gasping. The scent and sounds seeped deep into Sumiko and moved her to new tears. She wanted to go off and cry alone.

Seiko was angry. "You sure made some scene, didn't you?" she rasped. "They were all looking at us. How could you cry at such a crummy, low down ham show anyway?"

"I couldn't help it. I tried to stop."

"Sentimentality doesn't become our type. Now, me, you couldn't get a drop of tear out of me even if you shook me upside down. Seeing you cry just makes me sick."

Sumiko felt as if she had broken some unwritten law of her set. Seiko stamped off, her heels clicking sharply in the still night.

Sumiko walked on slowly, taking deserted side roads. She was trying to calm her nerves, but the thickly scented air only seemed to open old memories, and in her loneliness the feelings she had fought down these ten long years gushed out and took hold of her.

"Alone, all alone," she cried to herself bitterly.

As the little scooter came out of the night and stopped by the side of the house it sounded like the wings of a huge bird. Then Robert's face smiled through the window into the room. Sumiko was stretched out on the bed, but didn't get up.

Usually, she welcomed him with a hug and kiss, as she had learned from American movies. She knew if she didn't she would lose him, and with him her meal ticket. But today she just didn't seem to care. Ever since that night of the village play, she had felt accursed. She had been living, heart and soul, back in those dark days in that northern village where she had grown up. Remembering the hopes and aspirations of the young girl she had once been and looking at herself in her present state left her dispirited.

Seeing that she wasn't going to get up, Robert rushed into the room and with the extravagant physical demonstrativeness she felt so typical of Americans, he came toward her. He spread out his hairy arms to take her to him. She shook her head and fended him off. Robert winced and shrugged his shoulders. He took her hands and asked, "What's the matter, baby?"

"Nothing. I just don't feel so good."

She put her hand up to her temple, closed her eyes and turned her head to the side. But Robert put both his hands on her shoulders and sought her lips with his. He kissed her face, took her in his arms and pressed her close to him. Sumiko felt suffocated, and the smell of his body nauseated her.

Sumiko had black hair and black eyes and her face was yellow. Robert's skin, though sun-tanned, glowed pink like all those who eat meat regularly, and his body was covered with fine hair the color of corn. She had held many men like him these last several years, but today, for the first time, the foreign smell stuck in her nose. Their bodies were close, but the waters of the Pacific separated them. Sumiko closed her eyes and resigned herself to what she knew must follow.

Robert sought only to satisfy his own selfish desires and seemed to disregard her feelings altogether. But then it was his natural right. As an "only one" she was in no position to resist the desires of Robert. It was her lot always to submit to him, even though afterward she felt completely empty and drained. His emotions, penned up these last few days in the confines of a tiny cockpit, allowed only to press buttons and pull switches on his bomb runs over Korea, had suddenly found an outlet in Sumiko.

Finally, he rose and dressed. His wallet came out of his pocket and a roll of bills appeared on the table. It was the greater part of his pay, about fifty thousand yen, $140. He sat at the edge of the bed and lit a cigarette. Sumiko did not rejoice over the money as she usually did—she put it away and went back to bed.

Fifteen minutes later they were walking along the banks of the Tama River. Unable to stand the silence, she had suggested a walk and Robert had agreed. He was a happy-go-lucky sort, a sergeant in the Air Force who had been a clerk in a cannery firm at home. He was more than six feet tall and Sumiko, of average Japanese height, did not even reach his shoulders. Such combinations, though, were not uncommon in this neighborhood. They had already passed several similar couples as well as a few "butterflies," as the "only ones" called these transient dates dressed in butterfly-bright sweaters and skirts who flit from man to man, flitting by in contrast and seeming defiance to the peaceful scene of rolling hills and dark forests surrounding them. The couple passed a young Japanese farm boy, pulling a cart loaded with honey buckets full of human fecal matter for mulch. There was the same familiar accusing glare as the farm boy looked at Sumiko. She had beard that, to oppose the invasion of her kind of girls, the village had started a young people's movement. In the young farmer's eyes, behind his glare, glowed his dream of some day seeing tractors and combines running the fields of Musashino Valley.

The couple reached the river bank where the Tama divided, the larger branch flowing on to the great concrete and dirt channel that led it on to the great metropolis of Tokyo. In the shallow water of the other branch, the natural bed of the once great river, she saw some youngsters fishing. As she gazed at them, completely unconscious of Robert lying stretched out on the grass, the scene changed in her mind to the dirty little creek that had flowed by her house and she saw herself chasing *medaka* fish with her brother.

The little brook that ran through the *buraku*, the Eta or pariah ghetto where she grew up, was dirty and covered with oil, its bottom filled with garbage and the corpses of small animals. Sumiko hated to play in the dirty creek and wanted to go to the clear-water brook nearer to town, but her brother would not go because many town children played there. The wings of revolt that fluttered in Sumiko's heart were too small to make the flight alone.

She went on to the town high school, boarding at a distant relative's home, and tasted for the first time the free and happy existence away from the *buraku*. She decided to go far away from home when she finished high school and far, far away from the stifling *buraku*. She hated the outcast blood that flowed in her veins, hated the *buraku* with its stinking animal hides that hung in every backyard. The movement to liberate the people of the *buraku* that had started right after World War I had penetrated her district by that time, but she remained indifferent to it. She knew that centuries of prejudice could not be wiped out in a few generations.

The day after graduation she had gone to Tokyo to join a brother who had a job in a munitions factory. The war in China that had started in 1937 while she was in high school, developed into the Pacific war shortly after her arrival. Noboru, her brother, was soon drafted.

In the home where she boarded the young son was in a leftist literary group. Sumiko had no great intellect nor desire to join their activities, but among those who came to the house was one Wakabayashi Kazuo, college student. She was attracted to his clean, naive ways, and he to her passionate eyes and sensuous red lips.

Once the group was arrested and imprisoned for weeks. She didn't know why, but she took food and magazines to them. After their release, Kazuo came not only with the group, but sometimes alone to see her. Often they would go to the Rokugo Bridge across the Tama River, far below where Sumiko now sat with Robert. Airraid drills were commonplace and there was a feeling of urgency that had caused them to draw closer.

The big moment finally came, and Sumiko remembered how she wept alone, hiding from everybody. Her heart leapt with joy a few days later when she received a letter from Kazuo summoning her to his family home. His mother had consented to their marriage, and Sumiko rushed to her new life in a home bound with old traditions.

Sumiko wanted to return to Tokyo after the ceremony, but Kazuo wanted her to stay with his aged mother during his absence in service. His mother, old and proud, had dreamed of Kazuo taking a wife from a home of equal status, and had only consented to this marriage because she was convinced Kazuo would never return alive from the war. Even at that the old woman was prostrate with shock when the customary post-marriage investigation revealed that Sumiko was an Eta, a pariah. To this day Sumiko shuddered with rage when she thought back to those dark days after Kazuo left, just as she had the night at the play.

"It certainly was a good thing that there was no child. Our blood must be kept clean or the curse of our ancestors would be upon us," her mother-in-law would confide to her favorite niece, loud enough for Sumiko to hear. She had wanted this niece for Kazuo's bride. The particular ancestor, for whom the mother-in-law wanted the family's blood kept clean, Sumiko was always reminded, was some vague figure famous in Japan's dim past.

"That's right," the niece would agree sweetly, "the important thing is the purity of the blood."

Sumiko would shake with rage and pound her head against the stone wall, cursing her birth. Hot-headed, strong-willed Sumiko could not endure this treatment long and she fled to her own home. Mother-in-law considered it good riddance—she never came after her. But to one who despised her origin, the *buraku* was no place to start life again. While she spent her restless days under her father's roof, the war came to an end. With it, as if shaken by a violent earthquake, the world tumbled around her. Sumiko could not stay any longer shut up in the *buraku*, holding the picture of Kazuo.

She fled to Tokyo, the only place on earth where she felt she could spread the wings of freedom and revolt that had been held down so long. She was startled at but not afraid of Tokyo, with its streets filled with tall, blue-eyed GIs. She tried to get a job at a factory where she had worked before, but it had shut down when the war ended. She got a job as a bar girl, lowering herself to that only, she often thought, to spite her mother-in-law. She did not realize, of course, that it was a very perverted sense of triumph.

With their warped sense of newly gained freedom, the girls in the quarters where she lived sold themselves right and left for small luxuries. These things were scarce, she granted, but she remained faithful to Kazuo, dreaming of the day he would come back to her, as thin and wan as the repatriates she saw at the stations.

"Don't be old-fashioned!" the girls would say. "What's the sense of waiting for someone you don't even know is still alive?"

But she feared her faith was not true one night after she had been tricked by her best friend into a deal with an American. That night, she remembered vividly, she went back to her room and rolled over and over on the *tatami*, crying and laughing. When she got over her hysteria, she calmly burned Kazuo's picture.

"I can't face him anymore," she cried bitterly.

The way after that was preordained, and she followed it. Thickly but well made up, she picked her own customers and became an expert at the game. Her spirit of revolt would not allow the various social leeches to take nearly half her rightful earnings.

Four years after the war she visited her brother who, like many of his people, had gone into the black market after his return. She learned that Kazuo was back. He had been to her home seeking her, but they knew nothing of her. He'd become very active in the Communist movement and fallen out of touch with Noboru.

Sumiko felt a stab at her heart. "Too late, too late. I can't face him."

Robert had come upon the scene soon after.

A tear rolled down her cheek, her entire being embodied in it. Since the night of the play she had been existing almost as a living corpse. She could fight the accusing and hateful glances of her own people by glaring at them in return, or ignoring and pretending not to see them, but she could not fight back or run away from accusing voices in her own heart. She'd gone into this life to spite mother-in-law and the world, but wasn't there some other way out?

The days passed and with them her depressed feeling worsened. Robert continued to come and continued to release his pent-up emotions in Sumiko. Her long periods of dejection displeased him. She could neither muster the necessary feelings to hold him fast nor get up enough nerve to part with him altogether, for she had no other means of livelihood.

Robert was away when Seiko dropped in, dressed in a brightly printed skirt and loud makeup. Sumiko looked up at her and sighed enviously. Seiko was so full of life. At one time, Seiko had been a housemaid in Yokohama. She had learned enough pidgin English to get along, but could neither read nor write, which caused her quite a bit of trouble in keeping in touch with her boyfriend. In Yokohama, however, there were students who wrote English letters for the girls for a small fee, and Seiko patronized these as frequently as she did fortune-tellers.

"I just had my fortune read," Seiko snapped. "He made me sick. You know what he said?" Her ill-humor showed openly on her face.

"'You're not a bad girl,' he said, 'but you're too flighty. You should try to settle down.' Yeah, that's what he said," she pouted. "Imagine, he thought I was a butterfly. So I got mad and told him, 'Don't make me sick. You may not know it, but I'm an only one.'"

"Sure!" Sumiko said simply. She did not say more. Seiko seemed to think that there was all the difference in the world between a butterfly and an only one.

"Wouldn't you get mad too," Seiko continued, "if you were taken for a butterfly?"

"But if we couldn't be an only one, we would have to become a butterfly. "

"Oh, no, not I, never! I am going to get married and go to America. John always says so."

Sumiko envied Seiko. She was still capable of having dreams, of thinking of America as a fairyland where there were no problems. Sumiko had seen too many cases where young women, blinded by this dream, had been smashed by a sudden change of heart, an unsympathetic chaplain, or harsh immigration laws. The women had fallen still deeper into petty crime and greater vices or had committed suicide. Sumiko had no more dreams.

"You have no interest in what I am talking about, no sympathy," Seiko cried. "I can't imagine John having a change of heart. I won't."

For all her enthusiasm Seiko revealed between puffs on her cigarette that all was not serene and peaceful within her. Sumiko perceived that Seiko and John were not getting along as well as Seiko would have her believe. To lose their present men would mean for both the loss of their livelihood. Perhaps that's all the more why Seiko clung so fast to her dream, though even she must have realized that the dream was without foundation.

Sumiko had been playing a game of solitaire, a game of fortune-telling. Now, with a casual flip, the ominous ace of spades stared up at her. Seiko came closer to the table and stared at it.

"Whose is it?" she yelled.

"Nobody's in particular," Sumiko answered coolly. "It could be yours and it could be mine. Whosoever it is, we might as well face it. Neither of us will come to a good end, that's for sure." Sumiko threw down the cards and lit a cigarette.

Seiko's cheeks were white as she glared at Sumiko, "You sure are acting funny lately . . . depressed and mean." Then she quickly changed her mood and continued on in her old flighty tone, "Oh, yes, John has been transferred to the camp at Fuji and I'm going with him." She stood up, smiled, and strode to the door. Sumiko could tell she was only bluffing. Her defiant gestures confirmed how helpless her position really was.

Seiko turned when she reached the door. "Good-bye. We may leave suddenly, so I may never see you again."

"You will come to see me if you return, won't you?" Sumiko said, trying hard to be gentle.

Seiko went out without answering. Vain Seiko, poor Seiko, she is through with John. She must be going to Fuji and the new camp there to seek another partner, Sumiko decided. She had heard that already hundreds of women had gathered there.

Sumiko could see a bit of herself in Seiko and a cold chill ran down her spine. She lay on her bed, arms crossed on her breasts and eyes closed. If she had only waited for Kazuo . . . . She pictured herself in her mind's eye, baby tied on her back, shopping bag on one arm and worn-down *getas* on her feet, going from shop to shop looking for bargains, and she longed, with all her heart, to be as she pictured. "I wonder what he is doing?" and she felt a million little pangs in her heart.

The sound of Robert's scooter broke her reverie. Lately, she had noticed he was always in a bad mood. She knew it was not entirely because of her gloominess. The peace talks that had been going on all summer had gotten nowhere and the hopes that she was sure Robert entertained of going home to his wife and children had dwindled. Robert never told Sumiko that he was married, she just assumed it and felt a womanly sympathy towards him and his loved ones at home.

"Let's go down to the Ginza and have something good to eat," Sumiko coaxed.

"Okay, anything you want to do," Robert consented.

When they reached the station, Sumiko saw Harue, a butterfly, buying a ticket to Kure, Kyushu. When Harue saw Sumiko, she bowed, showing a respect a lower person always shows a superior. Harue had come to this base from Hokkaido last spring; now she was already leaving for Kyushu. What would become of these women? Sumiko sighed to herself.

Sumiko had heard that Harue had been a nurse once. Going home late one night, she was picked up and raped. Her parents never saw her after that. She was too ashamed to go home and had taken up the trade.

While waiting for the train, Sumiko and Robert met Robert's friend, William, with his Japanese girlfriend and their son. The boy, a beautiful child of four, had his father's features and his mother's complexion. Robert picked up the boy and held him high in the air, much to the child's delight. Sumiko saw in this how much Robert must be longing for his family. She felt cold and lonely inside.

The peace conference continued to drag on in Korea and Robert continued to fly on his missions. He never talked much about it to Sumiko and she never cared to hear about it. To live on the money he had earned by killing other people, was that all her life amounted to? The less she talked about it the better it was.

Then Robert stopped coming. It was not like him. It was not likely that he had gone on to another woman. Maybe, he had been shot down. No, not that. Still, she felt little emotion about the latter possibility.

Early one morning a note came from William's girlfriend. Robert's plane had not returned from the last mission. There was no way of knowing if he was safe or dead. He was merely listed as missing.

Her heart went cold, she could feel the blood leave her face. She felt dizzy and lay herself down on her bed. But she could not cry.

I am free, she thought. Then she thought of how she would have to make her living. She felt dizzy again, but still there were no tears. She felt sorry for Robert, yes. He had wanted so much to go home and with that close at hand to have to die seemed cruel and unjust. But there was herself to think of now.

She spent the following few days in a despondency never experienced before. She had lost all ambition to go find another partner, as Seiko had done; she knew there was nothing else she could do to earn a living—not the kind she had gotten used to since she had met Robert. One night an American plane crashed while landing nearby and burned several Japanese homes. That night she had a nightmare in which thousands of her own people stood before her screaming accusations at her for the accident. She woke up in a sweat. The dream shook her spirits, and she made up her mind to quit her present life forever.

She dressed as modestly as possible and went to visit her brother Noboru. He had recently found a job in a butcher shop. When she entered the store, Noboru threw down his butcher knife and hurried her out to a tea shop a few doors away.

"Good Lord, Sumiko. People can tell right away," Noboru began even before Sumiko sat down. "You just don't look like a decent Japanese girl anymore. Don't embarrass me."

"Don't be like that, please," Sumiko pleaded faintly. "I tried to dress sensibly, today."

Noboru dragged on his cigarette, his eyes cast downwards. "I went home the other day," he started, "they were worried about you. Cousin Taichi was talking about your Kazuo. It seems he's become a big shot in the Communist party . . . He's married again . . ."

Sumiko's breathing stopped. She could hear her pulse beating in her head.

" . . . Taichi is in a movement to liberate *buraku* people. Wants me to go in with him, but I'm not smart at all, you know . . ."

Noboru went on, but Sumiko only half heard. After the first of the shock was over, she was able to look into her own heart objectively and realized that she had still held a faint hope of going back to Kazuo or she wouldn't have been shocked so much.

"Why don't you wash your feet," Noboru suddenly remarked, "leave this life and start anew?"

Sumiko sat up. "That's what I came to talk to you about, but I have to think it over some more."

"What do you mean, think it over?"

"I just realized that life isn't as easy as it seems. I don't think I can ever lead a straight life again."

"You fool, you would continue being an embarrassment to your family?" Noboru screamed at her. These words stung deep and only served to wound her more. She went white with rage.

"What a thing to say. What a help you are. If that's all you're worried about, I'll never bring you embarrassment again. I'll never come to you again." And she walked out, her brother staring at her back, dumfounded as she disappeared from his life.

She went to the nearby house of Maki, a friend of hers. Maki had married a third national last year, but lived with him only three months. He was Taiwanese, a dollar broker. He also ran dope in the Tachikawa district and was hooked up with international gambling groups on the Ginza. Three months after their wedding, he got wind that the police had something on him and disappeared. Now Maki rented a room in Showa-machi, the tremendous new licensed quarter, and was in business again as a butterfly.

Maki was in her room. She greeted Sumiko sympathetically in her usual open manner. "You might as well realize, Sumiko," she started, while preparing tea, "yes, you'd better realize that once you fall into this life, you can't get out. It don't do you no good to yearn for a home life."

There was more truth in Maki's words than Sumiko would concede, or Maki, too, for that matter.

"Why, we can't even cook rice proper. We don't know how to sew or wash. Too much trouble to raise kids." She laughed hollowly. "All we know how to do is rub a man's back."

Yet Maki seemed to enjoy her life. Sumiko envied this, just as she had envied Seiko. Maki was the type born to the life. Even Sumiko, a woman, was aware of the sex that oozed from Maki's being. Sumiko watched the smoke of their cigarettes rise and disappear into nothingness and her own spirit went with it.

The realization that she could never go back to a decent life, that she could never walk the same road with the rest of her people, not even her own brother, let alone Kazuo, hit her harder than anything else had so far. The year was drawing to its end, and people everywhere hustled about preparing to greet the new year. The rush of their movement seemed to stir up cold breezes that flowed into Sumiko's already cold heart.

One day just before Christmas, she made up her mind to end her meaningless life. To her great disappointment, mingled, with a slight joy she could not deny, the overdose of sleeping tablets she took proved no poison to her system. Too long had she been addicted to the tablets for a normal night's sleep. When she came to this time, the sun was setting in the west and its faint cold winter light filled her drab room.

If I can't die, I must live, she thought to herself. And to live I must do the only thing I know. She closed up her house and rented a small room in Showa-machi near Maki.

"You can bring guests in," the landlady said, "but I don't want you bringing business." Sumiko didn't mind this. At least she could keep some remnant of independence and decency. She was through being an only one. Better to be a butterfly and free even if a butterfly of a cheaper type than she had been before she had met Robert.

She decided to make the Tama-no-ya her regular hotel. She took her first guest there and a boy brought in some cheap whiskey and a light snack. She got up and locked the door and went back and sat on the edge of the bed. Her guest poured a big shot of whiskey and downed it in one gulp. He glared at Sumiko and appraised her body, her past, her present, her future, and all its immediate possibilities and potentialities in one long lewd glance. Sumiko winced at the passion and violence she saw in that glance She expected him to pounce on her with a bestial growl and to give vent in one violent spasm to all that had been behind that long glance. All he required of her was a piece of flesh to get his money's worth. In her mind's eye she pictured the fight between some pre-human stone-age man and woman, and prepared herself.

He looked down at her, the soul of primeval male subjugating the female to his will reflected in his eyes. Sumiko killed all her emotions, coldly set about to calculate the other's ardor and desire. She would measure mechanically how animal-like are the desires of those who satisfy their hungers through money and superior physical power.

She despised more and more her inability to wash her hands of this life. She learned techniques to please men more. The hotels where she went with her guests took a large percentage of her earnings, but still she thought it better than suffering the loss of her last escape into decency and independence by using her own room.

The year ended and the world rejoiced at the new year, 1952, the year in which the peace treaty was to take effect and the Japanese would once again be free people. But to Sumiko it all made little difference. She stood at her street corners rain or snow.

One time she picked up a blue-eyed youngster who had no money to pay when the business was over. She had to stand the hotel fee. After that she checked, and when he came to the hotel looking for her she asked sarcastically, "Got money today?"

"Sure," and he patted his breast pocket.

"Let's see," she asked. But the bills he took from his pocket were all military scrip of small value.

"You think you can buy me with this?" she shouted in his face. "You must think you're some slick operator. Now, get out!"

She walked back to the kitchen, to the cupboard where she kept her bottle, lifted it to her mouth, sucked several gulps. She fell into bed in a heap, face down. She didn't want anyone to see her cry.

She stayed in her room for the next few days. In her veins a living venom, capable of rotting her very brain, was advancing into the final stage of its attack; a condition so inevitable she had never bothered to think about it.

Winter and spring came and went. On the first of May, not realizing what day it was, she went to a movie. On her way home, she saw a crowd gathering talking excitedly of what had happened in downtown Tokyo that day.

"It was awful. All those beautiful automobiles upset and burnt."

Sumiko could only catch fragments of their conversation. First she couldn't figure what it was all about, but as it gradually came to form a coherent picture in her mind, she trembled with fear.

You will be next, she heard the whispers inside, and she knew she couldn't run away this time.

"*Pon-pon!*" the voice inside her whispered again.

When news of the anti-American riot was confirmed on the radio that night, she groaned. She pictured herself being dragged about over flaming coals by a demon, tongues of hot flames licking at her face and body. She saw the flames engulfing her and the hideous grin of the devil laughing at her, his lips parted from ear to ear.

The laughter of the devil echoed sharply in her head as she staggered across the room to her bureau drawer. The cackle grew louder as she took Robert's old jackknife from the drawer.

Could it be that the venom had finally reached her brain?

She held it high, ready to plunge it deep into her throat the instant she heard the devil laugh again.

KOREA THROUGH JAPANESE EYES

by Yuasa Katsuei

THERE is a knock at the door, a visitor or a peddler? There is no one in the house but me. I go to the door, and open it a crack. A student stands there.

"Is the gentleman of this name plate at home?"

Purposely, I do not answer him. Lately I have been bothered by callers of all sorts. The student continues without looking at me.

"I am a student of Seoul University...came to Japan just recently. I've just read this gentleman's book *Isle of Tsushima,* and his short story "Woman Prisoner," in *King* magazine. He speaks low, still looking up at my name plate.

"If I may be permitted, I would like to see him and talk with him."

He is not a bit insistent. He merely wishes to be announced, yet I know that he saw my face.

I remembered there was a custom in Korea when a man calls on another. Even if the man he wishes to see comes to the door, the visitor pretends not to recognize him. If the man of the house does not want to receive that visitor, he calls into the house, asks himself if he is in, and gives an answer in the negative. The visitor goes away, and there are no hard feelings. Fond remembrances of this quaint custom struck me and I was touched by this young student's good manners and consideration. I let him in gladly.

He sits before me, and I notice that though he is very tall, he cannot be more than seventeen or eighteen. I soon learn that since the outbreak of the Korean War, he has escaped death four times, each time due to quickness of mind and body, acquired through

185

sports. Once he was taken for spy and almost shot to death by North Korean police.

With 100.000 yen in his pocket, he had left Seoul. Reaching Pusan he rejoiced when he heard a boat was to leave for Japan on Christmas day. Then news came over the radio that the Red Chinese Army had entered Seoul. He heard rumors that it was pretty rough going this time because the invaders were foreigners. He had told his mother and young brother and sister not to move out of Seoul no matter what happened. Hoping desperately that he will get there in time, he jumped on a truck in front of the Pusan station. His uncle lived in a little hot spring village nearby where he had left his 100,000 yen, but he had no time to go after it. In his pocket he had only two hundred yen, enough to buy a couple of candy sticks.

Threatened by thundering guns, the truck stopped many times but the boy had no money to sleep in an inn. Many a night he slept outside in the sub-zero temperature without food or drink.

Reckless—that's the only word to describe his action, yet in a few days, he ran into his family, who had been missing, near the old bridge. He was only fifteen then, yet his whole family depended on him. They ran to him, clung to him, and sobbed with joy. By hook or crook, he had to get them to safety, and succeed in taking them down to the south. How many times later he and his family fled back and forth between Pusan and Seoul.

By becoming an interpreter, and taking odd jobs, he studied and entered Seoul University, considered the most difficult to enter. If he had failed, he would have been taken into the army, and there, after half a year's training, be made a lieutenant, most expendable of all officers. The entrance exam was fierce and he succeeded in getting in, but he was too ambitious. He chose a harder and longer way—to smuggle himself into Japan and enter a university there. The boat met a storm on the way, and after a terrific voyage, all were caught. There were twenty of them like him. He escaped the hands of the police only because he spoke good Japanese.

While watching his own people being taken away like knots in a string, he made up his mind that next time he would bring his mother and sister and brother. What guts, what fire!

"How the students in Tokyo are enjoying freedom"—my young student says enviously.

"But jazz and dance? We have little of that." he continues. "My brother in Korea goes to see such movies as *Random Harvest* and

Waterloo bridge, as if touching a treasure, once in three weeks in disguise."

"Disguised?" I ask him in surprise.

"Keijo High School where my brother goes does not allow its students to go to movies. So my brother goes, disguised as a shoe shine boy."

"That so? But that's my school."

The school was first built by the Japanese community. After Korea became a Japanese domain, it became a state school. It was on a large estate, and employed about fifty male teachers. The school building itself was burned down twice—once during the Pacific War by American bombers, and once in this recent war. He shows me the picture and there is not much outward change. What surprises me is that he tells me that during the exams there is no one around to watch the students. Bread is sold at the canteen, but there is no one there to sell it. Everyone throws the money into the box. There has never been any cheating.

Even when the "heirs" of the rulers attended, there never was a system like that. Compared with Korea, Japan is far more fortunate in the food situation; yet can one find anything to equal this? I think how proud the students must be of this former school of mine.

I have used the phrase, "just like before" too much. The building is new, and the students are new. Both the grade school and the high school students and teachers each take a candle to school and stay in school until the curfew hour. They are trying to regain the time lost during the recent war.

They are all working hard with the will portrayed in our old Japanese saying, "Boys be ambitious—do not be overtaken by other students of the world."

The present teachers graduated from universities when they were under Japanese control. All the reference books are still in Japanese. There is an old English grammar, written by a famous Japanese professor of English, and although there is a Korean version of the same book on much better paper, and costing only two hundred yen, the students prefer the Japanese book even paying as much as six hundred yen, for a well-worn edition.

Lately, I meet people who often ask me, "Are you back already?" half jokingly.

This has been since a newspaper published a report that I had been invited to North Korea. I receive letters to be delivered to the Japanese prisoners in North Korea from their families. I receive callers, asking me to look up the addresses of these prisoners.

North Korea was very cooperative in returning Japanese, and those assumed to be still there are considered to be only about thirty. But then for those who are waiting their return, I should not say "only."

When I meet the families, some of them are even willing to join communism, if their loved ones be returned. Many of them were imprisoned for crimes not connected with the war, and their terms are long over, if they were able to live through the war. The families bear no grudges against the North Korean government, but they are afraid to be thought that way by others. A war widow confides that she realizes her husband was a scapegoat of war, but if she could only find out his whereabouts. I can appreciate her feelings fully.

Very few people even try to know of the place that would touch their forehead if they fell down flat on their faces. Whenever I write something about Korea, I usually receive letters immediately, mostly from Japan-born reared in Korea, or Koreans born and raised in Japan. They all want to know about the placed they lived when children. They all want to go back to Korea, some saying they dream about Korea almost every night.

But even if my checking revealed that some of those places have been bombed out beyond immediate reconstruction, I don't like to tell them so. I do not like to shatter their dreams.

As a result of the recent war, not only the scenery of Korea has been changed, but the people's thinking and their outlook have also been affected greatly. For only the two things I mentioned before, about the school examinations without proctors, and bread being sold without anyone guarding it, are enough to show that Koreans are trying to regain their national pride, even though I do hear that the black market is unchanged.

If circumstances permit, I would like to go to both North and South Korea, and see with my own eyes the changes that took place there. We need not have *Alilan* (Korean folk song) teach us that if one "walks with his eyes fixed on the star in the distant sky, he is likely to fall into the gutter."

LADY TARZAN OF KOREA

by Yuasa Katsuei

"I JUST can't believe it," sighed Yuriko, looking around, "that I should be here in this peaceful countryside again, talking and walking with you."

It had been just eighteen years since I last walked with her down this same road, looking at the same lovely hills of Izu peninsula; listening to the same sounds of little streams of hot spring waters that flow out of the Japanese inns, and which gather themselves to form brooks that weave in and out through this little hot spring resort town. Her father owned one of these inns, and on that day, eighteen years ago, we walked these hillsides, while she sought my counsel for her unusual love affair. She was then just out of a sewing school, a lovely girl of a little over twenty. 'Unusual love affair' I called it, because she had fallen in love with a Korean youth, Lee Min-young a musician.

She had sought my counsel, more to confirm her belief, rather than to receive impartial opinion, for she knew that I would not advise against it. She knew that I, having been brought up in Korea, would have nothing but the best to say for such an affair.

But now, seeing the same person in her prime, with two lovely children, a boy and a girl, not knowing whether her husband was dead or alive, yet none the worse for the extraordinary experience of having roamed through the densest mountains of Korea escaping death for having been taken for a spy by both sides, I wondered whether my advice had been just. It hurt me all the more, for there was not the slightest reproof in her tone as she recounted her blood-curdling tale of escape from war in Korea.

189

On that morning of June 25th, when she heard over the radio that the North Korean Army had crossed the 38th parallel, she could not believe her ears. She went to tell her husband, who had been playing his violin from early morning. But he only cocked his head and said,

"I wonder if it's true. There was no such report as far as I know." He put down his violin slowly, walked into the dining room.

The radio droned on, "The North Koreans have moved swiftly in their invasion. Having taken over most of the towns north of Seoul, are now heading toward the city from three sides. The UN Army is counterattacking." The radio urged the citizens to remain calm, and refrain from acts of rashness.

"I better gather up things just in case," and Yuriko started to collect her valuables. How she was unaware of the seriousness of the situation was shown when she gathered her photo albums together, and even thought of taking them. Photos of the time they were married in her father's home in Izu, her happy newlywed days in Tokyo and then Seoul, all the pictures of her children as they grew up. Not one photograph failed to reveal how happy she was in this marriage.

Just then her two children, Kyoko and Eiichi, came home from school and reported the goings on in the streets. They said that automobiles dashed about, and tanks and trucks were seen rushing north.

"Mother, is it a war?" asked Eiichi.

"Most exciting, isn't it?" squealed Kyoko.

They cried in unison, for they knew not the horrors of war, not any more than did Yuriko. Nevertheless, their eyes showed fear.

"We may have to evacuate," their mother told them, "so get your valuables together."

"Mother, may I take this drawing that got posted up at school?" asked Eiichi while Kyoko, had, among her valuables, her favorite French dolls.

"This is no time for trifles!" Yuriko admonished.

Yet she, too, was taking out pictures of her early married days from her albums.

But that night, when her husband came home, the situation had completely changed. Every vehicle, from truck to pushcart, had been taken over by the army, and it was impossible to evacuate with anything but the clothes on one's back. Min-young was inclined to stay put a while longer, and see how it would turn out, for he had heard that the US Air Force had entered the action.

However, in the morning reports came in that North Koreans were at the North Gate of the town, and that there were riots everywhere. Two Korean boys came to Yuriko's husband—boys he had saved from the hands of the government; they had been thrown into jail on suspicion of spying for North Korea. They assured her and her husband that they would do everything to protect them from the North Koreans. In spite of their assurances, however, they all felt uneasy, and taking meager food provisions and a few blankets, they left their home and went down from the hill where they lived. When they reached town, the North Koreans had already entered the city, and their tank-led troops were marching down the main avenue, while the citizens waved improvised red flags and shouted "People's Army, Banzai."

"Look at them," said Park, one of the jail-breakers. "We can't do anything but join them," he concluded.

Yuriko's husband put on Park's jail frock, and disguised himself as a jail-breaker reunited with his family. At first Yuriko could not shout the word "banzai" and only looked around her worriedly, but soon she got used to the atmosphere that surrounded her and was able to wave her arm with some semblance of sincerity.

When they reached Taekwan-moon there was a short skirmish between the North Koreans and a small band of the Republican, ROK, National Defense Army. The latter's vehicles were soon in flames, and the gunfire of the ROK Army from the city hall was soon silenced by the onrushing North Koreans. It was not long before the windows of the same building were filled by the citizens who welcomed the North Koreans.

Yuriko was surprised to see the quick change of heart of the masses.

There was no more fighting. They soon reached the East Gate where they met some more North Koreans entering that way, and both groups exchanged greetings with shouts of "Banzai,—live ten thousand years." Seoul was completely in the hands of the North Koreans. It was obvious that there was no escape.

"Madame, you must be tired," said Park to Yuriko. "Stay at our house tonight, and we'll think of our future plans."

When they reached Park's house, they realized how tired they all were. They had walked nearly twelve miles that day.

But the next morning, inspection of each house started. Yuriko's husband hid in the attic, but he could not stay there very long. He wanted to evacuate immediately. Park urged that they stay another two or three days, but Min-young insisted on going immediately. Yuriko's husband was a musician, but he was also registered with the ROK CIC—counter intelligence—and when the Northerners found that out, not only he, but the whole family faced the likelihood of being shot.

The great Han river flows south of Seoul and no matter which direction they headed, in order to reach Suwon where the government had moved the previous day, they would have to cross this river at some point.

When they reached Ojuri, they saw a store which had been made into an improvised inspection point.

Min-young turned pale. Then, composing himself, he took out his pistol, stuck it into Yuriko's skirt. He put up his hand, saying, "Well, then," and walked toward the store. It was over in a matter of seconds. Yuriko started "GO, run after him . . . " but was stopped by Sho.

Then when Sho saw Kyoko open her mouth to shout "Father," he jumped on her, putting his hand over her mouth just in time to silence her.

"Your father did that on purpose to save you all," he said. "If he passes in safety, then we will follow him. If not, we will have to find some other route."

They watched. Yuriko stared anxiously, and just as she most feared, he was stopped, and carried away by three men.

"Well that's that," Sho shrugged lightly so as not to make Yuriko and the children feel too badly. "Let's go to my relatives' house in Toksum. They will get a boat for us."

"Yes, but . . . " Yuriko still hesitated.

"Don't you see, your husband went alone to save you?" Sho said, gently but firmly. "If released, he will come to Toksum. We made plans, your husband and I."

There was no way out but to follow his direction.

On the way to Toksum, Yuriko accidentally dropped the pistol into a deep gorge, which helped her make up her mind. She thought it might help to protect her and her children, but in passing the check points in the future the pistol might arouse the suspicion of the inspectors. It was just as well that she lost it.

Sho's relative operated a plant manufacturing soy sauce, but the plant was already taken over by the North Koreans. Yuriko and the two children had to sneak in by the back door. They sneaked out again in the middle of the night, for they heard that a black-market boat was leaving, and Sho had gotten places for them in it. He took them to the boat, and after he whispered a few words to the boat-man, disappeared into the dark. Yuriko felt the lonesomeness as never before. She was alone with the children for the first time.

When they got out on the river they heard some commotion on the bank. Suddenly the terrifying crack of gunfire was heard, then the staccato rattle of a machine-gun. Yuriko and the two children ducked under the blanket. They heard the shots drop short into the water. A few of them hit the side of the boat, but they were able to sail out of range of the gunfire, unhurt.

After they disembarked, they walked and walked, heading for Suwon where the South Korean government had relocated. They had no certificate, so they had to take the back roads.

Yuriko did not speak Korean. It was Kyoko with her fluent Korean who always saved them and enabled their narrow escapes. "Father is a watch salesman, and is in the south. That's where we are going," was her line of talk.

But when they finally reached Suwon, the government had already been driven out and had moved to Taejon. No matter how much they walked, the onrushing Communists were faster and their passage was blocked by inspection centers everywhere. They detour-ed through rough mountain roads, to avoid these inspection post, and walked for nearly two weeks.

The roar of guns could be heard coming from the other side of the river. Then they heard stray bullets whiz overhead. There were many groups of non-certificated people, refugees, on this road ahead or behind them, but they suddenly disappeared. Yuriko grabbed her children and ran behind a hill. She continued to walk there in its seeming protection when suddenly they were challenged by a North Korean soldier.

"Halt!" he called. "Where are you going?"

"We are going back to Seoul," Kyoko answered, frightened.

"All right, pass," he said. "Take the little road down that way, and it will lead you to the highway to Seoul."

They knew that if they said they were going back to Seoul they would be freed to go on without inspection.

Thinking they had fooled him successfully, they took the road, but went the opposite way they had been told, and walked about three hours. Narrow roads, down steep cliffs, and crossing small but deep brooks without any bridges, and finally coming to a fairly good road . . . when again they were challenged by a familiar voice. Looking up, they saw the same soldier of three hours back. They had been walking around the foot of the same hill.

"You said you were going to the north," he said.

"Well, are you?"

"We have been going north," Kyoko replied feebly.

"I'll bet you have," he snarled, and jumped down the embankment with his companion and grabbed the trio. They walked, guns pointed at their hips, and reached the highway at exactly the same spot they had come to three hours before.

They were taken to a large gatehouse of a mansion which had been turned into an inspection point, off into a small room separated by a high brick wall.

"Say, you mute, you are a Japanese, aren't you?" the soldier said in Japanese as soon as Yuriko was made to sit down. "We can tell. You are spying on us, aren't you?"

"Oh no," Yuriko said desperately. "The father of these children is in Jirisan, and that is where we were heading."

"You say Jirisan?" he shouted. "But that's where our hero Balchizan is hiding."

"Yes, that's where father is, too."

"You are lying," he bellowed. "It makes you all the more suspicious." One of the two took Eiichi outside, and the remaining one told her to take off her clothes, pointing the gun at her.

"Please, that I can't," she pleaded in tears. "We are not spies. Who ever heard of a spy with children."

"What, you mean this young one is your daughter?" he said in disbelief. "You are lying again. Who ever heard of a woman in her twenties having a daughter almost twenty. All right, I'll see if you ever had a child or not." He stretched out his hand, and tore off Yuriko's skirt.

"Please, please, not that," and bending her body like a shrimp, she resisted the attacker.

"All right, if you won't cooperate ! " and he shot into the air.

It was only in threat, but it made a terrifying noise in the small room, and Yuriko fainted.

Just then Eiichi jumped into the room, and sitting astride his mother's body, he glared at the soldier. "If you want to kill mother," he yelled, "kill me first."

The two stood dumbfounded. Just then, hearing the gun shot, the master of the house and the commanding officer burst into the room. Kyoko, who was white with fear, suddenly became eloquent, and told in fluent Korean what had happened.

The commanding officer listened to her, and became very polite. He promised to give them a certificate, then offered them a meal of rice and meat soup. It was the first decent meal they had eaten in days.

"You say you are the mother of this girl, but you don't look it. It is no wonder my staff took you for her sister. I suppose you will be going back to Japan if you cannot find your husband," he said gently, and made out travel certificates for the three. "You will have hard times, no doubt, but good luck to you. These certificates should pass you through any inspection point. From now on, don't take the difficult mountain roads, stay on the highway."

And he told them that the war had spread throughout the country, "Therefore, it will be difficult for you to go down south direct. You had better go by way of Chungju," and he told them the way. Yuriko's Western-style skirt was torn, so they were given Korean clothes.

They encountered their first good luck most unexpectedly, all due to the desperate action of Eiichi, and Kyoko's eloquent Korean. After that the trip was much easier, thanks to the kindness of the North Korean officer. They kept to the highways, but everywhere they went they met fighting, small and big, and lost much time in turning back to take other roads.

One day they were taking the highway that led them to Umsong. Suddenly an airplane appeared, and it came in so low over their heads that they could see the blonde hair of the young American pilot.

"Look, an American airplane," Kyoko jumped up, and waved her arm violently.

"If he can pick us up, we can get to Pusan in no time," said Yuriko. She, too, was at the point of shouting, when suddenly they heard a volley of shots from the plane. Several people fell down ahead. Looking close they saw they were communist soldiers. Yuriko and her children were heading straight into a battle.

Those walking down the highway fled to the mountains, and Yuriko's party followed suit. The communists shot at them, and before Yuriko's eyes, their white clad bodies fell], stained scarlet with blood.

"We'd better take off these white Korean clothes," Yuriko suggested. "As long as we keep these on, we will be shot at for sure."

"But, . . . " Kyoko was young yet.

Just then a shot, evidently aimed at them, splanged against a rock nearby.

"We mustn't hesitate a moment," Yuriko urged.

"We must keep alive somehow and reach Japan." Yuriko took off her clothes, and covered her naked body with leaves and branches. Kyoko resigned herself, and took off her clothes too. They wrapped up their clothes in a bundle, and ran toward a big rock on the nearby hill.

"If we get behind those rocks we'll be all right," Yuriko yelled.

And they ran up the steep side of the hill. Taking off the white clothes had almost an immediate effect. Far fewer bullets came their way. They hid behind the big rock, and let out a sigh of relief, when suddenly Kyoko said, "Mother, where is the bundle?"

"Uh!" gasped Yuriko. She remembered hanging it on a branch when she needed both hands to climb over a rock on the way up. She had forgotten to retrieve it.

"That's all right, I remember where I put it," Yuriko assured her children. "We'll go back for it after it quiets down a little."

The fighting seemed to have moved away, and the three suddenly felt a great fatigue overcome them. They fell sound asleep.

When they awoke it was pitch dark. They climbed down with only the starlight to see by, but having run up the hill without any conscious effort to remember their route up, they could not find the place.

"What shall we do, Mother? Kyoko said in a tearful voice.

"I don't know, Kyoko," Yuriko sighed in despair.

The two wept in each other's arms. From now on they would have to live like mountain cats. They would never be able to go down to where people lived. Their certificates were with the clothes.

The three walked, avoiding the sounds of guns and bombs, over the tops of the mountains. They had to avoid people now.

On the second day they had better luck. They found a pioneer's camp, deserted by the inhabitants. They found a garden full of ripe cucumbers, eggplants and corn. They even found some matches, and that night they ate their bellyful of corn. They decided to make this place their abode and await the turn of the fates.

But it was not long before they had to leave the haven in the mountain. On the mountain side opposite them, across the valley, communists took up camp. They were sure to come this way, but still the trio could not make up their minds to leave. Then, one afternoon, the communist camps were bombed by US planes. The whole mountainside went up in flame, black charred human bodies hurtled into their garden. Hearing communist soldiers running behind, they too ran into the woods.

From then on their life was just like that of the Tarzan they had seen once in an American movie years ago, only minus tigers, foxes, or even tiny squirrels—these had all run north to the China mainland or Manchuria to escape the insane human war. There were still plenty of snowy heron, magpies, and crows, which the children learned to fell with stones. They also learned to cross rivers by jumping from tree to tree. Yuriko even learned to make fire from two hard stones. The meat of heron and magpie is not so bad after one gets used to it, especially when mixed with quail eggs, which the children occasionally found. It tasted out of this world to them at the time.

But, this life too, they eventually had to say good-bye to when the unmerciful north wind began to blow.

They could not burn camp fires to keep themselves warm at night for fear of attracting airplanes which were heard close overhead again.

One day, shortly after they moved to a cave facing south, they were discovered by young men of the village. However, much to their surprise, the boys were afraid of them, instead. Taking advantage of their fear, Kyoko demanded, in a very authoritative voice, why they had come up.

"We live in a village down below," one of them answered. "We came up here to escape being drafted by the communists." His voice quivered with awe.

"When did the Mountain Goddesses come down here?"

Yuriko now understood their fear. The boys took them to be the legendary Goddesses of the Taepaik Mountains, The Great Ever-White Mountains. Yuriko whispered to Kyoko to answer and to keep her voice ethereal.

"We Mountain Goddesses may come down further—even to your village. Therefore bring at once three well-washed white garments in three sizes."

The boys went down. Presently three elders of the village came up with the desired clothes, wrapped in white silk carrying cloths, and placed them on the rock as an offering.

"Leave them there, and wait under the tree with the heron's nest," Kyoko ordered them, as Yuriko whispered to her to say.

They were elated to put on clothes for the first time in three months, but when they were led into a room that looked like the largest and the best in the village they were frightened for not knowing what to do. Before them, large trays full of fruits, river fish and meat were laid. Eiichi almost pounced on the food and Yuriko had to stop him by pinching him hard. One of the older men came forward, and asked, forehead touching the floor.

"Please advise us," he said, "this village has always been highly religious from generations back. But now, we are surrounded by the communists. Please tell us what we should do, should we side with the communists, or should we remain secluded."

It was a hard question for Kyoko to answer. She asked Yuriko, who whispered back in Japanese. Then suddenly the surprised young son of the house, a man of about thirty, came forward and exclaimed in Japanese:

"You are Japanese, are you not?"

Yuriko turned pale. She had been certain that in this remote region no one would know Japanese.

"Please don't worry. I was with the Japanese Government in Seoul until the liberation of August 15th, 1945. I was an official of low rank, but after the liberation, was ostracized for being a pro-Japanese. So, I left everything, and came back to look after my aged parents." He said these things in one breath, then continued, "Your being here may well be the will of the Mountain God. I'll do all I can to help you. But first, tell me what brought you here."

Yuriko could not hide after that. She told everything.

Presently his father pulled at his sleeve. They conversed in Korean for a while, after which he turned to Yuriko with a troubled face.

"You see the big crowd outside," he said. "They are all here to look at the Mountain Goddess. If we tell the truth now, no telling what may happen.

"To fool them" he continued, "I will tell them that, in accordance with the will of the Mountain God, Yuriko the Goddess has been sent to marry me. A few days are necessary to prepare for the wedding, in the meantime, we can think of some way to set you free."

Yuriko could not refuse. The heat from the *ondoru*, heated floor, made her feel comfortably warm; there were 'foods of the land and of the water' before her eyes.

But, this suggestion was more than just a trick to fool the crowd, she learned later. The son began to make nightly calls to her room, urging her to turn the suggestion to reality. Her heart wavered a little. If settled here, her children need not know starvation and fear of death. But . . . .

"You see I do not know whether my husband is dead or alive. Please give me a few days to think."

*   *   *

"If you had married then," I said smiling, "you would have stayed in the mountain district of Taepaik-san and we would not have seen each other like this, would we?"

"That's right," answered Yuriko, also smiling. "He was awfully kind, but a bit off, in a way, too. We were, in effect, imprisoned, but fed well. We even got fat."

But, Kyoko was strongly against the idea of staying there. She wanted to come to Japan, go to a music school in Tokyo, and eventually become number one violinist of the world. But, her adamant attitude saved me. After I came back, I looked at the district on a map, and found out that it is the remotest section of Korea. You see, in wandering through the mountain district, we had traveled across the Korean peninsula, and were near the Japan Sea, while we had thought we were heading south."

"And how did you run out on him?" I asked.

"When the communist recruiting stopped, I figured that they had departed. So one night, when everyone was away for a village meeting, we ran away. We took the course to the south, but before long, we were caught again by the communists.

"We were again interrogated as spies; we were again made to take off our clothes. But, the company commander, about twenty-four or five, was a gentleman. He never did anything to us. He listened to us, understood our circumstances, and we were sent to the kitchen to work. It was then that the UN counter-attack began."

"That was in October, wasn't it?" I said.

"How should I know the date," Yuriko said. "The soldiers of North Korea began to move north, and pretty soon there weren't any familiar soldiers anywhere.

We,—that is there were several other women who were held by the North Koreans—were left behind. Then defeated 'Volunteers' began to filter in. They stole, they raped, they did everything to make our lives miserable.

"One night, all the women kitchen hands were huddled together, when suddenly some Volunteers forced their way in. There was one Korean girl among us who had lived in Japan, in Osaka. She was homesick for Japan, and often sang Japanese songs—sentimental tunes popular at the time she was in Osaka. When the Volunteers came in she stood in front of them.

" 'We'll cook a meal,' she yelled, 'but don't you dare put one little finger on these girls here'

"The ruffians winced, but a couple of them, unmindful of her, walked towards me and Kyoko. We were frightened speechless. Then, suddenly, this Korean girl started to pound the dinner gong with all her might.

" 'Here comes the UN Army. You better run,' she told them. Or 'if you must have women, you can have me.'"

So saying, she stripped off all her clothes and stood up stark naked. She was a big woman, and as she stuck out her belly in a vulgar challenge, she looked handsome.

"But you know, the men were frightened by this. They grabbed up rice sacks and ran," Yuriko said amused. "At a time like that, shock treatment is the way to go, isn't it?

"That was the last of the ruffians. After that came only wounded soldiers—without arms, or with a leg missing and who walked with the help of their comrades. These were the boys who were forced to fight at the point of guns by the previous ruffians. We went to our neighbors and begged for rice to cook for these boys.

"Kyoko and I were coming down a hill from one of these missions when we heard unusual noises down below. We peered through the crimson leaves, and saw trucks coming up the hill. We saw that the first of the convoy flew the Yin Yang flag of the Republic of South Korea.

"When I saw the flag, my knees gave way under me," Yuriko said. "Sitting by the road I waved my arms.

"'I am a Japanese from Seoul. My husband is a Korean, a member of CIC, and was arrested there.' I shouted, crying hysterically.

"A truck stopped in front of me, and a handsome young officer came down.

"'And what was your husband's name?' he asked.

"When I told him, he clicked his heels together smartly, and saluted me, saying, 'You mean that famous violinist Li Min-young? What a pity. But don't worry. My name is Lieutenant Kim Tu-kyom. I am in a hurry now, but you mention my name and you will be given all the facilities you need.'

"He told his soldiers to throw two sacks of rice to me, saluted and was gone. I thought I was in a dream. I gave away all the rice that was given us, and next day begged a ride of the UN Army truck going back.

"We headed for Pusan. The jeep must have raced 60 miles an hour. We passed through towns leveled by the war and reached Taegu that night. Next day we resumed our ride to Pusan. We covered the mileage that took us five months by foot."

"And after that it was an easy voyage back home . . . ?" I inquired, feeling the easing of tension that comes with the end of a long story.

"Yes, although we did encounter some trouble in Pusan," Yuriko said, with an expression that told that the hardships she encountered had been erased from her heart, that the only trace was the dark shadow that comes over her face, like the fleeting cloud shadows over a rice field in the early fall, when she thinks of her missing husband.

"We were detained once in Pusan on suspicion of being counter spies," Yuriko said. "But we were soon released"'

"And how are your children?" I asked.

"They are just fine. They go hunting everyday for pheasants, with stones, the art they learned in the Korean mountains," Yuriko laughed. "It seems that is the only thing they remember about their hardships."

They soon returned, and came before us. They were certainly lovely children, with no traces of their Tarzan escapade.

ECHOES FROM A MOUNTAIN SCHOOL

REFLECTIONS UPON MOTHER'S DEATH
AND HER HARD LIFE

by Eguchi Koichi

TOMORROW will be the thirty-fifth day after mother's death, and I have been thinking about her and the miserable condition of our home all day. We are so poor that after the funeral ceremony tomorrow my little brother will be taken away and adopted by our uncle. I hate to see him go. He is such a good boy and does everything I tell him. Tsueko, my little sister, is going to be adopted by another uncle, but she will not go until she gets over whooping cough, which she got after mother died. After that only grandmother, who is seventy-four and scarcely able to cook our meals, and I will be left. Mother did her best to keep us together, but now that she is dead, we have to be separated.

We have a two-third-acre field, our house and the land on which it stands. Ever since father died, mother struggled alone to make this land support us, and when I say support, I mean just that. Outside of public relief, we had no other means of livelihood. Now I have to work the land and support myself and grandmother. Mother's one hope was that I would soon grow up and help her. She was never very strong, but she worked all the time to feed us and to pay the taxes. Even after she lost consciousness, I heard her muttering, "Have you brought in the wood?" "Did you put the dried radishes into the salt and rice bran to pickle?" "Are the green vegetables washed, ready to pickle?" I am sure that she died more from exhaustion than illness. I did my best to help her, often staying home from school when there was work that required the strength of more than one person, but still I didn't realize what a burden mother was carrying until I heard her talking like that on her deathbed. Then I couldn't stand it and ran outside to work, even though I wanted to stay with mother.

On November 12, the day before she died, the neighbors came and helped me bring in the wood. I don't know what I should have done without that help. On the next day they sent word from the village hospital where we had taken mother that she was dying. When we were all gathered around her bed, I told her how the neighbors had helped me with the wood, and she smiled. I don't remember ever seeing her really smile before. Her lips rarely formed themselves into a smile, and when they did, it seemed that she smiled to keep from weeping. The expression that lighted up her face on her death-bed was something quite different. It was a grateful and contented heart that spoke. Her face with that smile upon it will remain in my memory forever.

Certainly she had had very little reason to smile. Ever since her marriage, and especially since our father's death, she had been absorbed body and soul in the losing struggle of trying to keep her family alive. Day after day, month after month, year after year, she struggled to improve our way of living. She fought with all her strength against asking for public assistance but the debts piled up. At last, in 1948, she and grandmother went to the village office to ask for help. She was never the same after that. She and grandmother never failed to remind us that our family was a public charge and could not be regarded like other families in the village who were able to support themselves.

A year and nine months later, mother became too ill to leave her bed. She insisted that she would soon be well, but she got worse and worse. Grandmother kept saying that we should send for the doctor, but mother stubbornly refused, saying that we could not afford a doctor.

"The time comes," said grandmother, "when the last field has to be sold to get medical attention."

But the field was never sold and mother got no better. One day Taro-san happened to drop in, heard grandmother talking about the doctor. "Do you mean to say," he exclaimed, "that you haven't had the doctor yet? Don't you know that everyone receiving public assistance is entitled to medical attention? I will send the doctor to you at once."

When the doctor examined her, he said that she had to go to the village hospital immediately. She had a serious heart condition. The word hospital always causes difficulty in a Japanese family, for it means that someone in the family has to go to look after the patient. I have heard that in some foreign-style hospitals, everything is done by nurses and that meals are prepared in the hospital kitchen for all the patients. This is a wonderful arrangement. I wish it were done in Japanese hospitals.

Our first problem was to decide who could be spared to go with mother to look after her and cook her meals. If I went, there would be no one to do the work. Grandmother was too old. There was no one left but little Tsueko; we wondered how a nine-year-old girl who had no experience in looking after a sick person, could possibly take care of mother, prepare her own and mother's meals and do all the other things which had to be done by a hospital attendant. There was no one else, so it couldn't be helped. Tsueko had to go.

After taking lunch with us, the doctor left, and grandmother and I got ready to send mother to the hospital.

The next day, uncle borrowed a two-wheeled cart drawn by a man on a bicycle. We piled the bedding on it and put mother on top of the quilts, covering her with one and spreading oil paper over everything as a protection against the rain. We then fastened an open umbrella over mother and at her back placed vegetables, rice, dishes, pots and pans. It was bumpy ride for her, but she endured it patiently. I was glad to have her in the hospital, but now the entire responsibility for the farm work rested upon me. I wanted to be with mother, but there was no time. Going to school was out of the question. There was nothing for me to do but work. That was when the people of the village came to help me. Then, on the thirteenth of November, mother died.

Two of our teachers came to the funeral with some of my classmates who had collected money from the boys for the funeral offering. When all the funeral expenses were paid, grandmother said, "We have seven thousand yen ($17.50) left. That is more than we had when your father died." When, however, we tried to pay off our debts, the seven thousand yen disappeared, and we found that we still owed four thousand five hundred yen ($12). How could grandmother think we were better off than when father died?

When my father died I was only six, but I knew all about it, for mother and grandmother told me so often that I could not possibly forget. After father's funeral, we had only five yen left (at that time, prewar, about one dollar and twenty-five cents), but even that had to go in taxes. We were in a dreadful state. Mother and grandmother didn't know each day where rice for the next day was coming from. Grandmother and mother made straw sandals which they traded for rice. The sandals made in one day could be exchanged for about six pounds of rice, a good price, mother said. We were small, so we could live on four pounds. This, in time, gave us a little reserve.

They worked so hard that they were able to save a little money. Mother hoped they could go on like that until I grew up, that we might be able to get along. Then the war came and everything became unbearably difficult. How often I heard mother say, "When Koichi grows up, he can help us and pay off our debts."

This was her only comfort, but she was never able to realize her dream. She was simply overwhelmed by poverty; all her labor got her nowhere. Why did it have to be like that? I wonder if mother really believed that things would be better after I finished school and began to work. After all, what could I do more than she had done? When I think of this, I can scarcely sleep. I thought so much about it that I decided to make out a plan and send it to our teacher.

Next year will be my third year in junior high school, the end of compulsory education, and I want to attend school every day without having to work anywhere except on my own farm.

The year after that, I will work as hard as I can and pay my debts. If I can ever save a little money, I want to buy a rice field, for with only a vegetable patch such as ours we can never have enough food. I want to see my family have a little comfort. I must continue to improve myself so that I can work like a man, not be fed like a sheep. This is what I wrote to my teacher. But as I thought the matter over, I found how mistaken I was. In the first place, how could I ever save enough money to buy a rice field? And in the second place, the rice field that I should buy would have to be taken away from another family who would then be as poor as we are now. At present our entire cash income comes from the tobacco we raise on one-tenth of our field, or one-tenth of two-thirds of an acre. The rest we need for vegetables for the family.

No matter how I work, there seems to be no way of increasing this income. In January of this year we sold our tobacco for twelve thousand yen. After paying seven thousand yen we had borrowed the year before, we had just five thousand yen left. This added to the one thousand six hundred yen a month we received in public assistance, was all we had to live on for the entire year, in all twenty-two thousand yen (about $60).

Is it any wonder that I could not believe it when grandmother said we were better off when mother died than we were at the time of father's death? I could see no possible way for the family to remain together and make enough money to survive. That is why it was decided to ask our uncles to adopt my brother and sister.

Even without the children, grandmother and I will need at least two thousand yen a month for a bare living. This does not count clothes and fuel, which would bring it up to two thousand five hundred yen (about six dollars) a month. These will just be covered by our tobacco and public assistance, but what about the debts we still owe? So my beautiful plan of buying a rice field is only a dream.

Our poverty is not due to inability or laziness. It is simply that we haven't enough land for our needs. How can a family of five subsist on two-thirds of an acre of land? There is nothing ahead but a losing struggle and final destitution. It was the fate of my father and my mother, and it will probably be mine.

When my teacher and the principal called on me a few days after the funeral, I intended to ask about my future, but before I had a chance to say anything, teacher Muchaku said, "Are you still carrying wood every day? How long will it take for you to get enough for the winter? What do you have to do next?"

I told him that, in spite of the help I received from the neighbors, I had a good deal more wood to carry, and after that I had to sort and smooth out the tobacco leaves.

"How long will that take?" he asked.

"I don't know," I replied.

"Don't you keep any records? Why don't you look at last year's record?"

I told him that there was no record for last year.

"No record?" he exclaimed. "That is no way to work. You should keep a record of the time it takes to do your work each year. How do you expect to make out a work schedule without a record? Begin from this very day to make a record. What do you do next?"

"I have to cover the house with straw mats before the snows come. After that, I think I can go to school."

"Which means that you will have only a few days at school this term," said Mr. Muchaku. "That will never do. Tomorrow when you go to get your rice ration, come over to school. You haven't been there for more than a month, and you have to see the boys and girls to thank them for what they did for you when your mother died. When you come, bring a plan of your work, written in a table form, and I will have a look at it."

When I heard this, a weight seemed lifted from my heart. When I finished my schedule, I found that, as my teacher had said, I had only a day or two in December for school. The next day I took my work plan to school and showed it to Mr. Muchaku. He looked at it carefully for a few minutes and then said, "Will you, Tozaburo, Soju, Shunichi and Tsutomu, go to the room of the teacher on night duty and wait there for me?"

When he went to that room, he handed my work schedule to Tozaburo, saying, "What do you think of this?"

Tozaburo read it and handed it to others. When they had all finished, the teacher said, "Well, how about it?"

"We can all finish up that work in no time," said Tozaburo, "can't we, boys? Then he can come to school like the rest of us." The boys smiled and nodded.

I couldn't say anything and had to blink hard to keep back the tears.

"Be sure you do the work systematically and efficiently," said the teacher. "Divide it up among you and get it done as quickly as possible." I could no longer keep back my tears, and they fell shamelessly onto my lap.

By early December, the boys and some of the villagers had finished up all my work, and I did not have to worry about not going to school. How happy I am to have such a teacher and such friends.

Tomorrow is the thirty-fifth day after mother's death. I will report all these things to her spirit. I will also promise her that I will study hard and try to find out why she had to work so hard with so little result and why people cannot earn enough to live on, even if they work every minute of their lives as she did. I also want to find out whether I can buy a rice field without causing the man who sells it to suffer.

In our school there is another boy, Toshio, who is even more unfortunate than I. He almost never goes to school, for he has to work nearly every day, rolling down logs and burning wood to make charcoal. Perhaps if we all get together, we can help him just as the boys helped me.

RICE WEEVILS

by Wada Den

THE GREEN LEAVES were all out. Sparrows played in pairs on the thatched roof, kicking up rotten old straws. When they fell, tripping over themselves, instead of landing on the grass, they fell right into the rice hulls. Surprised, they flew away. The pile of rice hulls had been made by Suke, who, of all things, had only now started rice hulling at this time of the year. It was an unwritten law among farmers that rice was to be hulled and packed away before the end of the year. Only lazy slowpokes left it unhulled over the yearend. If, because of some unforeseen disaster, the rice could not be hulled within the old year, it was usually finished within the New Year month. No one in his right mind left the task until this season of the year.

But Suke smiled at the sparrows that kept falling into the hull stack. It was a smile that showed complete contentment. It was nice to have everything working out as planned. It was not because Suke was an incurable slowpoke that he was doing what he did now. It was all included in his plan of things.

Last year his schedule had dragged nicely, or rather he had caused it to drag, taking only his son into his confidence; when he finally got around to the business of hulling rice, it was well into the month of December and time to prepare for the new year. Unmindful of his wife's cries of protest, he stopped hulling when he had enough for the government purchase quota and to last them until May. He told her that his hulling a little at a time from now on meant they would lose less each year to rats and rice weevils. It was true that the amount of rice lost annually because of rats and worms was considerable, but farmers had been losing rice like this for centuries. Lately everyone was putting their sacks in tin drums as a protection for the hulled rice. Suke not only gave no thought to buying such, but thought it a ridiculous idea.

Rats and rice weevils are ills ages old. There is nothing one can do about them. But at Suke's house the rats and weevils were not the same as those that bothered his neighbors or his ancestors; the pests demolished five and ten *sho* in one night, almost a sack a week. Suke remembered his own youth; when his son came of age, he was not so mean as to make much ado about the increased "rat" loss, but lately he had found out that the rats and worms were not his son alone.

When his son took on a wife, it became apparent. It was his son who started the fuss. He had stopped acting the rat when he married. Leaving the government rice aside, Suke measured out the rice for the family in front of them, telling them there was just enough to last them till May. That stopped the so-called rat raids.

Suke's wife, Ume, had gone to her brother's house that morning for three days. The brother's daughter was getting married. Suke was to follow his wife there on the day of the ceremony. "I'll take a present when I go," he said to Ume.

"Yes, that's fine," his wife answered. "But I can't go empty-handed today. I'd like to take some little thing, like cosmetics for the bride and sweets to the kids."

He should have given her money without being asked, but his innate stinginess, together with his suspicion that she might have some *hesokuri*, 'belly-button' money, secretly put away, kept him from offering. When he finally did put out some cash, with reluctance, Ume pouted at the small amount.

"It's different from an ordinary visit, you know," she whined. "I can't take any cheap stuff. There are no more share-cropping tenant farmers, don't forget."

He gave her a little more, but the way she had complained had angered him. Maybe it was this that had moved him to take out the milling machine.

Ume was his second wife, younger by ten years. He had a son by his first wife. Ume had married him in spite of this son because her family had been tenant farmers; Suke's family, on the other hand, had been landed farmers since generations back. It had been considered quite a Cinderella marriage. But her family held her good fortune against her, forever reminding her that while she had risen above her station, they had not; then the change in the land law, practically forced upon the Japanese by the Allied Occupation Forces, changed everything. It was ironical that it was Ume, for years the wife of a landed farmer, who had rejoiced over the new land law rather than her brother who, replacing his father as the head of the family, had benefited as much by the revolution as Suke and Ume had lost. Though it was now six years since the change, Ume rubbed it in every chance she had for the years of humiliation she had undergone. It infuriated Suke every single time.

"Enough to hold us till rice planting," Suke said to his son. "And about three sacks for selling should be plenty."

"I think so, if we can also sell some hogs," his son said.

Their minds were perfectly matched. Suke never mentioned to his son that he had intended to sell his hogs while Ume was away, but that too had been silently settled between them. "If we sell the hogs, then perhaps we need only about three bags." His son turned off the motor of the milling machine.

His son went to the hog dealer, who came by early the next day. The price of hogs was going down, he said, and told Suke to hang on a little longer until the price went up. Suke would not hear of it.

"You always buy high, sell cheap," the dealer remonstrated. "Then you blame it on me."

Suke saw the foolishness of selling his hogs now, but if he really wished to sell them without Ume knowing anything about it, now was the only time.

The dealer was telling the truth. But Suke said that it was only the rich farmers who could afford to raise hogs when feed was expensive. He wrapped a part of the money from the sale to take as the customary wedding present.

Ume was awakened by the noise her brother and his wife were making in the pigsty behind the house. Thinking maybe one of the litter was being squashed to death, she got up and went out to see.

The talk during dinner had been all about hog raising. Fifteen newborn was quite a litter in this time of low prices. "A mongrel may be cheap," her brother had boasted, "but mine are registered purebred hogs. They will bring not less than three thousand each."

"What happened, one squashed?" Ume shouted.

Her brother Kisuke looked excited, squatting in the middle of the pen. He held a tiny wriggling pig in his arms and his wife was counting the litter with both hands.

"What happened?" Ume asked again.

"What happened?" her brother repeated the question. "If someone had stolen one of my litter, I could understand it. But no we have sixteen instead of fifteen. How do you figure that?"

Kisuke babbled on. The one he held was the added member, he said. He had spotted it as a stranger and after a careful check, sure enough, he found he had one extra. A newborn like this couldn't have come of its own. Somebody must have planted it there. But what for?

"Maybe somebody came to change it for one of your good breed," Ume said, "then was interrupted and couldn't finish the job".

Her sister-in-law interrupted, saying, "That's just what I said my self, just before you came. It's better to have one stolen. This gives you a queer feeling."

Just then a man walked in and through the dirt-floored kitchen and came out back to where they were. "Say, Kisuke-san, you didn't have a baby pig stolen, did you?" He too held a baby pig in his arms.

"Nakatsugawa-san, it's the darndest thing, it's the other way around," Kisuke almost shouted. "They didn't steal one, they put one here instead."

"What?" Nakatsugawa exclaimed, round-eyed.

Nakatsugawa was a hog-raising specialist working in the Prefectural Domestic Animal Laboratory. He and Kisuke were on good terms because Kisuke was a conscientious hog raiser. Nakatsugawa said he had been awakened by the squeals of a baby pig in back of his house; when he went out to investigate, he found the piglet in the woods. Thinking it stolen from the lab, he had awakened the caretaker and checked, but the lab's litter had not been touched. Then he thought it had been stolen it from somewhere nearby and that, because it squeaked so much, the thief had left it where he later found it. So he came first to Kisuke to inquire.

Kisuke came out of the pen, still holding the baby pig he had just discovered in his own pen, and when he put his next to Nakatsugawa's, he exclaimed, "Look, it's from the same litter."

"So they have started throwing them away," Nakatsugawa remarked gloomily- "My gosh, Kisuke-san – – !"

"You think that's it?"

"But it's an interesting thought—instead of throwing them into a river or something, they do it this way."

"No concern to me," Kisuke grumbled. Only rich farmers could raise stray hogs at a time like this.

"What shall we do?"

"*Saah* . . . It's got me."

The sight of the bewildered twosome, each holding a baby pig, was so funny that Ume started to laugh.

Kisuke remarked. "Why don't you take it and raise it?"

Ume was thinking the same thing and was on the verge of speaking out her mind when Nakatsugawa joined Kisuke. "Don't buy a pig to raise," he said. "Raise a stray pig, that's the motto. In the fall, the price is sure to go up," he assured.

"When Suke-san comes, I'll speak to him for you," Kisuke said.

"At any rate, in this wedding uproar you must have your hands full, Kisuke-san," Nakatsugawa said, offering to take care of the stray pigs at the lab, and the two of them went across the field, each still holding the baby pig twins.

Ume's mind was made up to raise them. No matter what Suke said, she was going to keep them. Now that the rat holes were stopped up, she must think of some way to make her own spending money. She was tired of asking Suke to buy even her underwear. Unless she acted smart now, her stepson would be treating her the same way in her old age.

She waited for Suke to come. There were more reasons besides the question of the pigs that made her impatient to see Suke. Suke hadn't been here since the war ended. "When he comes, he will see with his own eyes how this place has prospered. Wonder what face he will make?" Ume chuckled.

"Huh, nothing but a tenant farm," he had often said derisively of the place before the new land reform law. But look at it now, a barn with an upstairs loft where they raised silkworms, the house newly roofed with zinc in place of thatch, with the whole south side porch enclosed by glass sliding doors, a chicken coop big enough to hold fifty, and a pigsty for four—all modern, up-to-date buildings. Suke boasted of being an independent farmer, but he can't even re-thatch his roof. Its rotten straw fell on her neck and gave her shivers every time sparrows took their exercise upon it and, worst, Suke did not seem to mind.

In this day and age when there was no longer any difference between the independent owner and the former tenant farmers, there was no reason still to have a feeling of inferiority, to feel Suke had rescued her from poverty and hopelessness; she was going to have it out with her husband once and for all. With that in mind, she went to look the place over just as Kisuke came back with a guest. "About the bride's escort, you don't mind going alone, do you?" Kisuke asked. "Suke-san doesn't have to go, does he?"

"Oh, it's all right, I suppose," she said readily.

"We have to match the number of our guests with the groom's, you know, and we'd be too many" Kisuke said apologetically.

The bride's escort party was composed of close relatives who took the bride over to the groom's house and stayed for the reception feast. Each side took pains to match the numbers as closely as possible since the wedding expenses were being split by the two families, as was the custom when the social and financial standings of the two families were on the same level. Ume, who was the bride's aunt, and her husband should be included in the party as a matter of course. In Kisuke's tone she noted that he thought lightly of Suke's position and his opinion reinforced her own feelings of a moment before. There now, you see? Ume said to herself, highly satisfied. The new guest who was to replace Suke was her youngest sister's husband, who, Ume had heard, was also making good lately because of the land reform law.

With the feast after the wedding ceremony over, Suke, who was not included in the escorting party, went home. He had come late and the house was already full of guests, Ume had not had much chance to talk to him about the pigs. She did manage to bring up the subject, but there had been no opportunity to discuss it at length. But she wasn't sorry. She couldn't expect much of an answer from him anyway.

During the three-mile walk to the groom's house her younger sister's husband came up beside her, saying, "Suke-san has sure aged lately, hasn't he?"

"Yes, all of a sudden," Ume answered.

"Like a father and daughter, with you," he remarked.

"Oh, you don't say." Ume laughed quietly.

"He isn't sixty yet, is he?" he asked.

"No, he is only fifty," she answered with emphasis.

"Well, he's sure aged."

"Yes, he's gotten so old, all the time he is worrying that rats and worms will eat his rice all up," Ume laughed openly. Remembering that this brother-in-law had been present when she talked to her husband about the baby pigs, she sensed that there was more on his mind than what he said.

"Is he the kind that leaves words written in the surface of the rice pile so no one can touch it without his knowing it?" her brother-in-law asked as her sister drew near too.

"That's not all," Ume answered, and then told them about Suke hulling just enough rice to carry over a certain period. Not only the bridal escort but the groom's party laughed, and the procession began to pass the joke around. People were still laughing as the procession, passing through several vales and over hills terraced in irregularly partitioned fields now sown in wheat, came to the village of the groom's house.

As they neared the outskirts, a group of men standing by the road—dressed in formal black attire of *haori* with family crest, and stiff silk skirt-like *hakama*, the groom's relatives who were not included in the wedding party, but who were invited only for the reception—were waiting for them. The waiting group stood rigid, and only bowed as the wedding procession passed in front of them.

Just then Ume saw a face. Startled, she looked away quickly. It couldn't—but then she saw him, she couldn't be mistaken. Why didn't she look at him closer, why did she look away so quickly? Yes, he must be Genji. What connection had he with the groom's house? He must have some or he wouldn't be standing there.

When the sake drinking started, Genji didn't even look at her. While the relatives were introduced, Genji stood back. The match maker was a poor talker and Ume couldn't understand half of what he said. Ume sat in the bride's group and Genji was sitting at the lower end at the groom's side. Ume tried to catch his attention several times, but he just sat drinking sake. He looked sturdy and with his healthy tan had the air of a well-to-do farmer. In his prime too. The way he drank his sake, too, reminded her of his aggressiveness of twenty years ago. She envied men, they didn't change as quickly as women, nor age as fast.

When the formality of the ceremonies began to break, it went down with the force of a landslide. Dancing and singing started and the seating places on both sides of Ume emptied quickly. The parties of the bride and groom mingled in merrymaking while twosomes sat here and there, talking loudly and exchanging drinks. Those who could not drink sat by the porch. Ume missed her younger sister, but soon found her talking among the women of the groom's side.

Not able to stand their open, ribald jokes, she was just getting up to join the porch group when suddenly, a sake bottle in one hand, Genji came and sat down in front of her. "Here, O-ume-san, have a drink on me," and he shoved a sake cup under her nose.

Overwhelmed by his insistence, all she could do was take the cup and utter faintly, "Why, it's Genji-san, isn't it?"

"Well, it's about time—I recognized you a mile away, and noded my courtesy then, a courtesy of twenty years. Anyway, drink it up," he ordered.

"Don't force me . . . please," she protested.

"But it's twenty years, isn't it? Haven't I got a right to force a little?"

Yes, it had been twenty long years, but Genji hadn't changed a bit. Ume looked at him with renewed interest. Genji, too, became a little sober and changing his sitting position slightly, started in on his tale. Genji now owned the house in the next village which Ume had passed on the way. He was a *yoshi*, a marriage arrangement in which the family name of the wife, who is usually the oldest or only daughter of a son-less house, is taken by the groom, who would be a second or third son because the first son must continue his own family name. Besides having quite a large farm, he was one of five big hog farmers in the village and quite naturally the conversation turned to the subject of hog raising.

"No, no, don't pick a stray pig to raise," Genji advised. "It can't be much of a pig. I'll give you a good one, a thoroughbred. You take it and raise it." He was dead serious.

"But I can't afford a thoroughbred," Ume replied.

"I said I'd give it to you, didn't I? For nothing. I'll take it to your place when it comes. My sow Yamabuki is expecting any time now. Yamabuki took a second prize at the county fair," he boasted. "A breeder from another prefecture offered two hundred thousand for her. But I didn't sell her. She is a beauty."

"But I can't take such a high-class hog. A cheap one is good enough for me," Ume said weakly.

"Don't be a fool. Cheap ones eat just as much."

When it came to hogs, Genji had much to say. He said he'd spent twenty years raising them. He had made his fortune with them, starting with only one sow, the sole inheritance that his brother had left him. The word brother, not father, puzzled Ume, but Genji's rapid speech left no room for her to ask questions.

"Anyway, it's right close by. Come and look at my place, will you?" He was already up, pulling Ume with him with one hand. The boisterous singing and dancing was still going on, no telling when it would end. Ume was thankful for the chance to get away.

Genji's house stood on the edge of the village, surrounded by zelkova and oak trees and, like Kisuke's house, it had been rebuilt after the war. She remembered that Genji's parents had been tenant farmers like hers. Walking close to the man she had once allowed to make love to her, she thought again of those times. At that time he had had Korea fever, like all the second and third sons of tenant farmers, thinking of emigrating to the then-colony where good land was available to homesteaders.

He had asked her to wait for him, he would come to get her when he had made his fortune. He had gone to Yokohama to make money to go to Korea, just about the time her marriage to Suke had been arranged without her prior knowledge. She didn't remember which happened first.

"And it was the damnedest thing," Genji started again. "Only about a half year after I got to Yokohama, my brother upped and died and I was called back to take his place."

"Then how came you to be a *yoshi*?" Ume asked, still puzzled.

"How come?" Genji turned to her. "It was second brother, who'd married into this family, that died, that's how come." He continued, "Left two kids. They'd lost grandpa the year before. Couldn't make a go of it for one day without a man so I was put there to take my brother's place."

"Oh! Now I understand."

"When I came, there were two kids, a woman fairly worn out by my brother, and a sow. But this sow was a beauty . . ." He disappointed her by talking some more about pigs. But then it didn't matter to her what he talked about.

"It's wonderful, your being so prosperous," Ume said, turning back to look at Genji's house again from the distance. But Genji started to laugh, but there was a faint hint of hollowness in his laugh.

"But look at me now. I've spent the best years of my life being a stud horse." There was even a bitterness in his tone of voice. "Just think. A young man of twenty-five, given a woman over thirty. She is seven years older. And as she is the head of the house, I cannot raise my head from my perpetual subservience to her all my life. Now that I think of it, the way I put my heart and soul into hog raising was maybe to distract myself and fill up an empty spot in my heart."

He continued brooding over it until Ume said, "If you've had no romance on the side, you regret your past. But now, you can't say that, can you?"

"Don't be a fool. I told you it was all hog raising, and nothing else. It was different then," he said.

The course of life was mapped out by one's parents. A boy replaced a dead elder brother, a girl took her dead sister's place. It was an unwritten law, he had had no choice.

"A big river dividing us, and I didn't know a thing." Ume blamed it on the river. Then she wondered if Genji had heard anything about her and she asked.

"If I'd heard anything, I suppose I wouldn't have let it go at that. You can't forget a person you once held in your arms." And without even a smile, he took hold of Ume's hand and squeezed it tight. She returned the squeeze and as if that were a signal, he stopped, pondered a second, changed their course and walked on into a dark grove of trees. After they walked a few paces into the darkness, through which Genji walked with sure steps, leading Ume by the hand, they came to an open space.

"An old race track," he explained. He kept on walking, and Ume followed blindly, her heart quivering with expectation. "Aren't you going to ask where we are going?" he asked, in a throaty voice.

Her heart was too full to answer.

Presently, he stopped at a spot where the grass was soft and dry under their feet, and put his arm around her waist. Without any hesitation, she threw herself into his arms.

Ume did not think Suke would consent as easily as that about the pig, but he simply said, "Okay, let's raise him, then."

"It takes guts, like the folks across the river." Folks across the river was a euphemism for her brother's.

"Yeah, some guts." But there was no sarcasm in his tone.

He certainly must have had his eyeful seeing with his own eyes the way her brother, whom he had always tended to look down upon, was doing so well. Then she got dressed to go to Genji, not listening to Suke's remark that she could send the reply by mail. Ume simply had to see Genji again.

Genji was working in the field. It was the biggest field she had seen and when she remarked about it, Genji said there weren't many fields as big as that in his neighborhood either.

"And it's all yours, too?"

He simply nodded, as if to say, of course. The fact that he said it so matter-of-factly reminded Ume that it had been some time since the new law went into effect. In fact, it could hardly be called new now. Yet it was just recently that she had begun to feel its effects.

"My, but it's wonderful," she said, half enviously.

"You too can do it," he added, half smiling. "Don't be taken for a rat or a rice weevil all your life."

"Then you know?" and she laughed. "Besides I'm not a daughter of a tenant farmer anymore, you know."

She said it with an implication, but she wondered if Genji could catch her meaning, or begin to understand the ordeals of the years of humiliation she had undergone. Then she was caught in the emotion of the loss of twenty years of happiness.

"You know, it was you I really came to see today," and she looked at him as wistfully as a maid of sixteen.

"You go ahead, and I'll follow you shortly," he said, moving the hoe all the while he talked.

She had walked about a quarter of a mile toward the town in the opposite direction from her village when Genji caught up with her on a bicycle. She got on behind him and the two rode toward the next big town where they would stop at an inn.

UPS AND DOWNS

by Shibaki Yoshiko

A LITTER of two-month-old pups, three in all, had just been fed their supper of ground meat and rice gruel. Their tummies full, they became lively and climbed all over her lap.

"No, no. Not till you get your mouths and ears wiped," and she cleaned gruel from their long ears and around their mouths.

Saeko was raising them to make some money, but she had a genuine love for them, too, so she wished to sell them to some nice people who would take good care of them. She thought of her many friends, not entirely without envy, who had married well. She herself was happy, if not nearl as well off as she would have been were it not for the war.

Her husband, a college professor, did not bring much money home. She had married him out of a girlish craving for a man who might gain fame through his intellect, rather than through physical prowess. But now, looking at the house under construction next door, the speed with which the man next door made his wealth—he was a taxi driver who only a few years ago had opened a small repair shop, and was now building a garage—and comparing it with her own house, she thought that being the wife of a taxi driver wouldn't be so bad. She wondered, at the rate they were going, when she would ever get a new house. That is why she had taken up puppy raising, to help ease the domestic finances. She was aware that to own a pedigreed dog had become a fad among social and well-to-do

219

people. As a prospective buyer of one of her pups she thought of Kuri Reiko, her old school chum.

Reiko, daughter of a well-known Doctor of Law, was married to the son of a prominent businessman. Two or three years after the war had ended, Saeko's graduating class got together. It was the first time in years. They had met regularly up till the first few years of the war. In the chaotic social conditions that followed the end of the war, social get-togethers were rare. For one thing, no one knew where anybody else was. But as things gradually returned to normal, the girls came together to talk over the hard times they had had. Most came dressed in drab clothes, but not minding at all.

Among this drably dressed group Saeko remembered how Reiko shone. She looked radiant, not only because of her natural beauty, but because she was dressed immaculately. Everyone looked at her with envy. She had come to the meeting in her own private car. Somehow, Reiko always had, even from their school days, a natural charm that prevented other women from being jealous of her good fortune. Maybe it was because she was not haughty, though she was proud.

Reiko told the girls gathered there that her husband was doing very well. But Saeko had since heard Reiko's husband was not doing so well, that they had sold their house in Tokyo and retired to their villa in Chiba prefecture.

"It must be a nice little villa by the sea," dreamed Saeko. "Just the home for one of my puppies."

The pups had played themselves out, and were now sound asleep, piled up on top of each other.

Her small son came running into the house. "A policeman followed me from the school, and he is now standing outside, Mummy," he told her.

Her heart made a small jump as she heard the word "police," and went to the door, wondering what he could want of her.

"You are Mrs. Suzaka, the wife of Suzaka Keitaro?" the young policeman asked her politely.

"Yes, that's right." Her voice shook a little as she heard her husband's name mentioned by the police.

"Do you know a woman by the name of Kuri Reiko?"

"Yes, I know her," she answered, relieved, but wondering at the odd coincidence.

"What has happened to Mrs. Kuri?"

"She's been arrested, but she's being released," he said, "She has to be released into the custody of someone, and she mentioned your husband's name."

"But isn't there some mistake?" Saeko said, unable to believe her ears. "She is not the type to be arrested. She comes from a very good family."

Yes, of course," the young policeman admitted, and looked ill at ease.

"Tell me," Saiko persisted. "What has she done?"

"I don't know the details," the policeman said. "I was sent here by my chief, but I heard it was a light offense."

"Well, I'll go to the police station," Saeko said firmly. "I have to first make sure."

The policeman thanked her and went away.

The atmosphere of the police station was oppressive, even to Saeko with her clear conscience. She could not enter into it as light-heartedly as she would a post office. When she sat before the officer in charge of Kuri Reiko, she had the feeling that she herself was being questioned, though the officer was very polite. She noticed the sharp difference between his manner and the cold arrogant manners of the pre-war police of the Imperial Government. The officer asked her about her relationship with Reiko, and about Reiko herself.

"Well, then it is true that she's from a good family, as she insisted she was," the officer said in the end. "Come to think, she does have that air about her."

"I have not seen her for two or three years," Saeko said. "What has she done?"

"Shoplifting," he answered. "Her second offense."

Saeko turned pale. She was astounded, it was the last thing she had expected.

"She did it twice in the same shop, a second-hand clothes shop. The owner wants her indicted but, being a wife and a mother, we decided to release her into the custody of some socially responsible person. She would not tell us the names of her own people, only yours."

Presently a haggard-looking woman was brought before Saeko. She wore a skirt too short for her and a faded sweater. Saeko could not recognize the woman at first. Then, as the contours of the woman's face became clear, she saw that it was Reiko, and she could hardly believe her eyes.

The officer gave a short lecture and said, after the brief procedure to effect Reiko s release, "Please take her home and have your husband give her a good talking to."

Once outside, Saeko took Reiko to a nearby noodle shop. After a bowl of hot noodles, faint color reappeared in Reiko's pale cheeks and she smiled for the first time. "Thank you very much," she murmured, "I have not eaten for three days."

"For three days?" Saeko was appalled.

"Yes, three solid days. You see, it was my only way to show my resistance. They called me a thief. I am not. How could I do such a thing, and disgrace my family and my parents' name? You know that, you know I am not that kind." She said these things in one breath, and her eyes shone in her otherwise dull face with outrage.

"Yes, yes, I know," Saeko said, trying to comfort her. "Tell me about it."

"I don't know where to begin," said Reiko, looking lost.

"The last I heard about you, you had moved to Chiba suburb," Saeko said, by way of helping her. She refrained from telling Reiko that she had been considering her as one of the prospective buyers of her puppies.

"That was such a long time ago," Reiko said dreamily. Actually it had been only three or four years.

Then Reiko began to explain. The last time she and Saeko had been together was about the time when her husband Kuri began to fail in his business. They had to sell their house in Tokyo. Immediately after the war ended, Kuri, who made use of his grandfather's connection with the pre-war government-subsidized South Manchurian Railway Company, supplied materials to the Japanese government railways. It was still the time when things were scarce and everything he touched made money. But as things returned to normal and pre-war companies got back on their feet, competition became too keen. As a last hope, he put everything into selling the railroad a patent. He spent a great deal of money bribing officials, dreaming that once he succeeded, his company would grow tenfold. He failed and lost everything.

Reiko took her two small children and went to Chiba. Kuri went to Tokyo every day to find some capital. He used to bring home men Reiko never saw before, men whose looks made her distrust them immediately, but her husband asked her to entertain them and she would sell her prized kimonos and obis to do it.

Some of her husband's friends tried to find him a job, but he would not let go his desire to have a business of his own. "My life is through if I have to be tied to somebody with a meager salary," he would say. When he told Reiko that he was sure to make good once more, she believed him and, believing him, did not hesitate to sell her clothes. Saeko remembered that Reiko's trousseau was the talk of her friends. Reiko sold her kimonos one by one.

"At first, it was fun to get cash for a kimono, a kimono I was tired of, or that I was too old for, I was not a bit sorry to sell," Reiko said. "The children were still small so I kept my maid. You see, I did not know what it is to economize," she said, laughing to cover her embarrassment.

She didn't know when Kuri did it but, after about two years in Chiba, she found out that the villa there had been mortgaged, and they had to move back to Tokyo. They found a small room in the suburbs of Tokyo, not far from where Saeko lived. She gave up her maid, but she was the type that could not call on her relatives without taking a present, even if she had to sell one of her obis to raise the money. It was the training she'd received from her grandmother, who had gone to Gakushuin Peers' school. No matter where she went, she met only criticism of her husband. Some even suggested that she get a divorce, though no one offered to take in her and her two small children.

She had no ability to earn a living. She had been trained to be a wife and mother. Piano, flower arrangement, tea ceremony and dressmaking, studied when a girl, were all useless as means of earning a livelihood. Her only hope was in Kuri. Kuri kept saying that he would make good once more and she blindly believed him. She was disappointed in him and no longer loved him, but she continued to believe, as he believed, that he would make a comeback. It was the kind of belief that only they could understand. They had to have it — it was all they had.

About three months ago, Kuri wanted to take a trip to Osaka in a desperate effort to find a backer. He had no money to buy a ticket, and as he told her that he was certain of the success of this trip, she took her last dress kimono and matched *haori* coat to the second-hand kimono shop she always dealt with.

"This kimono and this *haori* I don't want to sell," she told the shopkeeper "I want to borrow some money with them. As soon as my husband makes some money, I will come back to claim them, so please do not put them on sale until then."

"That's all right," said the shopkeeper, and gave her the money.

The kimono and *haori* she left at the shop were old; they were her mother's last present before she died. Reiko recalled the sadness she felt when she lost her mother. She consoled herself with the idea that they would be returned to her as soon as Kuri came back from Osaka. In spite of this sacrifice on her part, Kuri returned empty-handed.

"What are we going to do?" she asked her husband. "We have nothing to eat."

"Go to some relative or friend and borrow some money," he ordered.

"I have nothing to wear to go out."

"I'll make some money soon."

"Have you made any at all lately?"

"This time for sure," Kuri smiled. "The House of Kuri has a large piece of land in Aoyama cemetery. We don't need that big space. I am going to sell a part of it."

"What a thing to say," and she loathed her husband as she never had before, for even thinking such a thing.

She had to go some place to borrow some money, and to do so she needed decent clothes to wear. She went to the second-hand kimono shop, and asked the shop owner to let her have the kimono and *haori* for just one day. He refused and would not listen to all her pleadings. In the end, taking advantage of another client that came in, she made for the kimono and *haori* and started to go out. The shopkeeper grabbed her, took her kimono and *haori* from her, and knocked her down in the scuffle. She almost died of shame. She was furious when she thought of the money the shopkeeper had made through her kimonos during the past three years. She thought she would not hesitate to sell the family cemetery, even her life, to avenge this.

Kuri continued to dream of the great business he would again transact. "I am going to try once more," he said, and left the house without saying where he was going.

Kuri did not return. She spent a week as if dead. Then one night after a heavy snowfall she went out into the street. When she passed the front of the secondhand kimono shop, she saw her own kimono in the window, "for sale." It looked so forlorn to her, it seemed as if it were pleading with her, begging her, to take it away from the store. She went to it, absentmindedly, and held it tight to her breast. That was all she did.

"Did you tell all that at the police station?" Saeko asked.

"Of course I did," she said flatly. "But they would not release me unless someone with good social standing claimed me. I am sorry I made use of your husband, but I could not let this be known among my relatives."

They both looked up at the clock at the same time; they were both thinking of the children who must be waiting for their return.

"Please take something to your children." Saeko gave her some money, unobtrusively.

"Thank you for everything." Reiko bowed low, without looking at the money as she hesitantly accepted. "I shall never forget."

Saeko watched her walk toward the station and stood there until she disappeared into the crowd.

SAZANKA

by Kawachi Sensuke

MRS. NAKAGAWA SUMIYO, who arranged negotiations for this marriage, and Mr. and Mrs. Ikeda, who consented to be formal go-betweens at the wedding ceremony, all arrived right after lunch. The beauticians came soon after and started readying Miyoko for the wedding.

As the household got caught up in the excitement of the approaching wedding hour, Kosuke lost all his equanimity. He went to look in at the memorial altar of his dead wife, stood there for a moment gazing at its ebony black surface, its gold letters shone in the flickering candlelight. He went into his study to lie down, but could not stay more than five minutes. He got up and went into the dining room to get something, and quickly forgot what he had gone there for.

"Surely, I am not getting old," he muttered, and waved his hand before his face as if to throw off the idea. Coming from the dining room he passed in front of Miyoko's room. They must have forgotten to shut the door for he saw, reflected in the tall mirror, Sumiyo in her bright undergarment. His heart skipped; he swallowed hard, and walked quickly away. To his great surprise an old forgotten emotion was aroused and stirred within him. He blushed. His heart was still thumping when he entered the dining room for the third time and sat down.

"You look like a stray pup," his sister Katsue laughed at him.

"You know, aunty," his oldest son said, "There is a saying in Europe that when young grapevines bloom, old wine ferments also. Maybe father wants a new wife, too."

This, coming from his own son, embarrassed him and Kosuke turned crimson. "Don't say that," he said, weakly- "At a time like this, a father doesn't know what to do."

Katsue did not know that Kosuke was aroused and bewildered at seeing Sumiyo. She had only seen him standing forlornly before his dead wife's altar, *I suppose he thinks of her at times like this,* she thought to herself and, as soon as Miyoko's wedding was over, *I must settle the question of marrying Sumiyo off to Kosuke.*

"You had better get dressed too," Katsue said. "Miyo-chan will be ready before you are."

Kosuke had known Sumiyo thirty years before when he was still in college. Kosuke's family villa had adjoined Sumiyo's in Ashiya, the summer resort town near Osaka where the families used to spend summers together. They had been in love, but neither of them had confessed it to the other. In those days life was easy, not so rushed as it was now, and people took these things more leisurely. Kosuke had entered a university in Tokyo. Then one day in the autumn, as he was absently watching the fine, threadlike rain fall on the brilliantly yellowed gingko leaves in the backyard of the boardinghouse where he stayed, the mailman had rung. It was a letter from his sister, Katsue, telling him that Sumiyo had married a rich man's son to save her father's declining fortune. He remembered reading it as if reading a cheap pulp magazine story.

It was not very long after this that he fell blindly, madly in love with Aiko, daughter of the boardinghouse owner. His father took this as a disgrace to the family and disowned him. It was only because of his mother that he was able to finish university. His father's large store had been handed down through many generations. Being a merchant through and through, he did not like Kosuke's going to university. The only reason he did not oppose it entirely was because Kosuke was second son, and first son had given up schooling after he'd finished high school to help his father. Kosuke often thought that father would have been happier had he at least taken a course in business instead of literature.

"Ah well, I entered the university against my father's wishes," he had told Aiko. "I might as well go all the way and marry you."

In spite of Aiko's deep affection for him, he had been bothered for a long time by Sumiyo's image coming over the face of Aiko every time he held her in his arms.

After he finished university, he taught school to make a living. It was not until he became the father of four children that he was able to depend solely on his writing for his income. The war with China had then developed into the Pacific War, and in its third year his own first son, Ichiro, a student in college, was drafted. After being sent to the front, this son was missing for a long time, and it was not known whether he was dead or alive. One day, late in the spring of the year after the war ended, Ichiro came back. By then, both Kosuke and Aiko had turned gray with worry. And yet, Kosuke remembered, during the time Ichiro was missing, neither of them hardly ever talked about him. Perhaps it was because each knew what was uppermost in the mind of the other.

With Ichiro's return, the family suddenly came alive. It was as though oil had been freshly added to a dying lamp whose light, in its renewed strength, now reached every corner of the house. And yet, and yet, in spite of all this rejoicing, Ichiro silently and glumly turned his back to them all.

"Did you eat lizards, too?" Shinji, the second son, would ask.

"I bet you ate slithery snakes, also," Ryozo, the youngest, would pipe in.

"Oh, shut up and go away," Ichiro would finally shout. The little ones were just at that inquisitive age when they wanted to know every thing about strange lands. They would look hurt and disappointed at their brother's reaction, while Ichiro would look as though an old wound had been torn open. He was drunk most of the time and spent all the money his father gave him on drink and gambling. Whenever he ran out of money, he would sell his overcoat or other clothing on the spot. Although he lost some of his emaciated look as time passed, thanks to his mother's and sister's loving care, his behavior did not improve.

"Like a hoodlum," his mother said sadly. "If he should be led to take part in one of those robberies—."

Newspapers at the time were full of news about gang holdups and robberies by repatriated servicemen who had lost their spiritual sustenance in the defeat which came after they had been led to believe deeply in their country's final victory.

Kosuke and Aiko could not sleep on nights he was out.

The atmosphere of the family returned to darkness, darker than the time when he was missing.

"Father and Mother don't say much to you, but you have no idea how much they are worried," Miyoko said one night when she had him alone and cornered. "I think I can appreciate how you feel, but to me a life of nihilism is a living hell. It is only by fighting against this temptation that our lives take on any meaning. You know that without my telling you, and I know that you are not such a weakling."

At first Ichiro refused to listen to her, pretending that he didn't hear. But she kept it up, gently but firmly. Suddenly Ichiro's face took on an expression of extreme agony and he turned aside.

"No, I am a weakling," he said. "I just don't know how to continue to live in this topsy-turvy world of ours," and Miyoko then saw tears in his eyes, although Ichiro did his best to hide them. Miyoko felt that she had won.

It was not only Ichiro, but Kosuke too, for that matter, who had found himself unable to cope with a world that had changed so suddenly after the war. His being able to remain calm was perhaps due to his age; he was able to submit instead of straining against circumstances.

Even so, he remembered now on the wedding day how he used to sit all day, doing absolutely nothing but listen to the waves of the sea wash against the side of his house on the Kugenuma beach. He might have stayed like that until death claimed him had it not been for his wife Aiko's sudden death.

One day in autumn, when the sound of the waves was high, and the delicate pale pink blossoms of the sazanka tree quivered in the wind that had changed to the north, his wife Aiko came down with acute peritonitis. She suffered only one week. "I am so grateful that I saw Ichiro back and alive" began her last conscious words to the gathered family. "And I am also grateful that I am able to die on *tatami*. Please find a loving bride for Ichiro and a fine husband for Miyoko. Ichiro, my only worry is about you. You take care of Shinji and Ryozo, will you? And take care of father. Don't make him sad." After she fell into a coma, all she talked about was Ichiro. She died holding Kosuke's hand. She was fifty, and they had been married for twenty-six years.

For a while Kosuke felt as though he had lost his spiritual support, like a boat that had lost its rudder in the foggy sea. He would remain inert for hours on end—then suddenly a gust of sadness and misery would come over him and he would work furiously to overcome it. Above all, what hurt him most was the realization that he had not remained emotionally faithful to Aiko through all those years. He thought that he must live until all four children became independent and found their happinesses, that it was the only way he could repay his debt to Aiko's departed soul.

Three years had since passed since her death. Ichiro had gradually regained his composure, landed a job in a publishing company and was busy running about, getting articles and stories from writers like Kosuke.

"You have recovered from your repatriate sickness, haven't you?" Kosuke teased him one time.

"Repatriate sickness? Well, I wouldn't brush it off as easily as that—but—" He grinned sheepishly. "It was a form of psycho neurosis, I guess."

They had both laughed it off happily. Kosuke felt that it was Aiko's prayer on her deathbed that had saved Ichiro. Ichiro was now twenty-eight and Miyoko twenty-six. Kosuke told himself he had to find them good partners and life companions, as he had promised Aiko. He wished that they would find someone by themselves. Come to think of it, Ichiro seemed to have found a girlfriend, though he hadn't admitted it yet. But Miyoko had no opportunity since she kept house after her mother's death. She had by nature great perseverance. Aiko often used to say that she wished Miyoko and Ichiro were reversed in their nature. Miyoko would never complain about her own hard lot.

Then Kosuke took notice of Miyoko for the first time—that her hands were chapped, her complexion, which she never had time to look after, had coarsened, and all in all, she looked not at all the way a marriageable young lady should look. What chance had she to get a husband, looking like that? From the next day he put on his old clothes and helped her clean around the house, something he had never done all his life.

"Please father, don't," Miyoko teased. "Don't make it rain, I want my washing to dry."

One day Kosuke did his own washing and Miyoko was furious. She said he was doing it to spite her. Was he dissatisfied with her housekeeping? She burst into tears. Kosuke watched her cry herself into hysteria and decided that something really must be done.

He wrote to as many friends as possible, sending Miyoko's photos with his letters. An answer soon came back from his sister Katsue. She said that Sumiyo, whom Kosuke must remember, was in Osaka recently, though she really lived in Tokyo. She had become widowed and, when told about Miyoko, said that she knew of a young man who would be just the type for Miyoko. "At any rate she will call as soon as she gets back to Tokyo."

The letter concluded, "Sumiyo still uses her married name, but recently she was legally divorced from her former husband's family register. She also said that her folks want to marry her off again. When I told her about your being a widower, her face brightened and she hinted that she might refuse the marriage talk of her folks."

Kosuke had to smile at Katsue's usual busybody attitude, always meddling in someone else's affairs. And yet he could not really get angry with her. Why? Then he realized that he had not, after all these years, really forgotten Sumiyo; that it was she, or rather her image, that had always stood between him and Aiko.

Sumiyo came about ten days later. Kosuke received her full of anticipation, like a young boy meeting a girl for the first time. Sumiyo was reticent at first, but after their business about Miyoko's prospective husband had broken the ice, the talk turned to the old days. As the years disappeared, there hovered around her an air of womanly charm that was most bewitching to Kosuke.

"Do you have children?" he asked.

"No, I was never blessed with any," she answered, and the way she blushed when she said this intrigued Kosuke.

"No wonder you are still so young," he said.

That night his old heart itched for the first time since his wife died.

The negotiations for Miyoko's marriage were carried out smoothly. At first Miyoko had refused to be married off, saying there will be no one to take care of the family. "You marry first," she said to Ichiro, "then there will be someone, a woman in the house, to take care of you all."

"No, I can't agree with you," Ichiro said flatly. "Of course I appreciate . . . we all appreciate . . . how you took care of us after mother died. But I don't want you to stay with us at the sacrifice of your own marriage. I would feel obligated to you too deeply; the feeling would be a burden to me, to all of us, and would nag at us. I can't express myself very well, but father, you know what I mean don't you?" he concluded.

"Yes, yes," Kosuke said. "I know exactly what you mean."

Ichiro smiled at his father and said: "This is as good a chance as any, so I am going to tell you now and have your understanding, I am going to marry soon. You remember Matsunaga Shusaku, a college chum of mine? It's his sister. It's all right, isn't it, father?"

"Why, of course, if you like her," Kosuke said happily. "It's perfectly all right with me. But my finances aren't in good enough shape for both of you to get married at the same time."

"That you don't have to worry about," Ichiro said. "Miyoko has been working for our family for nothing, so you will naturally have to pay for her wedding. But I have been saving, and with my savings and my fiancee's savings together, we should be able to have our own apartment."

"Then what are you going to do about the *yuino* exchange of gifts and money between the families of the betrothed couple, and then the wedding?"

"I don't believe in *yuino*. That custom should be done away with," Ichiro said strongly. "The wedding ceremony—well, I am going to have a simple one, just with close relatives, a few friends. And the reception will be very small also."

Kosuke agreed with him in every way, but he felt as though there was an empty space somewhere in his heart.

Ichiro is terribly matter of fact, he thought to himself. But then I suppose you can call it American rationalism. Just then Miyoko looked up.

"I think I will marry, father," she said bashfully, but with a bright smile.

"By all means," Kosuke said emphatically. "Don't worry about us. We'll manage. I might marry too, who knows!" And they all laughed happily.

Yuino for Miyoko was exchanged and the wedding date set. The formal go-between was decided upon as Mr. and Mrs. Ikeda, old family friends, because Sumiyo, the actual go-between, was a widow and could not act formally in that capacity at the ceremony. While the wedding preparations were going on, Sumiyo practically lived in Kosuke's house and looked after motherless Miyoko. But nothing was mentioned about the marriage between Kosuke and Sumiyo, al though it seemed tacitly assumed by both.

Then, on the wedding day, his sister Katsue began to tease him again with her sharp tongue. "Don't sit there like a borrowed cat, have a cigarette."

Kosuke simply smiled and sat down by the *hibachi* to warm his hands over its glowing coals.

"What are you going to do about Sumiyo?" Katsue asked. "If you settle that, I can go back to Osaka in peace of mind. Sumiyo says that nothing definite has been decided upon."

"Yes, I suppose it really is the best, but—" Kosuke stammered, searching for words. Katsue looked at him uncertainly.

Just then the two younger boys came home. When he heard their happy young voices at the front door, Kosuke, undecided till now, suddenly made up his mind.

"I don't think I'll go through with it," he said decisively. "The two boys are at critical ages. I don't want to risk making them unhappy because of my marriage. Aiko would never forgive me if anything should happen to them."

He felt empty inside, but light. He felt a bit guilty toward Sumiyo, but then he had never actually proposed to her.

I shall continue to cherish her image deep inside my heart, he thought.

A slanting ray of sunlight filled their small dining room. The dressing of Miyoko for the wedding would soon be finished.

BRINGING UP MOTHERS-IN-LAW

by John Fujii

ONE OF THE PLEASANT THINGS about life in Japan are the unexpected complications. Just about the time I thought I had everything licked, comes this cable from the folks in the good old U.S.A.

Father and mother were born in Japan but spent the last forty years in California, with time out for an occasional excursion to visit their grandchildren in Washington, D.C. and Chicago. Now they had decided to see Japan before they faded away. So like a couple of "Urashima Taro," they returned to the land of their birth.

Urashima Taro was the legendary Japanese character who befriended a lonely turtle; the turtle took him to a fairy Neptunian princess who lived at the bottom of the sea. He went to live in that mythical wonderland until one day he got homesick for his old homeland and came riding home on the back of the turtle only to find that everything in his homeland had changed—he had been away too many years.

So father and mother came riding back to Japan—by Japan Airlines instead of on the back of a turtle—to find everything had changed except the smell.

Nothing was left of the Japan that mother knew as a girl except for Fujiyama, the Imperial Palace and Shimbashi Station. They *oh*-ed and *ah*-ed all the way into Tokyo from Haneda Airport and were happily pleased to find everything at my house in Stateside shape,

234

including the plumbing. Mother kept on saying that she would have made the trip much earlier except for the memory of going to the old *benjo* and the ordeal of a public bathhouse, while father kept on asking whether the tap water was safe to drink.

During the first few weeks and our daily brushes with the traffic, father was glad he had given up driving ten years ago. "Too many people on the streets and they drive on the wrong side anyway," he complained.

Every time we ate sushi, it was always the same routine, "Do you think the tuna is safe to eat raw?" I assured them that the only thing radioactive was their imagination.

In our trips around the countryside, it was all I could do to curb my unfilial temper. They compared the Kamakura Buddha with the Statue of Liberty, Kegon Falls with Niagara, the Tsubame Express with the Super-Chief. I finally squeezed a begrudging concession out of them: they admitted that Fujiyama was unsurpassed. I noticed that they stood stiffly at attention one morning at Shinagawa when the Emperor's special train roared through the station.

They burst out with such unexpected observations that it was hard to keep from laughing. They expressed surprise that their grandchildren, going on four and six, spoke such good Japanese. They wanted to know whether the fresh milk was imported and who baked the bread. Now that they've slept on *futon* bedpads laid out on the *tatami* and eaten off the floor, they remember the vivid colors and bright spring days of their childhood. They recalled some of the ethereal beauties of ancient Japan and faced the realities of modern Japan. In the brief three months they spent in Japan, I got them to admit that life in Japan was pleasant and comfortably leisurely for a couple of exiles, seventy-odd years old, even without color television.

If you think you have mother-in-law troubles, a Japanese mother in-law adds additional complications. All through the "beautiful friendship," one often wonders whether he is marrying the girl or her mother. Every time you go courting, the mother serves the tea and cooks the dinner. When winter comes, you get a hand-knitted sweater which old mama-san has produced.

After the first few weeks, if your intentions are not strictly honorable, mama-san is a pretty hard obstacle to face. If your intentions are on the up-and-up, you have problems, too. Mother treats you like one of the family already. Eventually, you break the news of the impending nuptials and mama-san rushes down to the nearest shrine to determine the best day for the wedding. It doesn't make any difference whether it's in mid-summer heat or winter cold, it's mother who arranges the wedding details.

Mother tells you where you should spend the honeymoon and looks a mite unhappy when you decide to leave her at home during the nuptial excursion. As soon as the newlyweds are back from the honeymoon, mother is back sniffing around to find out when the baby is coming. If you haven't quite decided on a family, mother goes back to her priests and then announces the most auspicious day for a son. The parents don't count at all. They are expected to cooperate fully.

If the prospective heir is delayed for any of a thousand and one domestic reasons, the mother-in-law flutters about with a determination to thwart any apparent catastrophe. She worships at a temple dedicated to the phallic deities, she consults her herb doctor for a bitter tea that is supposedly good for future fathers, and otherwise creates such confusion around the household that the parents finally decide that it's probably better to have the baby now than wait a year.

Once the fateful pronouncement is made by the doctor that the wife is pregnant, then the mother-in-law really gets down to business. She moves in bag and baggage to supervise the household. She directs the prospective father's diet and the future mother is forbidden to eat anything but tradition-prescribed food. It doesn't matter whether you get food parcels from the States or your friends help you with U.S. military or embassy commissary supplies. Food that was good enough for her and for her grandmother is good enough for her daughter and the cans of nutritious food go up on the pantry shelves. The next few months are pretty hectic and, rather than face the inquisition of an irate mother-in-law, it's recommended that the father stay out of the way.

You don't worry about a name—she's got one picked out for the future offspring, which she has already decided is a son. If the baby should turn out to be a daughter, then mama-san won't speak to you —until the next confinement. If you are blessed with a son on the second try, mother is all smiles.

Japanese mothers-in-law may be a nuisance when it comes to having babies, but they are sort of nice to have around when you have problems. If you want to buy a piece of property to build a house, they usually scrape up the collateral. If you even casually mention that it's difficult to get some item of food, the old mother shuffles in from the country on the next Tokyo-bound train laden like a an old-time black market peddler.

Once the youngsters are well on their way to adolescence, mother in-law limits her visits to the New Year's holidays or a children's festival, when she insists they have a new kimono. When you try to explain that your current income does not warrant such foolish fineries, she usually trundles in with a kimono she has stitched together herself or provides a bolt of kimono silk.

She insists that the Japanese customs be maintained and you reluctantly comply.

A good mother-in-law is one's best friend in Japan.

THE COMMUNIST

by Abe Tomoji

SUZUTA WAS A DEFENDANT in the 1952 May Day riot trial. He came out of the public courthouse and was walking toward Hibiya when he ran into Ino. "Why, Suzuta," Ino exclaimed, walking towards him smiling.

How he has changed, Suzuta thought. He had not seen Ino since a year ago, when he had had coffee with him; when he had last seen him Ino was dirty and miserably dressed. Now he is the picture of prosperity, he thought. Why, he even wears a red necktie. And he's smiling.

"I'm really glad to see you," Ino said. "But what are you doing in this neighborhood?"

"The public trial," Suzuta answered, irked at Ino's absent-mindedness.

"Oh, that's right," Ino smiled, a bit embarrassed. "I'm sorry. Well, I wish you all the luck. I suppose I shouldn't be walking through this neighborhood. They say they are still pinching those who 'went' that day."

"You'll be all right, I'm sure," Suzuta said.

"Anyway, have supper with me, won't you?" Ino asked. "I know a place near here—an inexpensive Chinese restaurant, but the food is excellent."

Suzuta looked at him, puzzled.

"Don't worry, I didn't rob anybody," Ino laughed. "I just happened to fall into some money."

Suzuta did not possess the power to resist. His stomach, too long used to poor food, stirred inside him; it would not allow him the luxury of refusing. He followed Ino until they came to the broad intersection of Toranomon, the Tiger Gate, when Ino suddenly stopped. "Hey, Suzuta, wasn't it around here where we started our zig-zag snake dance that day?"

"Yes, I believe so," and Suzuta remembered that day two years earlier as if yesterday.

It had been a bright day like this. He and Ino, their arms tightly interlocked, marched at the head of the students' section of the long parade that followed. They were covered with dust and sweat and their voices were hoarse from yelling the old country-festival nonsense rally cry "*Washoi, washoi.*" They passed by Toranomon, the 'Tiger Gate' of the Imperial Palace, and marched into Hibiya Park then rested a bit, harangued by leaders. They resumed the snake dance, its tempo rose and suddenly, as if possessed, they streamed out of the Park, past Hibiya intersection and the American Army of Occupation[1] G.H.Q. building, headed toward Babasaki-mon intersection to storm into the broad, tree-lined open space of the Imperial Palace Plaza. The last he remembered was being trampled by the counter-attacking police and struck on the back of the head by a night stick.

He lost his glasses, got up and tried to run away. Everywhere there were whirls of dust, and he heard a pistol shot. He picked up a bamboo stick and, waving it high in the air, rushed toward a group where several police had caught a rioting student. Knocked down again, he was grabbed by the police and arrested, taken to jail and indicted for trial.

Suzuta had first met Ino at a preliminary "warm-up" rally in the Palace Outer Garden. Seeing that Ino, too, was a student, Suzuta and he joined as new friends and locked arms together in the main march.

Suzuta was questioned many times and asked to reveal the names of those who were with him at the May Day riot, but he did not once mention Ino's name. Suzuta considered himself a true Liberal. He did not know anything of Ino's political ideology, nor

---

[1] The Allied, really U.S., occupation of Japan had ended formally only a few days prior.

did he particularly care. It was simply that he did not think it right
to reveal the names of those who were with him; his imprisonment
gave him a chance to nurture a long dormant fighting spirit.

Held for eventual trial, he was bailed out in the winter of the
following year, and that was when his fight for existence began. His
family, never well-to-do, stopped his allowance completely. His
body became run-down working at cheap manual labor. He was on
his way back from one prospective clerical job that he hadn't gotten
and was in extremely low spirits when for the first time since his
release he ran into Ino, who had stopped his milk delivery bicycle
in front of Suzuta, stuck out his hand and gripped Suzuta's bony
hand. Suzuta perceived that Ino was thanking him in silence for
having protected him.

"Come to my place for a minute," Ino said that day over a year
ago. "I ran under cover immediately after that mess and came here.
There is always a job delivering milk, thank god." Ino led him into
a back street that was dark and dirty and with the atmosphere of
the bottom of a gully. Suzuta guessed that Ino had come to a place
like this better to escape the police. That meant Ino knew where to
go to get away. Then, unlike himself, who had gone to the May Day
parade more out of curiosity than conviction, he thought this Ino,
dirty and disheveled, must be a regular member of the Communist
Party. I had better look out for him, Suzuta thought over his cup of
coffee.

Ino had gone on talking about the hardships of the life of a milk
delivery boy and had ended by saying that he was just about at the
end of his physical endurance. He had not attended school for
months, he said. "I appreciate your protecting me by not divulging
my name," Ino thanked him that first time, offering him a cake in
that small, dirty shop near the station. "I understand you're asking
for an individual trial, instead of a collective trial with the rest.
May I ask why?"

Suzuta wondered, How could Ino, living under cover in a place
like this, know such a thing so fast? He really must be a big figure
in the Party, he thought. Suzuta decided he would put Ino to a test.
"I wish to promote May Day as the day of peaceful festival for free
workers. And I wish to advocate this as a Liberal, and not as a
Communist."

"I wonder if that lot would understand such a subtle
distinction?" Ino answered.

Just then a tall young man walked in. His dark gold hair shone wet, his eyes were bluish, and his skin fair. He looked like a half-blood, a Eurasian, but he was as miserably dressed as Ino. The young man nodded to Ino and sat at their table. When the fair-haired stranger left them after a cup of coffee, Suzuta could not help asking who this strange-looking young man was.

Ino explained that Okijima Taro was half Japanese, half Russian. His father, a White Russian, had escaped the 1917 revolution by fleeing across Siberia and China to Japan where he had married a Japanese woman and taken her name for naturalization. Taro had lost his parents during the air raids and his aunt in Osaka had taken him in, but she had not been very kind to him. Eventually he left her and made a living as best he could—which included a number of fringe enterprises. He was a good fighter, as his fair features in wartime Japan necessitated, so everybody feared and respected him. He was always getting into trouble with women, too. He sold dope, but one of his partners cheated, ran away with all the profits.

"He must have done something serious, and come to Tokyo to take cover in this neighborhood," Ino added. "Taro got a job teaching Russian to a group of university students. I'm in that group. All the girls seem to fall in love with Okijima and I can't keep pace with the feverish way the girls study. One of the girls seems to have won out and at present Okijima is head over heels in love with her. But the girl's father is a very strict type, a government official, and has virtually imprisoned her in the house. Okijima goes near her house every evening, hoping to get a glimpse of her." Okijima had come in, Ino explained, to get a cup of coffee to fortify himself against the long hours of freezing vigil near her house.

While listening to Ino, Suzuta had been seized with an uncanny feeling that Ino was making up his story, that Okijima was actually more than just a teacher of Russian. He had thought that Ino himself might be trying to make use of the Russian class as a means of getting to the women students for political reasons. Suzuta had decided that day that he had really better stay clear of Ino.

The conversation in the coffee shop had taken place a year before. A short time after that first encounter with Ino, Suzuta changed his mind and decided to ask to be included in the collective trial instead. He has been attending court two or three times every week for the year since.

Now the twosome entered a small Chinese restaurant near Tora-nomon. "Please order anything you like," Ino said. "You will have some beer, of course."

Suzuta was still puzzled. Is this the same Ino that he saw over a year ago, on that snowy day, looking so gaunt? "Ha, Ha. Why do you stare at me like that?" Ino asked. "Is there some secret written on my face?"

"That's what I am trying to find out," Suzuta answered. "The change is so great."

"It's nothing. I just happened to fall into a little money," Ino answered cheerfully. "That is, I am going to. I think my *arbeit*, my side job, is going to make a hit."

Suzuta had an uncanny feeling again, that Ino must be doing something extraordinarily unusual. He was overwhelmed with curiosity. "What are you doing, anyway?" he asked.

"Well, I don't know quite how to explain—it's a sort of racket, frankly, with Americans as 'clients.' It's called 'consulter.'"

"Is there such an English word?"

"I think there is."

"Does that mean one who consults, or one who receives consultation?" Suzuta asked, curious.

"You are still the same. What difference does that make? A name doesn't mean anything, it's the business I'm interested in.

"I see. And what is the business?"

"We find, through classified ads, that there are people who want to sell their cars or something. We telephone them," he explained. "We call and say, 'you want to buy a dog,' or 'your dog has run away,' 'you need a maid,' or 'you have old books to sell,' or 'electric icebox to sell,' something like that. By the way—do you know of anyone who wants to buy an electric icebox?"

"No, I don't know anyone who wants to buy one. But you've certainly thought up some great business, haven't you?"

"No, I didn't think of it. I was working for a fellow until recently who thought it up. He made a mess of the business by getting himself tangled up with women. I took it over. I got the job through school. I saw a want ad for a student fluent in English. There were four who answered it. Two didn't pass the test. The other fellow and I passed the test, carried on the business, and for a while made quite a lot of money. You want to come in on it?"

"No, I'm no good at a thing like that."

"It's nothing difficult. Just a little bluff. I use 'living' English. Not the stuffy, dead English they teach in school. I call up U.S. colonels, majors, even generals. They call me back. I go to their homes, offices, wherever they want me to. Everywhere I go, I use 'living' English and I get what I want. I get my business done."

Suzuta was again caught with that strange feeling that Ino was making up his story, to cover up something else. Suzuta thought it was possible Ino might be thinking of something big for his Communist group, hiding behind the bourgeois capitalist cloak of this new consulter, consultant, or whatever he called his business, to gain access to American military officers and foreign businessmen[2].

---

[2] Looking back forty years later, one sees that it was just such youthful 'radicals' and 'revolutionaries,' who escaped arrest and later graduated to join the major trading companies and manufacturers and waged Japan's economic and trade revolution. [Ed.]

A DATE

by Saisho Foumy

IT BEGAN RAINING when Asa reached her flat. There was a strange intimacy about the somber, ivied flat in the rain, dimly lit from inside. She knew René was in.

"Bon soir, madame." René's resonant voice greeted her from the deep divan into which he was sunk, evidently reading. "I have just come in."

"How are you, René?" Asa said mechanically, feeling empty in heart.

"You look fatigued, *cherie*," René was quick to observe. "Let's have a glass of wine, it's six o'clock anyway." René got up, his well-shaped limbs emphasized by white shirt sleeves.

Tomorrow, ten o'clock, Asa repeated in her mind. Suddenly nothing seemed as important as that ten o'clock breakfast appointment with Yugo—she'd never had a date with Yugo before. It was impossible tonight to banter with René.

"You are day-dreaming. What happened?" he said, half seriously, half pretending to tease her.

"My dear man, I've never consulted you about the affairs of my heart before. Please don't expect me to now." Asa was surprised at her own tone.

"Oh, you have a heart?" René countered. "That's news to me." The patter did not quite come off. His eyes were not laughing, but gently apprehensive.

244

This was what Asa liked about René, about the French, they allow women freedom of emotion; they were not arrogant about love.

"Stop that. Maybe I need your wisdom, but just now I don't want to be particularly wise."

"That's better," René said, studying Asa with his fascinating black eyes directly on hers.

"René, would you object if I lived with a man?" Asa said suddenly.

"What sort of a man?"

"Oh, René, someone I like extremely well, and who likes me too.

"That sounds trite, doesn't it? You don't need any comment from me, do you? You are free, but I don't want you to be too foolish."

"You think I am? I don't want to be particularly clever with this man."

"Nor very proud?" René insinuated.

"Oh, I don't believe in marriage, you know that, René."

"And he doesn't?"

"I never asked. I met him only two weeks ago and spoke to him only today."

At this, René did not, as Asa had half hoped and expected, gesticulate to loosen the tension. He did not move. He looked straight at her. No chance expression on Asa's face could now escape his gaze now.

"Who is the man?"

"Sogano Yugo."

"Not that playwright?"

"Yes."

"Going in for reflected glory?"

"Why should I now? You reflect your glory on me already," Asa said tenderly.

"Enjoy yourself, then," René said. "Anything's a pastime in this floating life, this, what you call it, Ukiyo."

His deliberately chosen words—"enjoy yourself," "pastime"—outraged and hurt Asa and from this she knew that he was more hurt than she.

René reached for another glass of wine. The rain was getting heavy. Raindrops spattering against the window-panes emphasized the stillness and intimacy of the night. Rain spattering on the roof, Asa thought, is one of the few things I live for. There is a sense of gladness of the mere fact of living, however lived. Asa loved this moment—not yet committed to a new love which would no doubt bore her in the end, yet not yet terminating the old love still warm.

The one mortal fear Asa had was to be bored, to be bored of everything, including herself, bored of men she loved and everything else that was supposed to be good in life. Better buried than bored. That was the main reason she had stopped smoking—cigarettes only emphasize the emptiness of life. She did not mind dullness at all if it got anywhere, if it produced anything.

Asa could not bear the end of things but this was not quite an end or a beginning, that thin dividing line which allows you to linger between your remembered happiness and hoped-for moments. That too will end soon and we may become strangers, Asa thought and looked at René lounging gracefully on the sofa in his white shirt sleeves. The sardonic glint in his eyes was gone, and he was quite his usual self, oblivious to what had been said. Their eyes met and they unconsciously smiled.

ONE WORLD

by Serizawa Kojiro

THE 15TH OF AUGUST was here again.

Madame Abe Sonoko dreaded this day.

On this date in 1945, she had listened awe-struck to the voice of the Emperor over the radio, listened and cried over the sad fate of Japan. Her life, too, had gone topsy-turvy as of this date. Little did she realize it then, however, for she had been thinking only of her country, as befitting the wife of a high officer of the Imperial Navy of Japan.

But it is not because of the memory of this that she dreads the return of this day. It is the never-failing annual visit of Tokuda Kakuko that weighs most heavily on her heart, for Kakuko's visit always leaves a big ripple in the peace of this House of Abe.

On this day in 1945, while she was still wiping the tears that kept flowing, Kakuko ran in. "Madame, it's over! It's all over at last," she had cried. "His Excellency will return unhurt, and my husband too. It's peace! Peace has returned at long last." Stuttering excitedly, she bowed low before Sonoko, and cried tears of happiness. It was so unlike Kakuko to lose her composure so, but then, who was she to blame her? Sonoko took Kakuko's hands into hers.

"There will be no more Imperial Navy, Madame," Kakuko said. "His Excellency, and my husband, will leave the sea forever, and you and I can lead normal lives, free from worrying about whether they will be killed. We've had enough of it, haven't we?" And Kakuko's face looked infinitely bright.

247

She talked over and over about the return of peace and their husbands. Sonoko stared at her face, wondering if she had lost her mind. 'While I lamented over the fate of Japan, this woman cried in happiness because her husband was coming home unhurt'—this thought never once entered Sonoko's mind.

Kakuko's husband, Lieutenant-Commander Tokuda, had become her husband's adjutant some two years before, and the two left for a base in the Southern Islands. The women met often in Sonoko's house to console and to encourage each other. There never was any discord between them during those two years, but now . . . Sonoko was bewildered. She could hardly sympathize with the feelings of her good friend.

It was not until Kakuko went home and she was left alone on the upstairs verandah that the realization began to take form and make sense. She saw the ocean before her eyes, shining blue under the August sun, and saw its quiet waters for the first time in a long while. She had not seen it thus since the American air raids began. She realized for the first time that peace had really returned, for she saw it written over its surface, spelled out by the white ripples.

Yes, this was a part of the Pacific Ocean; Pacific, peace. . . .

And with this thought she was able to realize fully the meaning of the words which she said first to herself, then out loud. "He is coming home . . . ." And as she heard herself repeat the words, her eyes blurred, and she understood Kakuko's tears. Her own tears, this time different tears, flowed down her cheeks . . . warm, warming her heart. Suddenly she became hot as hot blood ran through her body.

Just as suddenly, she was chilled through, for her mother-in-law was standing behind her.

"Sono-san, even if Jusuke does come home safe," the old lady said calmly, "he must commit harakiri in apology to His Imperial Majesty, mustn't he?"

Her mother-in-law's late husband had been a civil official, and at one time a member of the Privy Council. Even when the air raids became severe, he turned a deaf ear to all their pleas to evacuate with the other aged folks. He insisted that as long as the Imperial Family remained in the capital, he could not quit Tokyo. On April 1945, in one of the worst bombings of the capital, his house caught fire and he was trapped. This old lady, a stout woman despite her small size, cremated the body of her husband in the blazing fire of her own home before she escaped to Sonoko's house here in this small town by Sagami Bay. "You must be prepared for it," the old lady continued.

"Yes, mother," Sonoko answered. But how was she to quiet her hot blood and her heartbeat. She blamed Kakuko for the loss of her own poise.

Just minutes earlier Sonoko had sat before the radio with this mother-in-law, who had changed into her formal kimono because she was going to listen to the voice of the Emperor.

A few days later, before Sonoko's son, Taro, and daughter Fumiko came home from their labor corps demobilization, Kakuko had come running in again, quite out of breath. She reported that she had been to General Headquarters. She was told that Sonoko's husband had left Keelung, Formosa, on a submarine headed for Japan, but that there were no reports of his having arrived anywhere in Japan.

"They said that he must have known of the end of the war. And so did the enemy, so it is not likely that he was bombed on the way home." She became indignant. "I realized then for the first time that we've lost the war. Everyone of them was at a loss as to what to do. Yes, those once high-and-mighty officers, such a poor lot. I was quite disgusted with them."

"You say Abe's boat was lost?" Sonoko mumbled, her face had turned pale.

"They couldn't even make that clear," Kakuko sneered. "'If His Excellency did arrive in some Navy yard, he should contact the headquarters.' That's all they said."

"If Abe left Formosa knowing of the defeat, he left but with one thought . . ." Sonoko's voice did not shake. "He would not have reached Japan."

"You mean . . . to commit . . . suicide?" Kakuko's voice was clearly shaking.

Sonoko nodded in silence and stood up. She must not lose her composure before this woman, mere wife of her husband's subordinate. A bag of this year's formal powdered *matcha* tea had been sent from the father of another subordinate of her husband. This may be the last grind of tea, the letter that came with it had said. She got her equipment out for a tea ceremony. The bowl was the favorite of her husband; it had been held lovingly in his hands often over many years. He had wavered many times over the decision whether to take it with him.

Kakuko remembered it, too. She had helped Sonoko in the packing. Kakuko now cupped the bowl in her hands and closed her eyes. Its smooth surface was soothing to her uprooted nerves.

"The tea was sent to me by First Lieutenant Oishi's father," Sonoko said, and prayed inwardly that the young lieutenant be safely returned to his father.

Kakuko drank the tea, and placed the empty cup before her on the *tatami*. Then she covered her face with both hands and began to sob. Sonoko's calmness touched her heart, and this time she cried in sheer sympathy for this senior wife. But, while crying, somewhere in her heart was a faint hope that His Excellency would not have taken her young husband on the journey of death.

On the 15th of August of the following year, Kakuko came in deep mourning.

Sonoko was taken by surprise. Defunct Navy Headquarters had not yet formally announced the death of her husband; she herself had not performed any of the Buddhist rites for the deceased. Her husband's smiling portrait still adorned her dining room. She had not yet removed it to the family altar room.

Kakuko clasped her palms before the altar for a while, then walked into the dining room.

"Is Taro-san home?" she asked in a most casual voice.

"No, he went to Hiroshima."

"To the Peace Festival?" Kakuko smiled. "So unlike Taro-san, isn't it?"

"I haven't the slightest idea what for," Sonoko answered with a slight bitterness.

Taro, her first son, had graduated that year from junior college in Okayama and entered the medical college of Tokyo University. But he seemed to have lost interest in his studies. He left home everyday, then instead of going to school he wandered the streets of Tokyo all day.

A few days before he'd announced suddenly that he was going to Hiroshima, and left. Not even a postcard had come from him. She had not had train fare for him, but he took his father's watch, a souvenir of his days as a navy attaché in London. Taro must have hocked it for his fare. When asked why he was going to Hiroshima and where he was going to stay, he simply stared at her with his huge eyes and muttered, "It was awful in Hiroshima, you know."

The year before, when the war had ended, he had not returned until late in September, thin and pale, his big eyes burning dark like two big holes in a skeleton's head. "I was in Hiroshima," he had said. "It was awful there," and gazing deep into her face, huge tears formed beneath his hollow eyes.

"What do you mean, 'awful'?" she had asked. "How come you are unhurt?"

But his lips only quivered, and no words came out of them. In the year intervening there was no further conversation between the two pertaining to Hiroshima, even after she had learned through newspapers about the "awful incident of the atom bomb." She had been too busy with the cares of living.

"Fumiko-san is out too?" Kakuko asked.

"She is at work," Sonoko answered simply.

"I wanted to ask the young folks' opinion. I thought it would be quicker that way." Kakuko took some American cigarettes from her handbag. "But if they are out, I am going to be direct, and ask you."

It was the first time Sonoko had ever seen Kakuko smoke, but there was nothing awkward about the way she smoked. She had rouge on her lips and her fingernails were manicured red. Kakuko looked infinitely young, and Sonoko stared at her, amazed. Unmindful of Sonoko's curiosity, Kakuko came directly to the point of her visit. The deep respect due to the wife of her husband's senior officer had disappeared from Kakuko in the course of one year. Sonoko's house was big and Kakuko wanted to know if she would let her two Western-style rooms to an American officer.

Sonoko had spent her days during the war without ever knowing the hardships and scarcity of food. From somewhere, someone always sent food that was hard to obtain. With the termination of the war all that favoritism had stopped, and almost every day someone's kimono went in exchange for more-needed everyday clothes, or a family treasure laden with past ancestral memories went for rice.

Kakuko, on the other hand, made use of her youth, her good looks, and some workable English. She had become a manager of a social club in Yokohama catering to American officers. It was no use hiding anything from this woman, Sonoko thought. She had come to the rescue of the Abe family's finances.

"He is a gentleman, and casual about money," she coaxed. "Take all the money you can. I haven't forgotten they were my husband's enemy. Our government won't take care of us. It is our only lot to take all the money we can from them."

Sonoko was amazed at the way Kakuko talked. When she finished, Sonoko told her that she must first consult with her mother-in-law and her children.

Ten days later Kakuko called and said she was bringing the American officer. Unmindful of Sonoko's protest that she had not yet talked with her family, Kakuko came about an hour later with a tall officer.

A year before, just before the Americans began their Military Occupation, Sonoko had, like everyone else, sent her only daughter Fumiko away temporarily to a relative in Shizuoka, for her 'safety'. The government had sent out warnings, telling the young girls not to smile at the American soldiers, that they must retain the pride of Japanese womanhood. When the streets and towns had become filled with GIs and sailors, Sonoko failed to hear of any dreaded incident. Not only that, the Japanese people welcomed the conquerors with open arms, saying the Americans had saved them from the long oppression of the Japanese warmongers and from hunger. Within a year, the same people watched, with no disgust, as their daughters walked hand in hand with GIs in broad day light.

But Sonoko could not receive an American into her home. He might not be a foreign devil, but he was—or had recently been—her husband's enemy. She went to the door with every intention of refusing him, but after the introduction Kakuko would not let Sonoko open her mouth.

"Shattuck-san loves the sea," she said. "He is happy also that he will be able to enter into a Japanese family." So saying she let the major take off his shoes.

"We have not decided yet," Sonoko sputtered. "And I have not cleaned the rooms yet," she added.

Kakuko ignored Sonoko's protest, and showed the major the two rooms that faced the sea. Then she took him to where the young folks were. After a short introduction, she started in with the financial advantages of renting the rooms to the American.

Fumiko ignored Kakuko's financial arguments, and tried her faltering English. "When you say you will use your rooms only at night," she asked with dignity, "does that mean you will bring your girlfriend here?" She looked directly into the Major's blue eyes "This is our home, it is sacred to us."

The major listened to her with a grave expression.

"No, I sleep alone every night," he said in slow, distinct English Fumiko could understand. "I want to experience the sanctity of Japanese home life. That is why I want to live in your home."

Sonoko stood outside the room, wondering anxiously over the conversation. She called Kakuko outside and told her she would give her answer in a few days. The Major bent over Sonoko's hand and kissed it. It might be an American custom, but her hand smarted a long time afterward. She felt she must refuse the Major no matter what.

Her mother-in-law came in. "Sono-san," she declared with dignity, "If you let an American into this house. I shall leave "

A year later in 1947, when the 15th of August came around again, Sonoko was sitting in the upstairs verandah with a pair of binoculars. She scanned the ocean for a boat which might possibly carry Major Shattuck and Fumiko. She dreaded this day, as she had in the past, thinking of Kakuko's inevitable visit.

When noon came, Fumiko did not leave for work. "I am thinking of quitting my job," she said when asked. Then she blushed and added timidly, "Shattuck-san wants to marry me."

Sonoko's heart stopped.

"But don't worry, mama," Fumiko continued. "I won't do anything rash. And I won't ask for your opinion until my mind is made up either. Only I didn't want to have any secrets from you."

"What did the Major say? You know it's against the American rules."

Fumiko only repeated, "I know, I know," and went out.

Sonoko wondered if Fumiko had made a rendezvous with the Major. She held her glasses close to her eyes.

In each boat was a pair or two of GIs with Japanese girls. They all looked so happy. Sonoko thought of her own youth, devoid of such freedom. The feeling of remorse for the freedom she never had, and apprehension for the youth of today passed intertwined through her own heart. She wondered if it had not been a mistake last year to let Major Shattuck stay in her house.

At that time a year ago, Sonoko and the old lady were dead against the idea, but the young people insisted. To be ostentatious was not in their vocabulary. They said they should be grateful to Kakuko.

The old lady had fretted and said she would go to the home of her second son, who operated a hospital in Shizuoka. In the end, Fumiko took her there.

"I don't think she will stay there more than a month."

To be sure, she returned exactly a month later. "I met Mr. Ando who was a member of the Imperial Privy Council at the time of grandfather," grandma said. "Mr. Ando had been to the Imperial Palace to pay his respects," and she told in detail what she heard from Mr. Ando, and about how the Imperial family live.

"The carpets are worn out and have holes in them. Mind you, holes. The Emperor tripped over one of them, looked at Mr. Ando, and smiled. Mr. Ando could not return the smile. Instead, he looked down and wept." The old lady wept anew as she told the story. "After I heard that, I made up my mind that I should be able to live with an American under one roof," and she bowed her head to Sonoko.

But she avoided Major Shattuck, and did not return his morning greetings, pretending to be hard of hearing. She ignored him completely. If Sonoko should tell her that Fumiko had been proposed to by him, she would surely have heart failure.

To Sonoko, Major Shattuck was a gentleman. He was polite and quiet, and not once was there any distasteful occurrence of any kind. He was humorous, too, full of fun. Takeo, her second son, regarded him as his idol. Not only that, but it was all due to his staying with them that her family of five had been able to lead a normal life. She wished that he would stay until Taro finished his college. Would he leave if she refused to consent to Fumiko's marriage?

But how had this romance happened? She thought she had watched over them very closely. She heard a rustle of silk and turned. Her mother-in-law was standing there. "Mrs. Okada is here," she said, formally announcing Kakuko.

Kakuko came not in mourning this year, but dressed in a white linen suit. She wore a strand of pearls and a pair of matching earrings—every inch the woman manager of a social club. She did not ask to be shown to the altar room, she was so excited.

"You did know all the time, didn't you? You must have," she said a little breathlessly. "Then please tell me, if it is true, that His Excellency and my husband are still alive, that their submarine did arrive in Japan."

Sonoko's body swayed forward involuntarily. "Who said such nonsense?"

"You know this is the third year, and I was about to hold the third-year Buddhist rite." Kakuko lowered her voice to show that it was a grave secret. "Mrs. Akutsu came in and told me the news. She said she even saw another of the crew, Lieutenant-Commander Ohba, selling old shoes in Shitaya. She said someone is sure to contact His Excellency's home."

"I have not received any information," Sonoko said.

Two or three months before, Taro had told her the same sort of thing, that he had seen Commander Haruki selling old shoes in Shimbashi.

"Kakuko-san, do you think such a thing possible?"

"The way things happen nowadays, anything is possible." Kakuko laughed. "Look at me, before the war, who would have thought that I could hold my present job, manager of a social club?"

"You actually believe they are alive?" asked Sonoko.

"I have to . . . There are many others who are waiting for the safe return of their missing husbands."

"But they can't, they are not the type to live under such humiliating conditions."

"You think not, Madame?" Kakuko's voice sounded strangely sarcastic. "We are not living in the Meiji Era. Remember how they used to love to get drunk and chase geisha girls? I no longer have the respect for them that I once had."

She got up and took up the binoculars Sonoko left on the table.

"Who knows but that they may be picking trash in someone's backyard right now, waiting for the peace treaty to be concluded, and for the return of their day once again . . . which even a ten year-old knows will never return . . . is gone forever."

Sonoko got up to get a cold drink for Kakuko, who stood, staring into the binoculars.

"Why, Madame, is Fumiko-san with the Major today?"

She must have found the boat. Sonoko thought as she ran downstairs, pretending she did not hear Kakuko.

Kakuko visited quite often after that, and each time brought different news. One time she brought a batch of letters, saying they were from either her husband or his associates. Once she came and asked Sonoko to consent to Fumiko's marriage to the Major.

The old lady always overheard everything. "If Jusuke should return safe and alive, I will assist him in committing *harakiri*," she said calmly. She always talked calmly, which sometimes aggravated Sonoko, but her dead seriousness was a joke to the young folks. Fumiko alone listened to her grandmother's lectures, and found in them cause to waver in her decision to accept the Major's marriage proposal.

One day, in midwinter, the old lady suddenly said she wanted to visit her second son in Shizuoka, and asked the Major to take her to Tokyo station. The Major was delighted at this sudden recognition. When they reached Tokyo, she asked through Fumiko that the Major drive around the Imperial Palace.

"*Sha-toku-san*, I love to watch these water birds in the moat," she suddenly spoke in English, to the great amazement of everyone. "I think this view of the moat around the Imperial Palace is the most beautiful scene in Tokyo."

Not only the Major, but Fumiko and Taro were taken by surprise at their grandmother's fluent English.

"I studied English from an Englishman back in the Meiji Era, your Victorian Age," she explained. "I am glad to find out that my English is understood by an American also."

Fumiko noticed that the old lady's accent was perfect.

A few days later she was found dead in their family cemetery in Shizuoka. No one could think of any reason why. There was only one tiny possible clue to the mystery.

When Taro went to get the body, he saw the priest of the family temple for whom his father had had great respect.

"She was in to see me four days before her body was found," the old priest said. "I was pruning my trees in the garden when she came. She stood watching me. Then she said, 'The old branches must be cut off to give room for the new.' Then she wanted to know if that was what I was doing. Come to think of it, these were the last words uttered by your grandmother."

For the forty-ninth-day Buddhist memorial rite for grandmother, held in Shizuoka, Major Shattuck was invited. After the ceremony Fumiko told her uncle, Dr. Abe, that she wanted to go to America to enter a college there.

"Does your mother know about it?" Dr. Abe wanted to know.

"No, I want you to tell her, please," she said.

In the car coming back, the two Mesdames Abe talked intimately.

"I am having such a time with Taro," Sonoko confided to her sister-in-law. "I never know what he is thinking."

"It seems that a big gap has opened between the young and the old since the war," the doctor's wife said. "We are having a hard time with our young doctors at the hospital, too."

"Well, the young ones are probably having a hard time with us, saying we have no understanding nor sympathy for them," said the good doctor laughing it off, and the gloomy atmosphere went out of the car with the breeze.

That night, after Sonoko got into her bed, she asked Fumiko, "Is what you told uncle true?"

"I don't know exactly what conversation took place in your car," Fumiko said. "Uncle may exaggerate, but he wouldn't tell a lie, I'm sure."

"Was your idea to go to America your own," the mother asked "or was it the major's?"

"No, I have not even told him," the daughter answered. "I will probably have to secure his help in obtaining my student visa, though."

"Did you give up the idea of marrying the major because of grandmother's suicide?"

"How preposterous," Fumiko cried. "What possible connection is there between the two?"

Sonoko could not explain her feelings very well. All she knew was that she wanted Fumiko to be happy. She had felt that Fumiko's hesitation to accept the major's proposal was due to grandmother. Now she had a premonition that because of the way grandmother had died, Fumiko had given up the idea entirely, and if that was so, Sonoko wanted Fumiko to know that she was sorry for everything she had done and said.

She was satisfied in the end when Fumiko told her that, before she made up her mind, she wanted to know the major better by going to America. Fumiko told her also that the actions of the young people nowadays might seem perilous and uncertain, but the young had at least learned to be responsible for what they are doing. This was true even of those young girls who walked the streets with the American GIs.

Kakuko came more often. She insisted each time that their husbands were alive, hiding somewhere, waiting for the Peace Treaty to be concluded. While Sonoko denied this, she still longed for her husband. She told him in her heart to come out of hiding, just for her.

One day, she was thus calling for her husband in her heart, watching from the upstairs verandah as the sun set over the horizon, when she heard her husband's voice in the *genkan* entrance hall.

"Where's mother?" he said. "Is she upstairs?"

She heard him come up the stairs, just like he always did when he returned unexpectedly.

Her knees shook, and the voice would not come out of her throat. Tears came down involuntarily.

"Oh, here you are," and before her stood her son Taro. She could not open her mouth. Taro stared at her tear-stained face in wonder.

"What happened?" he asked, still puzzled.

Sonoko told him for the first time what Kakuko had been telling her, that his father might possibly be still alive.

"Your voice was so very much like your father's," she said, shamefacedly. "I was seized by an illusion that it was your father."

"So you believe it, do you? You want to believe it, don't you?" Taro's voice was harsh. "You never knew the hardships of war, mother. You think you do, but actually you never suffered the way most people suffered. That's why you allow yourself to entertain such a dream." He looked at her accusingly. "Of course you had hard times . . . in your own way . . . but you didn't lose your house, you never saw death with your own eyes. I did. I saw with my own eyes two hundred thousand people die in one instantaneous flash. I can still smell their burning flesh. I can still hear young girls cry for 'water . . . water' . . . Sometimes I feel I ought not be living like this. So if father should suddenly appear before me now, alive and unhurt, I couldn't stand it. I don't think I could live with him in the same house. I would leave this house immediately.

"I am glad he is dead. I wouldn't have it any other way. It's your own fault to let him live in your heart. He is our enemy, and we should not let our enemy live."

The 15th of August has come around again. The peace treaty is be signed in a short while in San Francisco, and the whole nation is in a festive mood. But Sonoko tries to remain outside it, aloof, untouched.

She received a letter from Fumiko, who is attending Columbia University, saying that she is going to marry Major . . . Mr. now . . . Shattuck in a short while. He is studying anthropology at the same university, getting his Ph.D., and he will find Fumiko to be a good assistant.

Taro has finished his internship and is now in a lab in Nagoya, preparing his thesis on his study to free the human race from differences in color. It is his belief, however naive, that only by making all human races one color might world peace be realized, for then and only then could we live in one world, and will there be no more wars.

Her second son, Takeo, has a job as a live-in private tutor and is attending college.

Sonoko is now alone in the small house she has moved into, deep in the narrow alleys of a suburb of Tokyo. She waits for Kakuko's annual visit on this day, but she does not dread it as she had in the past, for no one else ever comes to see her and she is glad to receive her.

For some reason Kakuko is late. She usually comes early. Lunch time has passed, three o'clock tea time has passed, but still no Kakuko.

Sonoko confirms her husband's death in Kakuko's failure to arrive on this day. She changes into her mourning clothes, moves her husband's portrait to the *tokonoma*, and places some fresh flowers before it. Then she takes out the *matcha* and its special utensilss and slowly, painstakingly prepares a tea ceremony, and drinks deep its fragrant liquid from her husband's favorite bowl, as if receiving it from his hand.

"Where's mother?" she hears her husband's voice in the *genkan*. She starts and cannot get up. Her knees shake violently. She goes to the *genkan*, still shaking, but she only finds Taro taking his shoes off.

"I had to come to Tokyo on urgent business," he says, going into the dining room.

How the shape of his back has come to look just like his father's, she thinks.

Then Taro notices his mother's mourning.

"I was just informed of your father's death," she says quietly.

"Mrs. Tokuda was here?" he asks. "Then, Lieutenant-Commander Tokuda, too?"

"No, just your father," she lies. "Lieutenant Commander Tokuda is still alive, I believe. Your father committed *harakiri* as befitting the descendant of a samurai."

"I see," and Taro sits up straight, and prays in silence. Sonoko's conscience is clear.

"I didn't know that," Taro says. "I ordered a fish dinner be sent in from the corner restaurant, to save you the trouble. And some cold beer too. I am sorry," he apologizes in the realization that any meat, even fish, is taboo during Buddhist rites for the dead.

"That's all right," Sonoko says cheerfully. "I'll drink with you, to pray for his happy ascent to Heaven."

THE JAPANESE AUTHORS

KON HIDEMI (1903-), younger brother of avant garde Buddhist monk-author Kon Toko, he majored in French literature at Tokyo Imperial University, started writing right after graduation and soon became editor of the magazine *Comedy and Tragedy*. In 1929-30 he joined other artists in opposition to the Proletarian literature of the Marxists—because Marx pointedly ignored art. In 1933 he opposed as well the rising tide of nationalism, along with Abe Tomoji, Yuasa Katsuei and Serizawa Kojiro, who are represented in this book, and such writers as Kawabata Yasunari, Dazai Osamu, Takami Jun. Twenty-nine in all who called for a "tough and realistic prose," and insisted that art be "autonomous and integral." No strict policy was set down. Marxists denounced them as bourgeois, and the movement they had hoped to found fizzled into genre writing which did seem to fit the earlier Marxist denouncements.

Kon turned to what is classed as "midway literature," midway between writing for the masses and "pure literature" of the hermits.

Kon's other works include: *The Tragic General, On a Fine Day,* and *Wandering in the Mountains.* He won the 23rd Naoki Prize in 1950 with the short story 'The Emperor's Hat.'

MIYAMOTO YURIKO (1899-1951), born Chujo Yuriko in Tokyo, of noted architect father and mother of major intellectual family, started writing at 12 and published in *Chuo Koron* at 17, graduated from Ocha-no-Mizu Girls School in 1916 and studied English literature at Nippon Women's College for one term. She went to America with her father, attended Columbia University and married a student. She returned to Japan alone in 1919 and divorced in 1924. Her interest in Russian literature took her to Moscow in 1927; traveled through Europe until 1930. On her return to Japan she joined KOPF, Japan Proletarian Writers' group of bourgeois intellectuals led by Kobayashi, Kurahara, Nakano and Miyamoto Kenji. In 1931 Yuriko joined the Communist Party, married much younger Miyamoto in 1932, and like Kenji was herself imprisoned for short periods in 1933, 1934, 1935, and again in 1941 for opposing the war. Her writing was banned in 1938 and 1941. KOPF was dissolved in 1934 after Kobayashi died at the hands of the Tokyo police and the other leaders went to prison. Her husband's release in 1945 (purged by US Occupation in 1950, for most of the 1960s-1980s he was Secretary General of the Japan Communist Party) forms the core of the novel *Banshu Plain,* from which our selection is extracted.

The range of her themes is narrow, generally limited to autobiography. She is highly popular among present-day students. By Japanese critical standards, her "poetic technique" and "power of suggestion" are "weak"—by which is meant she is not ambiguous—and her directness is regarded as critically "uninteresting." Her odd tempering of the slow, interminable marching-forward-into-the-sun finale of socialist realism, with the Japanese sigh, almost of *mono no aware,* is poetically successful. She was one of the naive humanist communists, whose Western counterparts have long since been disenchanted with the Party.

261

ABE TOMOJI (1903-1973), born in rural Okayama, entered English Literature Department of Tokyo Imperial University in 1923. In 1927 as a graduate student he wrote A Gypsy in Japan, and 1930 *Intellectualist Theory of Literature*. He was especially active in the Proletarian literature movement and led the rearguard *Action* magazine in 1933-35 against the wave of nationalism. In 1933 he began teaching at Meiji University, where he was for years professor of English Literature. A humanist, he does not engage in dialectics as most of his so-called proletarian colleagues do, but fights issues. He is a crusader in the Occidental sense and is active in the Peace Movement, but he rejects the Communist-front line in favor of the Quaker approach. The range of his work is phenomenal, from heavy political and social criticism to literary scholarship, translations of major English authors, travel accounts, and humor.

The individualist and progressive-with-a-small-"p" is a *rara avis* in Japan and certainly needs a sense of humor to survive, as Abe shows in The Horse Manure Record and this collection's The Communist. Utter confusion of the characters, their ignorance, naiveté and suspicion, form a perfect portrait of the Japanese student who would rather prance on the palace plaza beneath pennants and police batons than tackle a real book or a smaller scale problem he might conceivably understand and attempt to solve—like my 1960s' students' vociferous concern for the plight of American blacks and simultaneous disinterest in problems of local native *eta* or *burakumin* untouchables, Koreans and their own war orphans. It is by far the best analysis and description of a mentality as slippery and as hard to grasp as soap, but, like it, the by-product rather than the source material of political TNT.

Abe has traveled extensively: to Java in 1941, to Europe since the war, and to mainland China in 1954 as part of a cultural delegation. Other works include: *Winter Inn, Wind and Snow, Doyle of Africa, White Officer, Alte Heidelberg, Peking;* the postwar *Flower Shade, Black Shade, Death Flowers, The Wanderer* and *European Journey.* Originally in *Bungei Shunju.*

SERIZAWA KOJIRO (1897-1993) was born in Shizuoka, south of Tokyo, where winter-ripening tangerines on steep-terraced, pine-topped hillsides instill an awareness of constant life and growth. He graduated from Tokyo Imperial University late at 35, worked for the Ministry of Agriculture for three years and then quit and went to Paris to study in 1935. He returned in 1939, and his maiden work, the autobiographical *Bourgeois*, based on his illness-racked life in France, won the *Kaido* magazine novel prize. His father was a devout adherent of the Tenri religion (often regarded as the Christian Science of Japan), which inspired his *A Believer* and *A Record of Conventions.* Their lack of deep religious insight may accurately reflect this religion's own philosophical poverty other than its doctrine of untutored, unselfish action. Serizawa is a romantic idealist usually classed with the Esthetic school. His main postwar writings include: *Anonymous Confession* (1947), *The Closed Door, Marriage, Hope, The State of Europe, One World* (1952-3, part of which appears in this collection, his sole translation into English, though he is much translated into French), *Repentance Record* (1961). After serious illness, 1980s into early '90s saw him revivified, again writing on self-religious attitudes. He is still one of Japan's principal Nobel prize hopefuls. Originally in *Fujin Koron.*

KAWACHI SENSUKE (1898-1954) died a few days after approving our condensation and translation of his novel *Sazanka.* He graduated from Osaka Koshu School of Commerce in 1916, and worked as a magazine editor. His first novel, *Gunji Yubin* (Military Mail), was serialized in *Shincho*. Later works included *Ishi* (Will), *Waga Ane-no-Ki* (My Sister's Story), and *Kaze Sayuru* (The Cutting Wind). Originally in *Shosetsu Koen.*

NAKAMOTO TAKAKO's (1903-) name almost didn't appear. *Gunzo* magazine in 1953 had a policy of running stories anonymously to encourage its public to read for the sake of the story, not the name of the author. *Kichi no Onna* (Camp Women, here translated as The Only One) appeared in July 1953. Nakamoto allowed translation only on condition that its author remain anonymous. Nakamoto was afraid that her story might be thought anti-American. In a way she was right, for most Americans in Tokyo were a super-sensitive (a form of insensitivity) lot, whether military, missionary, businessman or journalist. The title was changed to the corresponding local GI idiom—to Japanese *Kichi no Onna* carries other connotations as first US Ambassador to Japan, Townsend Harris, allegedly kept a mistress named O-kichi who has become titular deity of poor country girls sacrificed to the red-haired barbarians (*keto.* using the term for animal hair rather than human, thus pairing us with monkeys). The movie *The Barbarian and the Geisha* was a Hollywood perpetuation of this fully discredited story, which was given further life in its paperback PR-rewrite by Robert Payne, an otherwise exemplary interpreter of Asia.

Nakamoto's major prewar work includes *The Iron Kettle Tinkers of Nambu* and *White-Robed Workers*, which also deal with the affairs of people of the economic am social cellar. This appeared originally in *Gunzo.*

WADA DEN (1900-), scion of an ancient feudal family, graduate of Tokyo Imperial University's French Literature Department, was still resident on his ancestral estate when this story was translated. Wada joined *Nomin Bungeikai*, Agricultural Literature Society or "physiocrats." Agricultural literature was a pawn of both Marxists and the Ministry of Agriculture. The Ministry commissioned writers to do articles, in which their fiction training stood them well, of country boys who made good or who conquered the barren wilds of Manchuria—little that can be classed as literature.

Between 1945 and 1954 Japan underwent the most successful rural upheaval in mankind's history. The land reform of 1945 could not safely be considered a success until 1954, when the combination of technology, agricultural cooperatives and conscientious "traditional" farmers at long last conquered Japan's periodic famine. Yet this revolution has gone virtually unchronicled. Wada Den has managed to write of the farmer's life success fully, with sympathy and understanding and just that touch of humor so characteristic of village Japan.

His better-known works include: *The Last Grave* (1929) and *Fertile Soil* (1937). Originally in *Shosetsu Shincho.*

ISHIKAWA TATSUZO (1905-), born in Japan's far north, Akita, attended Waseda University, Tokyo, and made his mark early, winning the Asahi short story award in 1926. He came from a background of poverty and graduated into an emotionally nomadic life as dance instructor, writer-editor, pig farmer, very briefly emigrating to Brazil, and foreign correspondent, which probably accounts for the rapport which the foreign reader establishes with him even when he cannot "agree with more than half his statements, especially those on social problems."

In 1935 he started the magazine *Seiza* and received the coveted Akutagawa prize for his emigration period novel *The People.* Sent to cover the China fighting, he wrote articles that caused trouble with the militarists. In 1938 *Living Soldiers* earned him a criminal conviction—along with reinforcement of his own convictions to attempt "reform rather by goodwill than by wanton criticism." Other fiction from the China front followed. After the war his *It Isn't As If There Were No Hope,* serialized in 1947, was adapted for stage in 1948. Mostly it had to do with his own experiences in China, evidencing a desire to re-establish moral consciousness amidst postwar disorder.

He writes in tradition of the "I" novel, but rejects its usual preaching and subjectivity. Japanese critics note his directness, his avoidance of innuendo. He writes of China with just enough detachment and depth to allow Japanese to develop sympathy and understanding and a desire to rebuild and rectify, while avoiding saddling them with a "mournful awareness" of an unexpiable inherited guilt.

In the small Oriental literary world of emotional attitudinarians, Ishikawa persists as a "Moral Democrat." He writes what is classified as "mid way" and "adventure" literature and frequently, as with The Affair of the Arabesque Inlay, the story in this collection, adapts the detective story genre. Other works of note by Ishikawa Tatsuzo include: *Village in the Shadow, Green Grass of Wisdom;* the postwar *Wind-Swayed Reeds, The Last Republic, Pride of Three Generations, Tax Collector's Ballad, In One's Own Hole, Blue Revolution, The Joys of Evil,* and the especially noteworthy *Human Wall.*

In June 1962, despite Fascist threats against his life, he accepted editorship of the bankrupt weekly magazine owned by the Sohyo labor union. His rejoinder to the rightists accusations of Communism: "A liberal can be a nationalist too, and I shall prove it."

KOYAMA ITOKO (1901-) was born in Kochi, southern Shikoku, land of long-tailed roosters. Her education was limited to primary school plus five years at the old-style Kochi Girls' High School. She is primarily a novelist. In her early writing days she took a masculine pen name. Critics have called her style masculine, especially in her broad outlook—though on this standard the bulk of Japanese male writers could be classed as feminine. She stresses romantic love and adventure and prefers rather human, unconventional heroes, the sort of man who might be any one's husband, as in the story in this collection, Black-Out. She edited a women's magazine, *Bird of Fire,* in 1918, often appears in women's magazines like *Shufu no Tomo* (Housewives' Companion).

Her better-known works include: *Hot Wind, Village, The Daughter's House, Koya Monastery, Putting off the Action,* and the very successful serial which ran for two years in *Shufu no Tomo,* My Empress. Originally in *Bungei Shunju.*

KOH HARUTO (1906-) was born in Kumamoto, westernmost Japan, an area never thoroughly brought under repressive thought control of the Shoguns in Tokyo. Kyushuites to this day stand out among other Japanese for their independent ways, their individuality, their directness, which other Japanese consider coarse but which the Occidental long in Japan finds refreshing, if at first somewhat shocking. Yet they are conservative, clinging to old ways the central areas of Japan have given up.

Koh majored in English Literature at Meiji Gakuin—a school well suited to his personality, where English was taught by such iconoclasts as Dr. Saeki Paul Yoshiro, OBE (to whom this book is dedicated)—Christian, Confucian sage, world traveler, a plague on narrow-minded militarists and missionaries alike, and himself a country boy from western Japan.

Koh is of the same age group as such "Lost Generation" stylists as Hemingway, who brought conciseness and directness of language into our literature, with whom English Literature buff Koh was certainly acquainted and whose directness and simplicity and humanity would appeal to the same innate qualities of the traditional Kyushu cuss. The humor of futility in Black Market Blues appeals to our Western taste. Yet Western as story and treatment and style may seem, it is typically rural Kyushu, a modern version of what Kyushu farmers do to their ancient heroes and gods in the age-old autumn amateur performances of the Harvest Plays, *kagura.* Japanese college students whom I have assigned to read Koh were unanimous in praise of his simple, direct language and rapid development of theme. They especially noted the absence of any dialectic, of any attempt to explain or preach— further reasons why they had not earlier been introduced to him by their captive Japanese teachers. Yet they felt nothing "foreign" about him, felt at ease while reading him and, when finished, as several pointedly stated, "much refreshed." To the Westerner, this is especially evident.

Other untranslated works include: *Marriage, Mulberry in Water, Delinquent Girl, Ticket, Dangerous Experiment, Fire, Clear Eyes,* and *A Certain Gorge.*

Appeared originally in *Bungei Shunju.*

MISHIMA YUKIO (1925-1970), born Hiraoka Kimitake, was given his pen name at age 19 in 1944 while in middle school, by editors of a prestigious literary magazine in publishing his first book *Hanazakari no Mori.* Began prodigious rise with publication of novel *Confessions of a Mask* in 1949. A graduate of the Peers' High School and Tokyo University (1947), he was principal literary spokesman for Japan's "Lost Generation," and has been compared with Truman Capote and France's Raymond Radiguet. His stories deal mostly with homosexuality, as well as demented love, religious and political dementia—the full armory of a youthful literature of shock, symptomatic of a more general cultural malaise and certainly autobiographical as we would see in his own theatrical samurai-oiserie-*hara-kiri* death. His samurai pedigree was claimed from his grandmother's line (militarist by mannerism only, he dodged the draft in World War II) and he hid his grandfather's peasant origin though he admirably had risen to become governor of Southern Sakhalin. His earlier work especially was noteworthy for its irony, as *Minister* (1949) and *Revenge,* herein, which appeared originally in *Bungei Shunju.*

In 1954 we conferred with him to translate this piece, he had not yet been translated, though there was talk of it, as much talk of his meteoric reputation. Our policy was to have each translation approved by the author, and we sent his to him with questions about the ambiguity of the ending, which we felt we did not understand completely. He came to our office unannounced—it was an unheated mess, but so were all Japanese offices then. He was unfriendly, haughty and uncooperative, even insulting. He "could not allow" this ending to be published. We implored his help,

"Your English is excellent, you were an English Lit major in college, couldn't you translate those few lines? Or at least show us the way?"

He sneered, "I am an artist, not just some mere translator-word mechanic. That's your job."

After much fruitless exchange I said, "If the translation is not acceptable to you, we cannot print it. Our policy is to respect the original author."

He exploded. "Who the hell are *you* to reject my work!"

"I'm not rejecting your work, I am rejecting Grace's and my own sad attempt to render it into comprehensible and literate English. I will not insult you by printing a translation of your work you don't approve."

"It's your rag, print any damned thing you want!" And he stormed out, shouldered-topcoat flaring out behind him like a charging cavalryman's cape."

By then he had already produced over 70 volumes of novels, short stories, poetry, plays in old, new and mixed genres, much of which he did not take seriously himself and confessed through his journalistic mask to be plain pulp. A good bit is deservedly successful; some, as his modern Noh Plays, noble experimental flops but which indicate future promise, for their new forms perhaps more than for the author. Thankfully, he slackened his pace. Though he had long been discussed admirably in international literary circles, Revenge was the first of his work to be translated, followed 1956 by Meredith Weatherby of his major novel *The Sound of Waves*. Several more followed and Off-Broadway has tried his modern noh. He has been called the "exemplification of postwar conservative resistance." He was from the early 1960s, long a Nobel-prize hopeful and probably only his repugnant politics kept it out of his reach. Foreign critics stress his "alleged political ideas" (to use Luis Canales' words) and his homosexuality, while Japanese ignored both and emphasized his "pro-emperor ritual suicide." Such English texts are virtually banned in Japan, and Paul Schrader's film *Mishima* was banned from the 1985 Tokyo International Film Festival and never distributed, even in tape rental.

MIZUKI YOKO (1913-), born Takagi Yoko and raised in Tokyo, reflects the temperament of the Edo-ko, child of Edo (Tokyo). She majored in Japanese literature at Nippon Women's University and later took up drama at Bunkagakuin, and radio script writing. After the war she wrote movie scenarios, her first being *Onna no Issho* (Life of a Woman). She has been far less loath than most Japanese writers to tackle the broader social problems. One of her first movies to gain international attention, if not notoriety, was *Himeyuri no To* (Tower of Lilies), about the idiotic sacrifice of a large group of young Okinawan school girls during the American invasion.

Kiku and Isamu was a movie about two illegitimate children, product of a Japanese dalliance with a Black GI. The Black parentage was chosen because Caucasian-Japanese offspring are often able to pass for Japanese, or at least evade serious persecution. Where most Japanese writers drown in maudlin sentimentality, Mizuki manages to express sympathy. Her works include: *Tide*, *Mother*, *Here Is a Fountain*. She was awarded the eleventh Kikuchi Kan Prize and the Geijutsusen Award.

SHIBAKI YOSHIKO (1914-), born in the heart of the old woodblock-print Floating World, Tokyo's Asakusa district, graduated from Tokyo Girls' High School and attended Surugadai Women's School of the YWCA. In 1942 she married, published *Vegetable Market* and won the cherished Akutagawa Prize. In 1944 a stay in Japanese-occupied Manchuria provided the basis for several stories, including *Journey's Start* in that same year and the delayed *Song of Wandering in a Strange Land*, 1949. She wrote her first long novel, *Flowing Days*, during the war. Other short stories include: That Day (1947), Hope, and Truth (1948). In 1956 she traveled through India, Pakistan, Thailand and Indochina. Recent work includes serials *Springtime of a Woman* and *City*

Without Sea. Her stories Suzaki Paradise, Woman of Suzaki, Suzaki Area and Black Flame were published together as a novel entitled *Suzaki Paradise.*
Appeared originally in *Shosetsu Shincho.*

YUASA KATSUEI (1910-19-) noted author on Korea and Koreans in Japan, crusader for better cultural relations with Asia, he championed this book with Japan PEN Club, of which he was a long-standing member and prime mover. Both stories are reportage (in which he excelled) rather than fiction, and "Tarzan" was a favorite of his and is based on an actual experience of his friend, the heroine. Appeared originally in translation in *Korean* and *Orient Digests*, "—Eyes" ran in *Tokyo Shimbun,* translated in *Orient Digests*

THE MILITARY DIARISTS

YOKOI TOSHIYUKI, Rear Admiral, graduated Naval Academy 1919, trained as a pilot, and went to the Naval War College. He became skipper of the aircraft carrier *Hiyo* in 1943, extending his command to the entire 25th Air Fighter Wing for the crucial battle of the Marianas and the loss of his ship recorded in this selection. At war's end he was Chief of Staff of the Fifth Air Force. Later he turned to recording the war. *The End of the Japanese Navy* became a best-seller in Japanese, and was translated by the United States Naval Institute in 1954. He personifies the flowering of British Naval tradition as grafted to a Japanese root.

TSUJI MASANOBU (1902-1962?), while a staff colonel, exerted personal influence far outweighing his rank and earned a niche in history worth at least three stars: credit for blue-printing the conquest of impregnable Singapore. Tsuji was a fanatic, dedicated to the idea of a Greater East Asia as a common-wealth of colored equals, with Japan as first among equals. His sincerity and naïveté (traits necessary to a successful zealot) earned him many friends on both sides of the battle line and his efforts to bring about rapprochement with the Nationalists were received with enough good will to earn him protection of Chiang Kai-shek after the war. When the Imphal campaign fell apart in 1943 he was given a command on the Burma front. Wounded, he was transferred to Bangkok to purge the geisha-house command and stave off threatening revolt of Japan's only "ally," Thailand, with her 150,000 troops. It was futile. Thailand changed sides, Tsuji disguised himself as a Buddhist monk and Thai friends helped him escape, as did former enemies among Cambodians, Annamese and Nationalist Chinese. He eventually ended up as a secret advisor to Chiang. His first book, a runaway best-seller, recounts this trek of 7,500 miles, over two years in duration. Our selection is a composite of two parts from this *Senko Sanzenri* (literally Disguised Flight of 3,000 Leagues, but published in English as *Underground Escape*) (1950).
In 1952, consulting with Tsuji was like living a pulp magazine cloak-and-dagger thriller. Everyone suspected him, everyone wanted to hear what he had to say and no one wanted him to talk. The whole procedure was further flavored by his own obvious savoring of excitement. He stood for election to the Japanese Diet and won, and each re-election was a record breaking land-slide. In 1961 on a "congressional junket" to Vietnam he contacted former Imperial Japanese Army colleagues still in the area variously serving any and

all factions, then disappeared. Attempts to trace him have been futile and he is now believed dead.

His second best-seller, *Singapore*, was translated into English and published in 1960. Both *Underground Escape*, herein, and *Singapore* are among the principal historical works to come out of Japan recounting the loser's story.

Many of the older group of nisei—Americans of Japanese descent—born before World War I, opted for Japan, for the most part well before Pearl Harbor, out of varying degrees of reaction to their rejection by Caucasian American society. The job shortage, aggravated by the depression of the thirties, was especially hard on non-assimilated minorities, the "different." Japan's expansion needed skilled linguists, people with knowledge of the Western world, and Japan offered the rejected bi-nationals a haven. Many returned; some for jobs their superior education entitled them to, some seething for vengeance. Out of these came much of the staff of Japan's overseas propaganda bureaus, those several people known collectively as Tokyo Rose (one of whom took the whole rap), some of the most sadistic prison camp executives and some of the most sympathetic. Most important, these hardy graduates of the American and Japanese schools of hard knocks were among the first to rise like flowers out of the ashes of defeat, to serve as pontoons for the bridge between the derelict Floating World and the new reality. They were the editors and writers of local English-language newspapers, the interpreter-translators who were virtually the sole link between our linguistically deaf-dumb-and-blind American press, occupationaire educators, reformers, cultural missionaries on the one hand and the equally parochial Japan on the other.

YAMAMOTO TOMOMI, a *kibei* (American-born nisei but college educated in Japan), served as intelligence officer in Harbin, Manchuria, where he received word of the Russian invasion in sufficient time to cover up his identity. He had worked with, and later shared imprisonment in Siberia with, "Harvey" Fukuda, the "Taco" Fukuda of Kaplan and Dubro's book *Yakuza* who was go-between and interpreter for Kodama Yoshio and Tanaka Kakuei to the bribers of Lockheed in the scandal which brought down the Tanaka government. Captured by Russians and sent to Siberia, he served in various camps for four years. His repatriation was delayed, at one time seemingly canceled, because of his political obstinacy.

He wrote of his ordeal in both Japanese and English, the latter, published by Fukuda (who also published the Tsuji and Kodama books, as well as many others and a group of translated True Romance American women's monthlies) as *Four Years in Hell*, from which this excerpt, "Damoi—Homeward Bound," was taken. His was the fate of hundreds of thousands of Japanese military and civilians, tens of thousands of whom have never been our accounted for officially (in 1992 after the Soviet collapse, Russia delivered documents on deaths and burial locations to Japan, but no more survivors). It is the description of one half of the pincers in which the Japanese people were trapped; the other half is shown by Miyamoto Yuriko's *Banshu Plain.*

OKA MASAMICHI is a diarist, though no amateur, being a working journalist for the *Asahi* Newspapers, Japan's journal of record. Originally in *Asahi Weekly.*.

FUJI SEII was an amateur diarist and stringer photographer for *Preview* magazine. While our two projects of collecting, editing and translating Japanese non-fiction war accounts and postwar literature were in full swing, he showed symptoms of the endemic human ill, "Now I really have a story, if only I could write it." The story Captured by Americans was written for this translation, in which he cooperated.

THE CIVILIAN DIARISTS

This category, strictly speaking, would include many of the professional authors; but it is here arbitrarily limited to those who did not write primarily for commercial publication. The professionals, by the very fact of being trained writers, consciously affected techniques of fiction writing to varying degrees; fictionalizing to make facts more palatable and more believable, to contribute more directly to a specific end (*The New Yorker* calls this reportage); or embellishing an essential fiction with decorative accessories of miscellaneous facts to lend greater credence to a representative tale.

EGUCHI KŌICHI, at 14, was a student in an isolated mountain school, a poor boy even by the standards of his impoverished community. His teacher embodied most of the ideals that colleagues working in far more comfortable conditions claim to find unattainable. Teacher Muchaku Seikyo was impressed by his wards, aware of the inadequate material at hand, conscious of his duty to them. "Simply reading textbooks on social science did not seem sufficient," he writes in the introduction to his book *Echoes from a Mountain School* (Kenkyusha, Tokyo, 1953). "I received the idea of having pupils write compositions about their own special-problems and their thoughts on life in general. I tried to encourage them to make these compositions a part of themselves, a real study in the social problems of our community." His selection became a best-seller and full-length movie. Eight pieces were translated into English in 1952, the one included in this collection having been circulated by UNESCO in 1954.

SETO NANAKO (1932-1959) is an atomic age representative of one of the oldest forms of Japanese literature, the lady's diary. Seto Nanako, nee Hayashida, 13 years old when the atom bomb leveled Hiroshima, seemed unscathed. At 18 she opened a beauty parlor and at 21 married Seto Tsuyoshi, soon giving birth to a daughter, the Mami of the diary. In July 1957, she suddenly became ill. In October she entered the A-bomb Hospital. The following April, released to out-patient status, she suffered a relapse and was re-admitted. The diary takes up from August 25th of that year and continues on through February 22, 1959. She died on April 10, 1959. The diary was found by the translator among some books owned by a friend. After translation it was privately published by a special committee of the Hiroshima YMCA, July 15, 1961. I discovered it a few days later, as did the Pravda correspondent who arranged for its translation into Russian the very week Russia suddenly resumed atomic testing unannounced. The success of the English edition prompted a Japanese edition of the entire diary.

There is a literature on the atomic bomb, notably by Ota Yoko and Agawa Hiroyuki. The latter's novel *Devil's Heritage* has excellent English translation and I had intended to include an excerpt from it in this collection. I was on my way to the offices of the Hiroshima daily, *Chugoku Shimbun*, for which he wrote (and to which I contributed cartoons), when I discovered *A Crane*.

JAPANESE LITERATURE IN ENGLISH

An amazing facet of Japanese publishing for almost a century has been the English language press. This may not seem surprising at first glance, when one considers that Iran's finest modern author wrote simultaneously in French, that India and Pakistan have long supported numerous and healthy English publishing industries, that Southeast Asian and Black African and Moslem African authors excel, if only locally circulated, in the languages of their occupiers. Then recall that Japan's local English press dates back almost to the day English was openly allowed (a few special interpreters had studied it before Commodore Perry came). Japan's excellent English dailies are supported by a readership well over half of whom are Japanese. Japanese is the language of a vibrant and highly literate people, but the language is of no use in international communication. Japanese must use English (or some other Western tongue) to explain themselves to the world. Locally published magazines have usually (as with those I myself edited or published) been foreign-run—but not always, and far less so today.

But whatever the proprietorship, a fair block of internal circulation and a major segment of the contributors have from their very earliest issues been Japanese. These writers may be foreign-educated or repatriate second-generation Japanese. Some may be writing in their second language. Some are native-born but educated overseas by diplomatic or commercial-émigré parents, speaking English as their mother language. A number of these, several working today on the English dailies, are illiterate in Japanese. There are also the Eurasians and Japan-born (BIJs) and naturalized Caucasians, several of whom are working journalists. And Japan has perhaps as legitimate a claim to Lafcadio Hearn as has America (never an American citizen, he was naturalized as Japanese).

And in the nineties we have the twin phenomena of a native Japanese—Ishiguro Kazuo—writing in English (his Japanese is next to nil) winning the Booker Prize in Britain, and an America-born Caucasian with, prophetically, a Japanese given name, who learned Japanese in college—Hideo Levy—winning the coveted Noma Literary Prize for 1992 for new writing in Japanese.

While this is also a part of the literature of the English language, it is legitimately an aspect of the literature of the Japanese culture. It is written by men and women of that particular culture and about that culture. Nor is it exactly minor from a physical standpoint, for the circulation of some of the periodicals in which it appears is often as large as or larger than that of the vernacular literary magazines in which some of the major literature of the native language has gained recognition. Some of the non-fiction from Japan which has had the greatest impact on the West in recent years has appeared originally in English, since being translated "back" or re-rendered into Japanese—for example, the highly popular, yet scholarly, Zen philosophical works of Daisetsu T. Suzuki.

TAGUCHI SHU (1905-1956) born in Tokyo, finished primary school and entered Mitsukoshi Department Store, attended night school then disappeared, turning up after Great Quake with Eimo movie camera and made great documentary. Became a writer-director-producer of documentary movies, almost as much at home in English as in Japanese. The autobiographical piece in this collection is biography enough on him, except to say that as an artist with the camera he was superb. He adapted this, his own story "Three Unforgettable Letters," from an earlier scenario for a never-completed short documentary film.

SAISHO FOUMY (1922-1988): personally epitomized the Edo free spirit of the 'floating world', was long resident movie reviewer for *The Japan Times* and highly-regarded reviewer and in-theater bilingual commentator-translator of classical kabuki,also a member of the Tokyo-based editorial staff of *Reader's Digest*.

JOHN FUJII (1914 –) was taken to the USA as an infant. After completing college, returned to Asia in wave of backwash reacting to US racial prejudice to work at various English editorial jobs and in 1942 edited captured Singapore English daily. Returned to Japan after the war he has held numerous editorial posits on local papers, international magazines, and for American wire services. His ignorance of Japanese script has earned him the nickname of "World's Only Illiterate Journalist." His clipped and acid style owes more to his Edo-Tokyo environment than to American journalistic experience and he reminds one, for both his subject matter and style, of popular *kiroibyoshi woodblock-printed*-paperback hacks (literary companions to the Ukiyoe woodblock prints) of the Floating World of 17th–19th century Edo (and of whom he would be ideal translator, were he able to read them—almost no scholar can read their period slang). He later purchased my *Orient Digests* and edited several issues. At present, he lives in Tokyo, editing and free-lancing.

ABOUT THE EDITOR

JAY GLUCK born in Detroit, Michigan in 1927 grew up on New York's East Side (with time in mother's hometown of Newcastle in northern England), attending its excellent public schools as far as City College. At 17 he joined US Navy Air Arm to escape college and spent two years in schools. After war, roamed universities—George Washington, Columbia, graduating in Archæology-Middle East studies 1949 from Berkeley. After year in Greenwich Village buying beers at San Remo to hear recitations of *The Oral History*, he matriculated to The Asia Institute School for Asian Studies, completing two-year MA degree in half time, while Deputy to Director Arthur Upham Pope.

Before Asia or Japan Societies were active, at Institute he initiated public programs of stage performances paired with art exhibits, serial conference for Asian problems: India-Pakistan, Iranian oil nationalization, Israel-Arab, etc, bringing both sides to the public forum. At Japan Night of his *Thousand and One Asian Nights* series he met his future wife, a Nisei, and soon (1951) sailed for Japan for self study of its art as guest of a noble art family, the Sens, Tea masters in Kyoto. Intending to study two years then enter diplomatic service, has lived in Japan or Iran ever since. Spent final months of the U.S. Occupation in unscathed Kyoto, then four-plus years in ravaged, apres-guerre (*apuré*) Tokyo, two in old home in farming village, seven teaching (and learning from) Japan's most radical student body at Wakayama National University. Was regularly on Radio Japan Overseas doing third-person interviews, and when in New York as guest on all-night Long John Nebel show.

Back to entrepreneurship as publisher and art dealer, moving nomad-like on the silk road of the sky between first-love Persia (Iran) and Japan.

He persuaded Shah to move Pope to Iran for his final years and reestablish Asia Institute with himself again Deputy Director in the ancient cultural city of Shiraz in century-old *Narenjestan*, Palace of the Khamseh tribe of nomads —he and wife restored its polychrome-tile and mirrored halls to academic use. Pope died at 88 in 1969, was buried in nation-built monument, honored as no other Westerner in Asia. Back and forth to Japan, he twice (1964, 1977) republished Oxford University Press masterpiece *A Survey o f Persian Art* in 12 and 13 volumes, co-edited three additional volumes and with wife co-authored supplement on *Handicrafts*, and is working on *Pope Memorial.*

Author of several books on Japan—*Ah So*, his cartoons of "Misadventures of a Foreigner in –" to 1340-page "most remarkable travel guide to Japan" *Japan Inside Out* and best introduction to Japan's martial arts *Zen Combat*,. Lives in Ashiya near Kobe, Japan, writing, presiding over two museums housing the bulk of their collection of Persian antiquities and folk arts in old designated buildings he and wife restored, as well as originating and directing Japan's sole international festival in a Shinto Shrine.

First non-Japanese to receive Kobe City's 'International' and Hyogo Prefecture's 'Order of the Crane,' their highest civilian awards.

Two multicultural sons born in Wakayama, work in movie production in Hollywood; younger Garet co-authored 1992 new edition of *Japan Inside Out.*.

KYOTO INSIDE OUT

MARKING THE 1200TH ANNIVERSARY OF KYOTO

and inauguration of the New Kansai International Airport
Excerpted from JAPAN INSIDE OUT covering historical heartland of Japan,
with further details—ENTRY International airlines into Osaka, Nagoya
airports for—YAMATO HEARTLAND OF JAPAN **Ise Daijingu** Home of
Sun Goddess–**Ise Shima** of Diving Girls–**Great Tombs** Bigger Than
Egypt's Pyramids–**Tenri:** Navel of Earth–**Horyu-ji** world's oldest wood
building to–**NARA** City Imperial Walking–**En route Kyoto** Mt Yoshino
–**Koya-san** Real Life Shangri-la–**Kii Peninsula** Rugged and Rustic—
KYOTO: Where to Stay: Western Style Hotels–Ryokan, Japanese Inns–
Shukubo (Temple Stay)–**Pageant Of Ages:** Planning our TILT–**Rakuchu:**
Old City, Mirror of Ancient China–Heian Jingu–Gosho Imperial Palace–
Purple Period Western Outskirts–Heian Touch–Offbeat North–Hozu Rapids–
Uji Southeast Outskirts–Coming From Nara–**Decline, Fall & Renaissance**
1000-1500 AD–**Bells, Drums & Marrying Monks:** (South Central)–Nijo
Castle–**Tea Time** Reactions–**Ceremonial Sandpiles** Rambles Northeast–
Hiei-san Cold Mount–**Biwa:** Lake of Lute–**Museums–Personal Datebook–
Chopsticks–How to Get Your Geisha–Shoppers' Paradise:**
With supplements on modern entry cities of Nagoya, Osaka, Kobe.

ISBN4-89360-036-2

ZEN COMBAT
by Jay Gluck

THE FIRST — THE MOST COMPLETE — AND STILL THE BEST

Introductory Guide to the Oriental Martial Arts
Karate - Kendo - Tessen - Bo - Sumo - Fire-Walking - Kyudo - Aikido
*Over 400,000 copies sold and now a new expanded edition with an exciting
new chapter on KI ENERGY (alias Ch'i or Qi)*

Profusely illustrated with drawings by the author.

ISBN4-89360-038-9

YOU MEAN TO SAY –
–YOU STILL DON'T KNOW WHO WE ARE?
7 Classical Kabuki Plays Edited & Translated by Cellin Gluck
As performed by the only Japanese-speaking Foreign Kabuki troupe in a
remarkable experiment at a Kobe International High School

ISBN4-89360-033-8

PERSONALLY ORIENTED GUIDEBOOKS
by Jay & Sumi & Garet Gluck

JAPAN INSIDE OUT

Library Journal revised for the first time since initially appeared in 1964
—refreshingly frank, opinionated, and sometimes passionate personal
comments ... contains so much information (with 135 maps) that it should
be almost every library's next selection for an introduction to Japan.

Academic Library Book Review "...more than a guidebook...a riotously
pleasant treasure chest of information." **Asiaweek, Hong Kong,** It helps
to consult a good guidebook, and this title is an excellent new entry. The
authors cram a vast amount of information into the book. Covering almost
every nook and cranny of the land, Tokyo is left till last."

Japan Times Weekly, BIG. THIS BOOK IS big. Huge. Do not take it with
you on your travels unless using sherpa. That, apart from a few stylistic
quibbles, is the only complaint one can level against this encyclopedic
guide to Japan. Jay and Sumi first published Japan Inside out in 1964—in
five volumes but this version is fully revised and consolidated: hence the
heft... 1,286 pp, 220 maps, sketches, 2,099 festival dates. Glucks have put
virtually all of Japan between the covers. The introduction ... sets the
tone: personal... a labor of love, a sharing of the Japan the Glucks have
come to savor, and like all truly intense emotional experiences, once
unleashed, it's hard to keep under control.

City Life News, Tokyo: In recent months three major paperback
guidebooks to Japan have been published ... *Japan—A Travel Survival Kit,*
... *Japan Inside Out,* ... *Japan Inside Guide* ... closest to all-encompassing is
Japan Inside Out... .a 'personally oriented guidebook'... full of myriad
little details that enable a traveler to make a trip special just for him or
her. For example... fire-walking without burning your feet –It's also more
complete than its two new rivals in the number of places around Japan
that are included... If you want an accurate and in-depth travel guide, it
will have to be *Japan Inside Out.*

Chanoyu Quarterly the gift they have given us ... an irresistibly talented
trio that are a pleasure to know in print ... all the major cities as well as
some of the tiniest backwater towns ... 'Personal Datebooks' exhaustive
list of festivals and dates ... meticulously indexed and cross-referenced.
Filled with wit, irony. At first I thought I would never carry it with me
when I travel—it's so heavy. But ... it has been my constant companion.
Who needs pulp fiction to kill time on the road... sprinkled with insights
into comparative culture... I am humbled... by far **one of the most
amazing guidebooks ever written on Japan.**

ISBN4-89360-035-4